JAMES BEARD'S
ALL-AMERICAN
EATS

RECIPES
AND STORIES FROM
OUR BEST-LOVED
LOCAL
RESTAURANTS

FOREWORD BY **ANDREW ZIMMERN**

EDITED BY ANYA HOFFMAN ⌐ INTRODUCTION BY JOHN T. EDGE

PRINCIPAL LOCATION PHOTOGRAPHY BY JAMES COLLIER
PRINCIPAL FOOD PHOTOGRAPHY BY BEN FINK

RIZZOLI
NEW YORK

New York · Paris · London · Milan

CONT

CONTENTS

Foreword

JAMES BEARD ONCE SAID, "I don't like gourmet cooking or 'this' cooking or 'that' cooking. I like good cooking."

I love grand restaurants, I love seeing what the world's most highly motivated and inventive culinarians can do pushing themselves to the outer limits of their potential. I am one of those people who adore being dazzled for hours, sucking down course after course, getting a food high from twenty-four plates that all look like children's portions designed by interior decorators. I want to see what the greatest chefs can do with a foraged matsutake mushroom and a frying pan, or an anti-griddle and immersion circulator. I am guilty. I'm that guy. And yet I would trade all of that in, every tasting menu, every fought-over reservation, every fancy-food feather in my cap, every fancy-pants nibble notch on my edible bedpost, for a plate of Doe's Broiled Shrimp (page 29). Head down to Greenville, Mississippi, dig in for yourself, and call me if you don't think it's toe curling in its deliciousness. As complex, as deep in flavor as any food on earth. That's all Jim Beard cared about. Getting the toes to curl.

As for Beard, and all of us who love to eat, cook, and talk food, the flavor is the thing. And so is the place, the memory, the find, the smell, the smile as it's served, the hunt, the company, and about a thousand other variables that have nothing to do with the number of epic Barolos on the wine list. Some of the restaurants represented in this book have pretty nice wine lists, but if you're hung up there, you miss my point. I've had the *honor* of eating in most all of the eateries that share their histories here. I have history in them, too. I've had Tadich's sand dabs in San Francisco about forty times (page 258), fried tomatoes at Arnold's every time I'm in Nashville (page 49), and the *bureks* at Three Brothers in Milwaukee every year for the past twenty-four (page 118). Doesn't matter whether I'm a regular or a first-timer, the experience is the same. The food is sublime, the ghosts can be felt, the legends continue.

The restaurants in this book have all been open for a long time. A real long time. That's a rarity in the food world. That means they're special and that they have set the bar for generations of cooks not only to be impressed, but also to go off seeking excellence in simplicity, the hardest achievement in our business. These institutions have depth, they represent our nation's struggles, and they tell stories to hundreds of customers every day when they open their doors. That's the difference-maker.

Are the crabcakes at Joe's Stone Crab (page 52) the best of all time? They are when I'm sitting in that ancient dining room with the swirl of Miami pulsing all around me and the smell of icy piles of cracked crab whisking past our table on the tuxedoed arms of a waiter who understands that this is called the hospitality business for a reason. Did you know that Joe's owns its own crab boats and controls their product from the moment the crabs come on board to the time you pay your check? Did you know the mustard-mayo sauce is never served the day it's made because it tastes best a day old? Did you know that the same man has made the key lime pies for the last seventeen years?

We can all relate to that, can't we? Seems logical. Dedicated resources; staff that stays on forever because the restaurant is a fulfilling place to work, a family, really; most run by families, too. Consistent, simple food tastes great. Food with a story tastes better. Food with a story you haven't heard before tastes better than that, and if you can connect to that story, well, that makes it an American Classic, one of our best-loved restaurants. You hold in your hand some great food, and some even better stories. Milunka Radicevic, one of the current owners of the Three Brothers Restaurant, put it in a way that I think Beard would have appreciated: "We want the restaurant to let people know that we hope you become part of our family. There's a sense of continuity, a message that says, 'Welcome, sit down. Have a meal with us. Share a glass of wine with us.' My family has taken such great pride in becoming part of America's food landscape, and continuing the tradition of providing home-cooked meals."

Beard stood for American home-cooking at its best, neither "this" nor "that" cooking. Simply "good." He would want you to know the stories—he loved stories—but he would also want you to cook out of this book most of all. And so do I.

—ANDREW ZIMMERN

Meet the Classics
A Short History

AS WILLIE MAE SEATON, owner since 1957 of Willie Mae's Scotch House in the Treme neighborhood of New Orleans, walked from the rear of the auditorium to the stage at the 2005 James Beard Awards, men in black tie and women in sparkling gowns clapped and stomped and shouted their approval. Before the eighty-eight-year-old fried chicken cook accepted her beribboned medallion, embossed with the likeness of James Beard, before Seaton spoke one word, the audience had already clambered to its collective feet.

When the standing ovation quieted, Seaton spoke eloquently and honestly. "I'm just so full," she said as a second wave of applause rippled through the auditorium. "I didn't want to break down. It's just so great. It's just such a good feeling. I just can't explain it. I do my best to try to serve the people."

Restaurant professionals in the audience recognized their own ethic and aspiration in Seaton's pledge to excellence and service, her commitment to community and longevity. They heard, in her cracking voice, the clarion call of humility and hard work that has been a hallmark of the America's Classics Awards since their inception. "I get up at four fifteen A.M. every day to do what I do," said Bill Smith of Mustache Bill's Diner in Barnegat Light, New Jersey, after he won in 2009. "I knew there was a James Beard Award. I just never knew it was something we could win."

Since 1998, the James Beard Foundation has recognized our nation's vernacular restaurants with the designation America's Classics. Honorees that first year included Joe's Stone Crab of Miami Beach, Florida, the swanky clubhouse that opened in 1913 as a fried fish counter, and Tadich Grill, the sand dab emporium founded as a San Francisco coffee stand in 1849, before California was even a state.

In the years since, the foundation has celebrated a diverse roster of beloved restaurants. From the Oyster Bar at Grand Central Terminal in New York City, to the H&H Carwash & Restaurant in El Paso, Texas. From the Brookville Hotel in Abilene, Kansas, to Hamura's Saimin Stand in Kauai, Hawaii.

Some restaurants claim tenures worthy of Tadich. Others better measure their import in the devotion of their customers. Guelaguetza, a 2015 honoree from Los Angeles, made its reputation serving *tlayudas* and *huevos enfrijolados* to homesick Oaxacans. The Anchor Bar, a 2003 winner from Buffalo, New York, introduced chicken wings to the beer-drinking faithful.

The official awards criteria are august and serious and specific: Classics are defined by the Beard Foundation as "restaurants with timeless appeal, beloved in their regions for quality food that reflects the character of their communities." There's fine print to read too: "Establishments must have been in existence for at least ten years and be locally owned."

The operative definition is inclusive. Classics turn a mirror on our nation. They broadcast where America eats Tuesday pancake breakfasts. And Thursday lunches of burgers and fries. Classics are where church softball teams gather for fried chicken and sweet tea. Classics are where synagogue soccer teams huddle over pizzas after practice.

Through the years, the roster of Classics has grown to more than a hundred restaurants. No matter the style of food cooked, no matter the pomp or circumstance of service, Classics are restaurants where humility and excellence abide. In 2006, Bowens Island Restaurant near Charleston, South Carolina, celebrated its sixtieth anniversary. That year, proprietor Robert Barber, a minister and politician, ambled onto the same stage that Willie Mae Seaton claimed before.

Like many in the audience, Barber wore a black tux. Like no one else in the audience, he wore a pair of white fishing boots to honor the men and women who work the pluff mud of South Carolina, harvesting the oysters he steams. "We should remember that we drink from wells we did not dig," Barber said that night, quoting the Bible as he received his medal. "We warm ourselves by fires we did not build."

With each restaurant honored, with each film tribute commissioned, and now with this book, the James Beard Foundation fosters our nation's appreciation for culinary traditions and their stewards. The restaurants whose profiles and recipes follow do good work that is integral to sustaining America's diverse food cultures. This book celebrates their legacies and prospects and import.

—JOHN T. EDGE
Director, Southern Foodways Alliance

SOUTHEAST

PRINCE'S HOT CHICKEN SHACK

NASHVILLE, TN

2013 AWARD WINNER

Hot fried chicken, long popular in towns across the South, has become synonymous with Nashville. A visit to town doesn't count unless you make the pilgrimage to this joint, set in an abbreviated strip mall alongside a nail salon, for crispy yardbird with a cayenne-soaked coat of armor. The signature dish, as the story goes, owes its existence to a jilted lover. The original owner, Thornton Prince, was a handsome fellow who never lacked for female companions. One of his girlfriends grew weary of his late-night carousing; to get revenge, she doused his Sunday morning favorite, fried chicken, with cayenne pepper. But her plan backfired: He liked it. By the mid-1930s, Prince and his brothers had perfected the process and opened a café, which they originally called the BBQ Chicken Shack.

Current owner André Prince Jeffries, great-niece of Thornton Prince, continues the family tradition. She brines her chicken, flours it, fries it to order, and coats it with a secret layer of hot spices. You can order it from mild (don't be fooled: "mild" is still pretty damn hot) to extra-hot (reserved for people with an intense disregard for their digestive tract). As Ms. Jeffries likes to say, her chicken "burns you twice." The stack of crinkled dill pickle chips and slices of white bread that come with your chicken are the closest things to life rafts your taste buds will find.

I GREW UP ON THIS CHICKEN. I really didn't know it was peculiar to Nashville; I thought everybody had it. My father always had it; he'd go down late on Saturday nights and when we woke up on Sunday morning it was always on the stove.

We get people from all walks of life come in here and a lot of them, they'll tell you the story of how they grew up on this chicken, their parents took them to get the chicken when my great-uncle had it. I remember when my great-uncle started it, the Caucasians ate in the back and of course the black people ate up front. A lot of people, especially the older people, can tell you about it. They would pass through the kitchen on the way to the very back of the place. They had a separate dining area. That was wild—I thought that was really weird. They would come from the Grand Ole Opry, after the show, and just feast because, like I say, we were known for late-night business. I just try to keep up the family tradition of keeping it open late.

Women eat it hotter than men and I don't know why that is, but they do. So maybe that's something the scientists can look into—how women can tolerate that heat more so than men. Men will start out hot, but they quickly fade back down to medium. Not that many men get it hot. One man said it took the hair *off* his chest and another one says it put hair *on* his chest. I didn't want to see that chest. You hear all kinds of stories. One of our customers gets it and he says he eats it in a tub. He fills his bathtub full of cold water and that's how he eats it. I think I have just one customer now that's been getting it hot for a long time, but those women—I don't know what it is.

We have a regular customer that we think might be a "lady of the evening." She's been coming for as long as I've been in business. She brings her suitors down here—different suitors. She comes on the weekend and gets the chicken hot. One night she just couldn't wait to get out—the finale was on the hood of a car. Have mercy, it was good that it was late. We've had a couple of people like that, she's not the only one. We can see feet flying, doors not open. We just shut our eyes and continue to do our work, what we're good at. Yes, some strange things go on associated with hot chicken.

They say it's addictive. They say it's addictive, and I have some people who come every day I'm open. They come every day. I don't know how they do it, but they are chicken-holics; there are truly some chicken-holics in Nashville. People will be waiting for chicken and a complete stranger—they don't ask you if they could sit down; they just come and sit down and think nothing of it and just start talking to someone. We're definitely not a fast food. This chicken cannot be rushed; it cannot be rushed. To be right it takes time. Sometimes when we give it to the customers too fast they don't want it; they think something is wrong with it because they're used to waiting. It takes time to cook the chicken right.

Oh me, but it has a world of its own. Hot chicken has a world of its own—real hot chicken, the true hot chicken.

—ANDRÉ PRINCE JEFFRIES

THE BRIGHT STAR

BESSEMER, AL

2010 AWARD WINNER

A clump of feta tucked in a salad of iceberg and cucumbers. A stipple of oregano on a broiled snapper fillet. At the Bright Star in Bessemer, Alabama, an old steel town southwest of Birmingham, the vestiges of Greece are few. Greek immigrants built the Bright Star, a vintage dining hall with intricately patterned tile floors, nicotine-patinaed woodwork, WPA-era murals of the Old Country, and brass chandeliers, that opened in 1907. Descendants of the restaurant's founding fathers—Tom Bonduris and his cousin Bill Koikos, natives of the farming village of Peleta in the mountainous Peloponnesus region—still work the floor. Jimmy Koikos, a septuagenarian, and brother Nicky, seven years his junior, are in charge now. The menu is an honest—and very old—fusion, Greek meets Southern, as interpreted by African American cooks: Fried red snapper throats, house-cut from whole Gulf fish, are on the menu. Okra in a cornmeal crust, too. And field peas with snaps. In the Birmingham area, many of the best barbecue and meat-and-three restaurants are Greek-owned. And the Bright Star is the oldest and most storied of the bunch.

THE RESTAURANT WAS OPENED BY TOM BONDURIS, a great-uncle of my dad's, who came to Birmingham from Greece in the late 1880s. He came to this country as a young thing. He worked as a waiter. And then he opened up a restaurant in Birmingham called the Bright Star, but it didn't last long. He heard about Bessemer being the young, mining, progressive town, so he came here and opened up the Bright Star in 1907. We now have four locations.

Back in the early 1900s, they were opening a lot of restaurants in Birmingham. There was a restaurant called Gold Star, one called Silver Star. Another one in Talladega called some kind of "star"—they were named "star." So Tom Bonduris, he was a very smart man. Not very educated—no, he couldn't get educated—but smart and a good businessman. And he looked around and he said this restaurant is a "Bright Star," with a vision of nothing but a land of opportunity.

My daddy came to Birmingham in 1920 from a place called Peleta in Greece, just a country town. He came to New York, and then to Birmingham. There were Greek immigrants in the late 1800s, early 1900s, coming to America for better opportunity. He came here and walked through these restaurant doors and started working as a young immigrant to learn the language, to send his mother back everything he made.

My daddy was here in 1929 when the stock market crashed. They could hardly pay their rent. Nobody was doing well—sometimes they would just feed people. Nobody was doing business. The economy was zero. They made it from year to year until Roosevelt got elected and things picked up in '45.

Things have changed a bit since then. We've got some 1920s and '30s menus. Soup was a nickel. Ten or fifteen cents for hamburgers and chili. They had chili back then. The Bright Star became a seafood and steak restaurant in the 1930s, when we started getting fresh snapper. And it's still a specialty today, called "Bright Star's Snapper, Greek-Style." It's still one of the drawing cards that we have. You know, a guy called the other day and wanted to sell me some fish prefrozen. I said, "You're wasting your time and mine, too." All our pole beans—we shell them. The squash is fresh. The cream potatoes are not instant. That's what we believe in.

We make all our pies here. We got two pastry people who do nothing but make our pies, you know. And we make them every day. Lemon icebox pie—we serve a lot of them to go. Then you've got your peanut butter pie, the pineapple cream cheese pie, and coconut pie. Chocolate almond cream pie. They're made from the finest ingredients.

Oh, and we've got some great people. We've got one girl's been here thirty-five years, and one twenty-seven years. That's a success of the restaurant, to have people like that. We take a lot of pride in our people. And we've got really good people, so of course we try to take care of them.

We have a lot of memories. A tornado came through here and blew a sideline down and closed us for a few days. We went through the Depressions. And there's good times. Now, I think, we're fighting the chain outfits. There's a new restaurant on every corner, you know.

We're blessed, though. We've been here for a century. There was a woman in here. She was eating one Saturday. She said, "Aren't you the owner?" I said, "Yes, ma'am." She said, "I just want to know one thing: Is there going to be a Bright Star in Heaven? Because your place is just so wonderful." And that's one of the nicest things that I've heard.

—JIMMY KOIKOS

WILLIE MAE'S SCOTCH HOUSE

NEW ORLEANS, LA

2005 AWARD WINNER

In 1957 or thereabouts, corner tavern Willie Mae's Scotch House opened in the Treme neighborhood of New Orleans. The proprietor was Willie Mae Seaton. Born in 1916 in Crystal Springs, Mississippi, Mrs. Seaton moved south in 1940 with her husband, L. S. Seaton. Mrs. Seaton earned her keep tending bar at local watering holes—she won neighborhood fame for a signature cocktail of Johnnie Walker Black and milk—before opening her business and moving into the kitchen. By 1972, Seaton had converted a beauty salon in the front half of her double-shotgun home into a seven-table restaurant. Working with her daughter, Lillie Mae Seaton, she honed a repertoire of country-come-to-town standards: paprika-spiked chicken sheathed in a diaphanous crust, white beans with pickled pork, and a bread pudding that limned the Platonic ideal. Over a career spanning fifty-plus years, Willie Mae Seaton earned a reputation for forthright cookery of unimpeachable quality. She did so quietly, one platter of deep-fried chicken at a time. And in the process, she transformed her restaurant from a place where one eats to a place where one belongs.

At no time was this clearer than in the aftermath of Hurricane Katrina, which hit New Orleans just a few months after Willie Mae's visit to New York to receive a 2005 America's Classics award. The restaurant was completely destroyed by the storm. Regular Lolis Eric Elie, founding director of the Southern Foodways Alliance, organized chefs, food lovers, and Willie Mae's many fans in a massive effort to rebuild the iconic eatery. Two years later, with the help of more than two hundred volunteers, Willie Mae's Scotch House reopened. Willie Mae Seaton passed away in 2015, at the age of ninety-nine. Her great-granddaughter, Kerry Seaton Stewart, is now at the helm.

I'VE BEEN IN NEW ORLEANS SINCE 1940. I raised my children here, but Mississippi is my home, right this side of Jackson. My grandmother partly helped to raise me because my daddy died when I was six years old. And so my mother came back home, you know, and I was the only child. I just went from there—just watching them, and I did like a little child and tried to learn how to cook and do this and that. I've been cooking all my life. I had four children I had to cook for. I had to work and I had to cook. And my daughter could cook as good as me. She worked in the restaurant with me until she passed away.

My husband come here to work and he was in the shipyard and that's what brought us here. I was a silk finisher at a cleaners. I went to school to get a beautician license. I drove a cab about six years. Then I opened my bar in 1957, I believe. When I first went into business I had applied for my license. I got my liquor license but my beer license hadn't come and the federal people, they'd come around and check to see—nosy, you know. And they came around and I didn't have my beer license and I had a couple of guys around the bar there drinking beer, and they stopped me selling it 'til my license come. Those guys said, "You got your liquor license up there; we're going to buy all the Scotch on the bar," and they started drinking Scotch. They run an ad in the paper—my customers ran an ad, they paid for it—and in there they named my place Willie Mae's Scotch House.

When I come to Louisiana the food was a little different. It's Creole cooking. They use lots of seasoning. Garlic. Garlic plays a big role here in this city. It's good for your health . . . this is a garlic place, baby. Red beans. Honey, I just love me some red beans. This is a real red bean city. I know better than to put a pot on the stove unless I have red beans. If you cook them, baby, and cook them right, that's some good eating. That's what carries our city. They say New Orleans has the best food in the nation. This is called the Creole City, and they say Creole cooking—it means all of that good seasoning that you put into it. And everybody eats my food—black and white. Baby, we just have a bunch of precious customers. Oh, I have the top of the line.

But that storm put a hold on us. Pressure will wear the iron out. I don't have pictures here. A lot of my pictures got washed away, too, 'cause I couldn't get them out of there. We had to get out of there and they were screaming and hollering for me to come on out. We went to Mississippi and we was lucky enough to get a place there, went on to Houston. We tried to get back around here three or four times, but the water was still up there and the police turned us around on the high-way. Couldn't get to it. And there it is, baby; I just got to pick up the pieces and keep walking. 'Cause God was able to save our life. That's the main thing.

But I feel at home here. I thought about relocating and going back to Jackson and getting me a place up there, but my little place is so nice and the people treat me so nice. I been here all my life.

—WILLIE MAE SEATON

Fried Chicken

Brined or wet-battered. Fried in peanut oil or crisped in lard. Sprinkled with cayenne or soaked in buttermilk. There are as many ways to make fried chicken as there are country songs about infidelity. The dish is closely associated with Southern food culture, and for good reason: Fried chicken appears on countless menus across the region, from roadside stands to four-star restaurants. It's been perfected by several America's Classics winners from the Southeast—Beaumont Inn, Mrs. Wilkes Dining Room, and Willie Mae's Scotch House among them—each of whom swear by their personal (and often secret) time-honed techniques. But the dish also appears in distinct and delicious iterations throughout the rest of the country, from Anchor Bar's legendary Buffalo wings in upstate New York to Frank Fat's soy-marinated fried chicken in California's capital.

Region	Fried Chicken	Where to Get It	Words of Wisdom
SOUTHEAST	Fried Chicken	**WILLIE MAE'S SCOTCH HOUSE** New Orleans, LA	The standard-bearer for Southern fried chicken, Willie Mae's has perfected its yard-bird technique over the course of almost sixty years at the stove. The recipe may be a closely guarded secret, but the juicy, shatteringly crisp–crusted chicken is known throughout the world.
NORTHEAST	Buffalo Wings	**ANCHOR BAR** Buffalo, NY	They're not called Buffalo wings for nothing. Though it's hard to imagine there was ever a time when people *didn't* deep-fry chicken wings before dousing them in butter and hot sauce, the dish has only been around since the 1960s, when it was first served as a late-night snack for hungry customers at this legendary bar in Buffalo, New York.
MIDWEST	Pan-Fried Chicken Dinner	**STROUD'S** Kansas City, MO	The folks at Stroud's have long been known for having a sense of humor (their motto, which the restaurant sells printed on T-shirts, is "We choke our own chickens"), but when it comes to their family-style chicken dinners, they are dead serious. The golden-brown, perfectly seasoned chicken is pan-fried to order in a cast-iron skillet and served with homemade chicken noodle soup, big bowls of mashed potatoes, porky green beans, and a creamy, pepper-flecked gravy made with chicken cracklings.
SOUTHWEST	Jason's Crispy Chicken Sandwich	**PERINI RANCH STEAKHOUSE** Buffalo Gap, TX	Sometimes even cowboys need a break from beef. Fortunately, Perini Ranch has poultry-loving patrons covered with this lunch-menu sandwich. The chef layers crispy fried chicken breast on a soft burger bun with lettuce, tomato, and a dollop of housemade spicy chipotle mayo.
WEST	Brandy-Fried Chicken	**FRANK FAT'S** Sacramento, CA	Tender and tasty, the brandy-fried chicken at Frank Fat's has long been one of the Chinese-American restaurant's most well-known dishes. Before frying, the chicken pieces are marinated in soy sauce, fresh ginger, garlic, and, of course, brandy.

TOMATO-WATERMELON SALAD

CROOK'S CORNER

CHAPEL HILL, NC

A perfect end-of-summer dish, this recipe makes the most of those glorious weeks when tomatoes and watermelon are both in season. Chef Bill Smith cautions against making this quick and refreshing salad ahead of time—the dish is best when eaten the same day it's made and tastes even better when served very cold. To add a salty counterpoint, top with a handful of oil-cured black olives.

SERVES 4 TO 6 AS AN APPETIZER OR SIDE DISH

5 cups cubed and seeded ripe watermelon

5 ripe medium summer tomatoes (about 1½ pounds), cut into wedges

1 tablespoon sugar

½ teaspoon salt

1 small red onion, peeled, quartered, and thinly sliced (about 1 cup)

½ cup red wine vinegar

¼ cup good olive oil

¾ cup oil-cured black olives, pitted (optional)

GENTLY combine the watermelon, tomatoes, sugar, and salt in a large bowl. Let the mixture sit at room temperature for 15 minutes. Add the onion, vinegar, and oil and gently stir to combine. Refrigerate until very cold and top with the olives, if using, before serving.

"We make homemade everything: ice cream, pie crust, crackers for the soup, cookies for the ice cream."
— BILL SMITH,
Crook's Corner in Chapel Hill, NC

PIMENTO CHEESE SPREAD

SALLY BELL'S KITCHEN

RICHMOND, VA

One of the longtime staples of the boxed lunch at Sally Bell's is this creamy pimento cheese spread, which the proprietors slather on soft white bread and serve with a deviled egg, potato salad, and an upside-down cupcake. The piquant pimentos lend the rich, addictive dip its signature light orange color, and a pinch of cayenne supplies just the slightest hint of heat. Try it spread on crackers or, better yet, buttermilk biscuits.

MAKES ABOUT 5 CUPS

1 pound extra-sharp cheddar cheese, shredded

⅔ cup cream cheese

½ cup mayonnaise

⅓ cup diced jarred pimentos

½ teaspoon salt

¼ teaspoon cayenne pepper

COMBINE the cheddar cheese, cream cheese, mayonnaise, pimentos, salt, and cayenne pepper in the bowl of a food processor and blend until smooth, stopping to scrape down the sides of the bowl when necessary.

FRIED GREEN TOMATOES

ARNOLD'S COUNTRY KITCHEN

NASHVILLE, TN

At meat-and-three eatery Arnold's Country Kitchen, customers pile their trays with crisp fried chicken or rare roast beef and Southern sides like macaroni and cheese, squash casserole, cornbread, and these crisp, tart, fried tomatoes. A not-unsubstantial dash of hot sauce gives the tangy, cracker-crusted tomatoes a welcome touch of heat. If you can't find cracker meal, pulse a sleeve or two of saltines in a food processor and use the crumbs instead. Leftovers—if there are any—make a life-changing BLT.

SERVES 4

1 cup all-purpose flour

Salt and freshly ground black pepper

2 large eggs

2 tablespoons red wine vinegar

1 tablespoon hot sauce

2 cups cracker meal

1 tablespoon dried basil

1½ teaspoons dried oregano

1½ teaspoons sugar

Canola oil for frying

4 large green tomatoes, stem and blossom ends removed and discarded, cut into ½-inch slices

---

COMBINE the flour with salt and pepper to taste in a wide, shallow bowl and mix well.

IN a medium bowl, whisk together the eggs, vinegar, hot sauce, and ½ cup water.

COMBINE the cracker meal, basil, oregano, sugar, 1½ teaspoons salt, and 1½ teaspoons pepper in a separate medium bowl; mix well.

IN a large cast-iron skillet or heavy frying pan, heat ¼ inch of oil over medium-high heat to about 325°F. Line a plate with paper towels.

WORKING in batches, place a slice of tomato in the bowl with the seasoned flour and coat both sides. Shake off any excess flour. Use tongs to dip the floured tomato slice into the egg mixture and then dredge in the cracker meal mixture until thoroughly coated. Place the tomato slice in the hot oil. Repeat until the pan is full but the tomato slices aren't touching. Fry until the crust is golden brown and the tomato has softened, 4 to 6 minutes per side. Remove from the pan and place on the paper towel–lined plate to drain. Repeat with remaining slices of tomato, adding more oil to the skillet between batches as needed. Serve immediately.

CRABCAKES WITH RÉMOULADE

JOE'S STONE CRAB

MIAMI BEACH, FL

One of the house specialties at Joe's Stone Crab are these moist, tender crabcakes. The secret is not to overmix and to let the patties chill thoroughly before cooking so they don't fall apart. A large offset spatula will also make them easier to handle. Leftover crabcakes can be transformed into phenomenal sandwiches; top with lettuce and serve on rémoulade-slathered rolls. The rémoulade can also be used as a dip for shrimp cocktail or cracked stone crab claws, the restaurant's signature dish.

MAKES 8 CRABCAKES; SERVES 4

CRABCAKES

1 pound jumbo lump crabmeat, picked over (about 2 cups)

½ red bell pepper, finely diced (about ½ cup)

¼ cup finely diced onion

¼ cup minced fresh parsley

4 scallions, trimmed and chopped

1 garlic clove, minced

1 large egg, lightly beaten

2 tablespoons Dijon-style mustard

Juice of 1 lemon (about 2 tablespoons)

½ teaspoon Worcestershire sauce

½ teaspoon Tabasco sauce

¾ cup fine unseasoned bread crumbs

4 tablespoons vegetable oil, plus more if needed

Lime or lemon wedges

Rémoulade (recipe follows)

LINE a baking sheet with waxed paper; set aside.

IN a large bowl, combine the crabmeat, bell pepper, onion, parsley, scallions, and garlic. In a small bowl, combine the egg, mustard, lemon juice, Worcestershire sauce, and Tabasco sauce. Using a rubber spatula, gently fold the egg mixture into the crabmeat mixture. Add ¼ cup of the bread crumbs, mixing gently to combine.

USING ½ cup of the crabmeat mixture for each one, form eight oval patties about ½-inch thick and 3½ inches long. Coat the patties on both sides with the remaining bread crumbs and place them on the lined baking sheet. Refrigerate for 2 to 3 hours.

HEAT 2 tablespoons of the oil over medium-high heat in a large, heavy sauté pan or cast-iron skillet. Place four of the crabcakes in the skillet using a large offset spatula and cook until golden, carefully turning once, 3 to 4 minutes total. Repeat with the remaining oil and crabcakes. Serve with lime or lemon wedges and rémoulade.

RÉMOULADE

MAKES 1 CUP

½ cup mayonnaise

2 tablespoons ketchup

1 small celery rib, minced (about 2 tablespoons)

1 scallion, minced

1 tablespoon minced fresh parsley

Juice of ½ lemon

½ teaspoon Cajun seasoning

¼ teaspoon dry mustard

¼ teaspoon salt

⅛ teaspoon Worcestershire sauce

COMBINE the mayonnaise, ketchup, celery, scallion, parsley, lemon juice, Cajun seasoning, dry mustard, salt, and Worcestershire sauce in a medium bowl. Mix well and serve. Store leftovers in a sealed container in the refrigerator for up to 1 week.

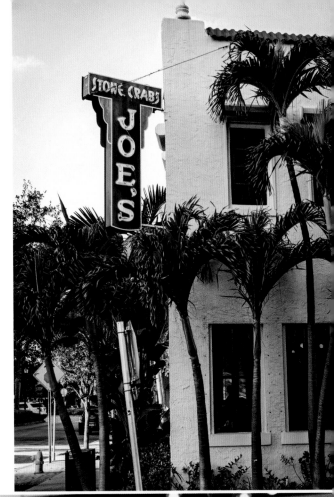

BROILED SHRIMP

DOE'S EAT PLACE

GREENVILLE, MS

The menu at the original Doe's Eat Place is simple: hot tamales, chili, salad, several cuts of steak, and shrimp, which diners can order either broiled or fried. The broiled shrimp is generously seasoned with garlic butter and lemon juice before going under the heat; as the shrimp cooks, the butter melts into a heavenly sauce. The restaurant serves the dish—which comes together in less than ten minutes—with a side of garlic toast perfect for sopping up every last drop. When buying the shrimp, ask your fishmonger to clean and devein them but to leave the shells on the tails for easier handling.

SERVES 4

2 dozen jumbo shrimp (21- to 25-count), cleaned, with shells on the tails

Juice of 1 lemon

1 tablespoon Worcestershire sauce

Kosher salt

6 tablespoons (¾ stick) unsalted butter, at room temperature

2 garlic cloves, minced

1 tablespoon Spanish paprika (*pimenton*)

1 teaspoon Italian seasoning or dried basil

1 tablespoon Creole seasoning (or a mixture of 1 teaspoon garlic powder, 1 teaspoon onion powder, ½ teaspoon dried thyme, ½ teaspoon dried oregano, and ¼ teaspoon cayenne pepper)

PREHEAT the broiler.

PUT the shrimp in a single layer in a baking pan; add the lemon juice, Worcestershire sauce, and salt to taste and toss to combine.

IN a small bowl, use a fork to blend the butter and garlic. Spread the garlic-butter mixture over the shrimp and sprinkle the Italian seasoning, paprika, and Creole seasoning over the top.

PLACE the pan under the broiler and cook until the shrimp is pink and slightly charred, about 3 minutes, turning the pan halfway through. Serve hot.

...itional Southern ...ice Dishes

CAROLINA RICE

From Louisiana's gumbos to the Lowcountry's hoppin' John, rice is a central ingredient in Southern cooking. One of the area's earliest crops, the grain played a complicated role in the South's history both as a crucial commodity and as an integral part of slave culture. Rice cultivation took place in snake-infested Carolina swamps; it was dangerous, backbreaking work performed almost entirely by slaves, taken from West Africa and exploited for their knowledge of rice production. Today, rice remains a staple of Southern cuisine; the traditional and modern rice recipes served in Southern homes and restaurants are at once a living reminder of the region's history and a vivid example of the enduring role food has in cultural preservation.

THE PERFECT POT OF RICE

MAKES 3½ CUPS; SERVES 4 TO 6

When cooking Carolina Gold or any other long-grain Carolina white rice, the name of the game is fluffy. Unlike sticky, short-grain varieties like sushi rice or Arborio, Carolina rice is prized for its light, delicate texture—but only when it's not overcooked. The trick, according to *New York Times* writer Kim Severson, whose recipe this is based on, is to start the rice on the stovetop but finish it in the oven.

1 cup long-grain white Carolina rice

1 tablespoon unsalted butter

½ teaspoon kosher salt

PREHEAT the oven to 350°F.

RINSE the rice well in a colander. Put the rice in a Dutch oven and add 2 cups cold water, the butter, and the salt.

BRING the water to a boil, cover with a tight-fitting lid, and place in the oven. Cook the rice for 17 minutes. Remove from the oven and let the rice sit for an additional 15 minutes before fluffing with a fork.

Hoppin' John

Sauté onion, celery, garlic, and thyme in butter or bacon grease until soft and golden brown before adding 2 cups cooked black-eyed peas and 1 cup chicken broth. Simmer for 10 to 15 minutes and serve over a bowl of cooked Carolina rice.

Charleston Red Rice

Pan-fry bacon or salt pork, removing the meat from the pan when crisp. Sauté onion, red bell pepper, celery, and garlic in the pan grease until soft before adding 2 cups uncooked Carolina rice, 2 cups crushed canned tomatoes with juice, a healthy dab of tomato paste, 1½ cups chicken broth or water, a pinch of cayenne, and salt and pepper to taste. Bring the mixture to a boil, cover, and place in a preheated 350°F oven; cook until the rice is tender and the liquid has been absorbed, 20 to 25 minutes. Top with the cooked bacon or pork before serving.

Gumbo

Heat 3 tablespoons vegetable oil in a heavy-bottomed pan; add ⅓ cup flour and cook, whisking constantly, until golden brown. Add onion, celery, green bell pepper, fresh or frozen okra, crushed tomatoes, garlic, a bay leaf, thyme, oregano, a good pinch of salt, and 4 cups chicken broth. Bring to a boil and simmer for 15 minutes before finishing with cubed cooked chicken and sliced cooked andouille sausage. Serve over a bowl of cooked Carolina rice.

Red Beans and Rice

Sauté onion, bell pepper, and celery until soft; add cubed boiled ham, andouille sausage, garlic, a bay leaf, dried thyme, a pinch of cayenne, and salt and pepper and cook for 5 minutes. Add 3 cups cooked red or kidney beans along with 3 cups chicken broth. Let the beans simmer, uncovered, stirring occasionally, for about 1 hour, adding more broth or water if the mixture becomes dry. Serve with cooked Carolina rice.

Dirty Rice

Brown ground pork and finely chopped or ground chicken livers in vegetable oil. Season the meat with dried thyme, dried oregano, garlic powder, onion powder, a pinch of cayenne, and salt and pepper. Add diced onion, celery, green bell pepper, and minced garlic to the pan and cook, stirring, until the vegetables are browned. To the pan add 3 cups cooked Carolina rice, 1½ cups chicken broth, and a small handful of finely chopped fresh parsley. Cook, stirring, until the liquid has been absorbed and the rice is heated through.

BOWENS ISLAND FROGMORE STEW

BOWENS ISLAND RESTAURANT

CHARLESTON, SC

A classic Lowcountry dish, frogmore stew is actually not a stew at all: It's a Southern-style seafood boil featuring sweet shrimp, bright ears of corn, and bites of potato flavored with sausage and plenty of Old Bay. The key to doing the dish justice, says owner Robert Barber, is to make sure not to overcook the shrimp; he takes the dish off the heat immediately after adding it. At Bowens Island they turn leftovers into a potato salad studded with corn, sausage, and shrimp, all cut into bite-size pieces and folded together with a spoonful or two of mayonnaise.

SERVES 6

3 tablespoons Old Bay seasoning

2 teaspoons kosher salt

Dash of Louisiana-style hot sauce, such as Texas Pete (optional)

1½ pounds small red potatoes (about 15 potatoes)

1½ pounds breakfast sausage links, cooked and cut into ½-inch-thick slices

6 ears of corn, husked and cleaned of all silk, broken in half

2 pounds large shrimp, shells on and heads removed

FILL a large pot one-quarter full with water and place over high heat. Add the Old Bay seasoning, salt, and hot sauce and bring the water to a boil.

ADD the potatoes and cook until they're beginning to soften but are not fully cooked, about 9 minutes. Add the sausage and cook for 1 minute. Add the corn and cook for 2 minutes. At this point the potatoes should be easy to pierce with a fork.

BRING the water back up to a boil, add the shrimp, and immediately remove from the heat. Let the pot sit, uncovered, stirring occasionally, until the shrimp are a little pink but not fully cooked, about 3 minutes. (The shrimp will continue cooking in the serving bowls.) Use a slotted spoon to transfer the shrimp and other ingredients into bowls, straining out the liquid, and serve immediately.

ARROZ CON POLLO

CHICKEN WITH YELLOW RICE

VERSAILLES

MIAMI, FL

There are few places that make a better version of this classic Caribbean dish than Versailles, which has been serving traditional Cuban fare to homesick expats and devoted locals for more than forty years. The entrée, which is served with a side of *plátanos maduros* (sweet fried plaintains), is one of the restaurant's most enduring, says Luly Valls, the daughter of owner Felipe Valls Jr. The restaurant goes through so many orders of arroz con pollo that they never have leftovers, but Valls notes that when her grandmother makes the dish at home, she adds chicken broth to the crunchy bits of rice stuck to the bottom of the pan to make a delicious, warming soup.

SERVES 6 TO 8

¼ cup olive oil

1 (3- to 4-pound) whole chicken, cut into 8 pieces; or 4 or 5 large, bone-in chicken breasts

Salt and freshly ground black pepper

1 large onion, coarsely chopped (about 2½ cups)

1 medium green bell pepper, coarsely chopped (about 1½ cups)

3 garlic cloves, minced

1 (8-ounce) can tomato sauce

1 tablespoon annatto-based seasoning powder (such as Bijol or Goya)

1 bay leaf

1 teaspoon ground dried oregano

½ teaspoon ground cumin

1 cup dry white wine, or 1 (12-ounce) can beer

½ teaspoon ground white pepper

1 cup Valencia or other short-grain rice

1 cup parboiled rice (converted rice)

3 cups chicken broth, preferably homemade

8 ounces frozen and thawed or fresh sweet peas (see Note, page 34)

1 (4-ounce) jar pimentos, drained and diced

PREHEAT the oven to 325°F.

HEAT the oil in a large Dutch oven or ovenproof pot over medium to medium-high heat. Season the chicken generously with salt and black pepper. Working in batches so as not to crowd the pot, put the chicken pieces in the pot skin-side down and sear until the skin is lightly browned, about 5 minutes. Do not remove too quickly, as it will stick. Transfer the chicken to a plate and set aside.

ADD the onion, bell pepper, and garlic to the pot and sauté over medium heat until soft, about 5 minutes. Add the tomato sauce and simmer for 5 minutes. Add the seasoning powder, bay leaf, oregano, and cumin and stir to combine. Immediately

(continued)

add the wine, white pepper, and salt to taste; cook for 5 minutes, or until the liquid has mostly evaporated. Add both types of rice and stir until it is fully incorporated into the tomato mixture. Add the broth and stir. Return the chicken to the pot, pouring in any juices that have accumulated on the plate. Make sure there's at least 3 inches of space at the top of the pot, as the rice will expand while cooking. Bring to a boil, cover, and reduce the heat to low. Simmer for 10 minutes.

TRANSFER the covered pot, lid and all, to the oven. Bake for 25 to 30 minutes, or until the rice is uniformly cooked. The liquid need not be fully absorbed for the rice to be ready. Remember that the liquid continues to evaporate with the residual heat, so remove the dish from the oven when it is a little soupier than you want it to be. Remove and discard the bay leaf. Adjust the seasoning to taste.

DECORATE the top of the rice with the peas and pimentos before serving.

NOTE: If using frozen peas, the pot should be uncovered and the peas added in the last 5 minutes of baking.

CHICKEN À LA GRANDE

MOSCA'S

NEW ORLEANS, LA

As Calvin Trillin wrote in a 2010 *New Yorker* piece about Mosca's, ordering the Chicken à la Grande on every visit to the iconic Italian restaurant is a must. The recipe is simple but requires patience— the cut-up chicken is slowly browned in a cast-iron skillet before being simmered with wine, herbs, and garlic (the restaurant's "devotion to garlic has remained unchanged" since opening for business in 1946, noted Trillin). The results are extraordinary: salty, crisp skin and moist, perfectly seasoned meat scented with rosemary and oregano.

SERVES 4

1 small (3-pound) whole chicken, cut into 8 pieces

⅓ cup olive oil

2 teaspoons salt

1 teaspoon freshly ground black pepper

6 to 10 garlic cloves, unpeeled and smashed

1 tablespoon fresh rosemary needles, or 2 teaspoons dried

1 tablespoon fresh oregano leaves, or 2 teaspoons dried

½ cup dry white wine

PAT the chicken pieces dry and place them in a large, heavy, unheated skillet (a 12-inch cast-iron skillet will work well). Pour the oil over the chicken, making certain the pieces are well coated. Sprinkle the chicken with the salt and pepper. Place over medium-high heat and cook until the chicken is brown on all sides, turning as needed, about 25 minutes.

ADD the garlic, rosemary, and oregano to the skillet, distributing them evenly over the chicken. Pour the wine over the chicken. Reduce the heat to medium-low and simmer, uncovered, until the wine has reduced by half, 8 to 10 minutes. Remove from the heat. Discard the garlic cloves and serve the chicken hot with the pan juices.

GREEN TABASCO CHICKEN

CROOK'S CORNER

CHAPEL HILL, NC

A lacquer of spicy green Tabasco and a rich giblet gravy set this butter-basted roast chicken apart. "This is one of my go-to recipes for times when I need to plump up the menu but don't have a lot of time for prep," says Crook's Corner chef Bill Smith. "It's a town favorite here in Chapel Hill. We serve this with mashed potatoes and a mixture of julienned leeks and cabbage that have been quick-sautéed in butter. As for the liver, I fry it up and smash it onto a piece of toast to eat while I'm cooking the chicken."

SERVES 4

1 small whole chicken (about 3 pounds), giblets reserved

1 teaspoon salt

½ teaspoon freshly ground black pepper

1 lemon

1 garlic clove, peeled

1 jalapeño pepper

Several sprigs fresh herbs, such as basil, parsley, thyme, rosemary, or oregano (optional)

3 tablespoons Tabasco Green Pepper Sauce or other green chile–based hot sauce

3 tablespoons unsalted butter, melted, plus 1 tablespoon unsalted butter

1 cup dry white wine

PREHEAT the oven to 450°F.

PUT all the giblets except the liver in a saucepan and cover with cool water. Bring to a boil over high heat, then lower the heat to maintain a simmer. Allow the broth to cook while you proceed with the dish, adding a little water from time to time if it reduces too quickly. Reserve the liver for another use.

PAT the chicken dry. Snip off the pope's nose and the last joint of both wings. Add these to the pan with the simmering giblets.

SEASON the cavity of the chicken with ½ teaspoon of the salt and ¼ teaspoon of the black pepper. Place the whole lemon, garlic clove, and whole jalapeño in the cavity as well. Add fresh herbs if you have them on hand. Truss the chicken with kitchen twine and place on a rack in a flameproof roasting pan. Using a pastry brush, coat the chicken with the Tabasco. Season with the remaining salt and black pepper.

ROAST for 20 minutes. You will probably hear sizzling. Baste the chicken with the butter and turn the oven temperature down to 350°F. Roast until the chicken is done (the skin should be brown and the legs will wiggle easily), 35 to 40 minutes more.

REMOVE the chicken from the oven and allow it to rest for 10 minutes. Lower the oven temperature to 250°F. Cut the chicken into 8 pieces and place on an oven-safe platter or baking sheet. Reserve the cooking juices in the roasting pan and set aside. Put the platter in the oven to keep warm.

TO make the sauce, skim as much of the grease as possible from the juices in the roasting pan. Put the pan on top of the stove over high heat. Carefully add the wine to the pan: It may spit and flare, so use caution. Bring the sauce to a boil while whisking or scraping the bottom of the pan with a spatula to incorporate all the browned bits. Add the giblet stock bit by bit, bringing the sauce to a boil each time. Stir constantly for about 6 minutes, or until the sauce has thickened to your liking. (You might not need all the stock; freeze the leftover stock for another use.)

REMOVE the sauce from the heat and whisk in the remaining 1 tablespoon butter until it is completely incorporated.

ARRANGE the chicken on a serving platter and pour some of the sauce over it. Serve the remaining sauce in a gravy boat at the table.

"YELLOW-LEGGED" FRIED CHICKEN

BEAUMONT INN

HARRODSBURG, KY

A historic bed-and-breakfast in the heart of the bluegrass region, the Beaumont Inn has been serving their famous "yellow-legged" fried chicken for almost a century. The chicken got its name from the owner's grandmother, who swore that yellow-legged chickens were the tastiest. It's likely, however, that it's not the color of the birds that make the Beaumont Inn's fried chicken so crisp, flaky, and moist, but rather the way it's prepared: generously salted, flour-dredged, and then pan-fried in hot, melted lard. You can find lard in many grocery stores, but it's worth the extra effort to find a butcher or specialty merchant that sells lard that's not hydrogenated. If that's not available, you can buy pork fat from a good butcher or pig farmer and render it yourself. To do so, chill at least 2 pounds of pork fat before finely shredding it in the food processor. Place the shredded pork fat in a heavy-bottomed pot with a cup or so of water and cook it down over very low heat. It should take about 3 hours for the fat to melt; strain the melted fat to remove the cracklings and pour the rendered fat into a heatproof jar. It will keep for months in the refrigerator.

SERVES 4

1 (3- to 4-pound) whole chicken, cut into 6 pieces (legs, thighs, and breasts with wing attached), backbone and wing tips removed

Kosher salt

1 pound lard

3 cups all-purpose flour, sifted

THOROUGHLY and roughly rub each chicken piece with salt. Set aside.

IN a 12-inch cast-iron skillet or heavy-bottomed frying pan, heat the lard to 325°F over medium-high heat.

PLACE the flour in a shallow baking dish. Heavily dredge the chicken pieces in the flour, shaking off the excess. Working in batches if necessary to avoid crowding the pan, use tongs to place the chicken pieces in the hot fat, skin-side down. Fry for 10 minutes, then turn and fry for an additional 8 to 10 minutes, or until the interior temperature reaches 165°F and the skin is crispy and golden brown. Drain on a wire rack or paper towels and serve.

ITALIAN MEATBALLS

DOE'S EAT PLACE

GREENVILLE, MS

"This is a family-style restaurant. People come together, never meet a stranger, and it's the American way," says co-owner Shug Signa of Doe's Eat Place. And in fact, in the establishment's early days, when it was little more than a grocery store with a limited menu of takeout options, some diners ate their meals at a small table in the kitchen of what was still the Signa family home. Soon couches and beds gave way to tables and chairs and Doe's Eat Place the restaurant was born. Italian recipes like this one, which will feed a crowd, have kept customers coming back for generations. The combination of ground beef and pork and the addition of Pecorino Romano make these hearty meatballs intensely flavorful. Pair with spaghetti and your favorite tomato sauce.

MAKES 32 MEATBALLS; SERVES 10 TO 12

3 pounds ground beef

1 pound ground pork

1 medium yellow onion, finely diced (about 1½ cups)

1½ cups freshly grated Pecorino Romano

1 cup Italian bread crumbs

5 large eggs, beaten

½ cup chopped fresh flat-leaf parsley

6 garlic cloves, minced

2 tablespoons salt

1 tablespoon freshly ground black pepper

Vegetable oil for frying

IN a large bowl, gently mix the beef, pork, onion, cheese, bread crumbs, eggs, parsley, garlic, salt, and pepper until evenly combined. Roll into balls about 2 inches in diameter.

HEAT 1 inch of oil over medium-high heat in a large, heavy skillet. Working in batches, fry the meatballs until golden brown on all sides and cooked through, turning once or twice with tongs, about 5 minutes on each side. Remove with tongs or a slotted spatula and drain on paper towels before serving.

The first item sold at Doe's Eat Place in Greenville, Mississippi: hot tamales.

GREEK-STYLE SNAPPER

THE BRIGHT STAR

BESSEMER, AL

When it first opened in 1915, the Bright Star welcomed diners around the clock, serving doughnuts, soup, hamburgers, and chili to folks from nearby mining towns. In the 1930s, the restaurant started bringing in fresh snapper, and this simple, Greek-inspired entrée was put on the menu. The snapper fillets are drizzled with melted butter before being pan-fried and finished with a citrusy, oregano-infused vinaigrette. Current owners Jimmy Koikos and Nicky Koikos recommend buying a whole snapper and portioning it yourself (in fact, one of the dishes the Bright Star has become known for is fried snapper throats, a delicious example of culinary economy). For those who are less intrepid, precut fillets will do just fine.

SERVES 6

Juice of 3 lemons

1 tablespoon dried oregano

1 teaspoon salt, plus more for seasoning

¼ teaspoon freshly ground black pepper, plus more for seasoning

1 cup extra-virgin olive oil

6 (8-ounce) snapper fillets

½ cup (1 stick) unsalted butter, melted

½ cup all-purpose flour

6 tablespoons vegetable or canola oil

TO make the sauce, whisk together the lemon juice, oregano, salt, and pepper in a medium bowl. While whisking, slowly pour the olive oil into the lemon mixture, until emulsified.

PLACE the snapper fillets on a large plate and drizzle with the melted butter, coating each fillet evenly. Lightly dust each fillet with flour on both sides and season with salt and pepper.

IN a heavy skillet or on a griddle, heat 2 tablespoons of the vegetable oil over medium-high heat. Working in batches, add two snapper fillets to the skillet and cook until lightly browned, about 5 minutes per side. Remove to a warm plate. Repeat with the remaining fillets, heating additional vegetable oil in the skillet as needed before cooking each batch.

POUR the sauce over the fish and serve immediately.

RABO ENCENDIDO
OXTAIL STEW

VERSAILLES

MIAMI, FL

The secret to this rich, hearty stew is low-and-slow cooking—the oxtails are simmered for hours until the tender meat falls off the bone. Versailles used to offer this dish as an occasional special, but it was so popular with native Cubans hungry for a taste of childhood that the restaurant added it to the daily menu. The stew can be made a day or two ahead of time; in fact it'll taste better if left to sit in the refrigerator overnight before serving. Pair with yellow rice and black beans.

SERVES 6 TO 8

3 pounds bone-in oxtails, about 2 inches thick, trimmed of all visible fat

2 teaspoons salt, or more to taste

1 teaspoon freshly ground black pepper, or more to taste

1 tablespoon all-purpose flour

3 tablespoons olive oil

2 large onions, finely diced (about 3 cups)

1 large green bell pepper, coarsely chopped (about 1 cup)

4 garlic cloves, minced

2 cups crushed tomatoes

1 cup dry red wine

1 cup beef stock

¼ cup dry white wine

1 tablespoon red wine vinegar

1 bay leaf

½ teaspoon dried oregano

½ teaspoon ground cumin

½ cup pimento-stuffed olives

¼ cup chopped fresh flat-leaf parsley (optional)

SEASON the oxtails with 1 teaspoon of the salt and ½ teaspoon of the black pepper. Toss the oxtails with the flour in a bowl to dredge lightly on all sides; set aside.

HEAT the oil in a Dutch oven or a large heavy-bottomed pot over medium-high heat. Working in small batches, sear the oxtails until browned on all sides, about 7 minutes total. Transfer the seared oxtails to a plate and set aside.

REDUCE the heat to medium and add the onions, bell pepper, and garlic. Sauté until the vegetables are tender, about 5 minutes. Add the tomatoes and cook for another 5 minutes. Add the red wine, stock, white wine, vinegar, bay leaf, oregano, cumin, and remaining 1 teaspoon salt and ½ teaspoon black pepper. Bring to a slow boil over medium-high heat. Add the oxtails, reduce the heat to low, cover, and simmer for 2 hours. Add the olives and continue cooking, covered, until the meat is falling off the bones, 30 to 45 minutes.

ADJUST the seasoning to taste. Remove and discard the bay leaf. Garnish with chopped parsley, if desired, and serve.

SOUTHERN GREENS

ARNOLD'S COUNTRY KITCHEN

NASHVILLE, TN

These tender, smoky greens are made wi[th a] base, a concentrated ham stock (sort of [like] chicken bouillon, but made with ham), w[ith] an extra layer of smoky flavor. It can be omitted if unavailable, or you could use pork stock in place of the water. The recipe calls for collard and turnip greens, but any combination of leafy greens (kale, mustard greens, Swiss chard) would also work well. Once cooked, the ham hock can be pulled apart and mixed in with the greens or reserved for another use.

SERVES 4

3 ounces applewood-smoked bacon, chopped into ½-inch pieces

1 (8- to 12-ounce) smoked ham hock

1 yellow onion, chopped (about 1½ cups)

3 tablespoons rendered bacon fat or vegetable oil

1 turnip, peeled and chopped into ½-inch pieces (about 1½ cups)

¼ cup prepared horseradish

1 tablespoon ham base (optional)

3 tablespoons sugar

1 tablespoon salt

2 teaspoons freshly ground black pepper

1 teaspoon red pepper flakes

1 pound collard greens, washed, stemmed, and chopped (about 6 cups)

1 pound turnip greens, washed, stemmed, and chopped (about 6 cups)

> "Nashville's a pretty small community—it's like one big family, really. Everybody knows somebody, and no matter what industry you're in, they all come here and eat."
>
> – KAHLIL ARNOLD,
> Arnold's Country Kitchen
> in Nashville, TN

IN a large, heavy pot, cook the bacon, ham hock, and onion in the rendered bacon fat, over medium heat until the onion is translucent, 5 to 6 minutes. Add the turnip, horseradish, ham base, sugar, salt, black pepper, red pepper flakes, and 6 cups water and stir to combine.

ADD the greens and simmer, partially covered, over medium heat until the greens and turnips are tender and the ham hock pulls apart easily, about 2½ hours, stirring occasionally. If necessary, add more water. The longer the greens cook down, the more flavor they'll have. Taste for seasoning and serve immediately.

LEMONADE COOLER

HANSEN'S SNO-BLIZ

NEW ORLEANS, LA

Drizzled over shaved-to-order ice, sweet-tart lemonade syrup makes a refreshing summer treat, but it can also be mixed with sparkling water for a simple but utterly satisfying homemade soda. Proprietor Ashley Hansen prefers to use fragrant Meyer lemons when they're in season.

SERVES 4

1 lemon
1¼ cups simple syrup (recipe follows)

Sparkling water
Sweetened condensed milk or whipped cream (optional)

USING a Microplane or other fine grater, zest the lemon. Cut the lemon in half and use a reamer or juicer to extract the juice. In a large liquid measuring cup, stir together the zest, juice, and simple syrup.

FILL four tall glasses with ice and fill each halfway with the lemon mixture. Add a splash of sparkling water to each and top with condensed milk or whipped cream, if desired.

SIMPLE SYRUP

MAKES ABOUT 1½ CUPS

Make a double batch of this versatile sweetener to use in cocktails and iced tea or coffee. Keep extra syrup in a glass jar in the refrigerator for up to a month.

1 cup granulated sugar

COMBINE the sugar with 1 cup water in a small saucepan and bring to a boil. Simmer until the sugar has dissolved, stirring occasionally, about 3 minutes. Remove from the heat and let cool completely.

Ernest Hansen of Hansen's Sno-Bliz built one of the first electric ice-shaving machines, receiving a patent from the U.S. government for his creation in 1934.

"EF'S BIG LIE" BANANA PUDDING

BOWENS ISLAND RESTAURANT

CHARLESTON, SC

Bowens Island insiders swear by this creamy layered dessert, which is the perfect ending to a meal of the scenic spot's locally harvested oysters, fried shrimp, hushpuppies, and cold beer. The dish was created by chef Robert Barber's wife, LaNelle, who combined two recipes in a local South Carolina cookbook to replicate a dish described by a friend; food writer Jane Kronsberg published a version of this recipe in her 1997 book, *Charleston: People, Places, and Food*. It's not hard to imagine where the dish gets its name; made with instant vanilla pudding and Cool Whip, the dessert requires assembly more than it does cooking. (We prefer it made with whipped cream, but the restaurant swears by Cool Whip.) But when the dish is this good your guests won't care that you took a few shortcuts—and, better yet, they never need to know.

SERVES 6 TO 8

2 (3.4-ounce) packages instant vanilla pudding

3 cups whole milk

3 cups whipped heavy cream, or 1 (12-ounce) container Cool Whip

1 (8-ounce) container sour cream

2 teaspoons vanilla extract

1 (11-ounce) box vanilla wafers

6 ripe bananas, peeled and sliced into ¼-inch-thick disks

Spray-painted on the side of the cinder-block bunker that houses Bowens Island Restaurant are portraits of Jimmy Bowen and Sarah May Bowen, the husband-and-wife team who bought the island in the 1940s.

COMBINE the pudding mix and milk in a medium bowl. Using a rubber spatula, fold in 2 cups of the whipped cream (or half of the Cool Whip), the sour cream, and vanilla extract.

LINE the bottom of a 9-by-13-inch baking pan with a layer of vanilla wafers. Top with a layer of bananas and a layer of pudding. Repeat layers. Top with the remaining whipped cream or Cool Whip.

COVER and refrigerate for at least 2 hours before serving.

ATLANTIC BEACH PIE

CROOK'S CORNER

CHAPEL HILL, NC

Similar to a key lime pie, this citrusy dessert boasts a crisp, golden crust made of crushed crackers, which gives each bite just the right touch of salt. Many seafood restaurants on the North Carolina coast serve a version of the dish, but chef Bill Smith tops his with fresh whipped cream rather than the more traditional meringue. The result is a showstopping finale made from, as Smith puts it, "the easiest recipe in the world."

SERVES 10 TO 12

1½ sleeves Saltine crackers

3 tablespoons sugar

½ cup (1 stick) unsalted butter, at room temperature

1 (14-ounce) can sweetened condensed milk

4 large egg yolks

½ cup fresh lemon juice or lime juice (or a mix of the two)

Fresh whipped cream

Coarse sea salt

PREHEAT the oven to 350°F.

USING clean hands or a food processor, crush the crackers finely, but not to dust. Put the cracker crumbs in a medium bowl and add the sugar, stirring to combine. Using your fingers, knead in the butter until the crumbs hold together like dough. Press the crumbs into a 9-inch pie pan to cover the bottom. Chill for 15 minutes.

TRANSFER the pie pan from the refrigerator to the oven and bake until the crust begins to color, about 18 minutes. Set the crust aside.

IN a medium bowl, beat the condensed milk and egg yolks with a whisk to combine. Add the lemon juice and whisk until thoroughly combined. Pour the filling mixture into the pie shell (the crust need not be completely cooled) and bake until the filling has set, about 16 minutes.

LET cool to room temperature, then put in the refrigerator to chill (the pie needs to be completely cold before slicing). Top the chilled pie with whipped cream and a sprinkling of coarse sea salt.

The Award Winners

ARNOLD'S COUNTRY KITCHEN

605 8th Avenue South
Nashville, TN
Owners: Jack and Rose Arnold
2009 AWARD WINNER

Co-owner Jack Arnold, who favors overalls and foulard bow ties, began his restaurant career as a dishwasher at the age of twelve. While studying art at Vanderbilt University, he managed the campus cafeteria. By 1983 he had his own place, Arnold's Country Kitchen, a concrete block building outfitted with a steam table and a tray line. Along with his wife, Rose, and his son Kahlil, Jack has won a citywide reputation for excellence in meat-and-three fare. Although he roasts a beautiful haunch of beef, vegetables are Arnold's specialty. His long-simmered greens, perfectly crisp fried green tomatoes, and tender cornbread have won the allegiance of downtown business types, country-music show folks, and workaday Nashvillians alike.

BEAUMONT INN

638 Beaumont Inn Drive
Harrodsburg, KY
Owners: Dedman family
2015 AWARD WINNER

Founded by Glave Goddard and Annie Bell Goddard in 1917, the Beaumont Inn, which opened for business in 1919, is still operated by their descendants. Set in a former women's college built in 1845, the Beaumont main house is columned and formal. And the menu is deeply rooted in Kentucky. The Dedman family, now at the helm, serves Kentucky products with pride, including Weisenberger meal, Meacham hams, and bourbons from the best distillers in the state. Recipes for dishes like corn pudding and fried chicken, handed down through five generations, form the core of the menu. As their forebears did, the Dedmans serve two-year-old country ham, which they bring to maturation in their own aging house. Little has changed since the days when the pioneering critic Duncan Hines was a regular.

"Now write this down for the people in Kentucky," he told a reporter back in 1949. "[Say] I'll be happy to get home and eat two-year-old ham, cornbread, beaten biscuits, pound cake, yellow-leg fried chicken, and corn pudding. And you can say what I think is the best eating place in Kentucky: Beaumont Inn at Harrodsburg."

BOWENS ISLAND RESTAURANT

1870 Bowens Island Road
Charleston, SC
Owner: Robert Barber
2006 AWARD WINNER

Drive the lane that branches off the road from Charleston to Folly Beach, South Carolina, and as you wend your way through a thicket of palmettos onto Bowens Island, you'll spy a dock jutting into the marsh. At the heart of the island is a restaurant, a cinder-block bunker ringed by oyster middens. Decorations include decommissioned televisions scrawled with graffiti, a jukebox or two, and a rusted-out blow-dryer liberated from a beauty parlor. Spray-painted on the side of the building are portraits of Jimmy Bowen and Sarah May Bowen, the husband-and-wife team who in the 1940s bought the island and, in what seemed a quixotic move, constructed their own causeway leading to the mainland. Alongside is an aerosol-rendered likeness of John Sanka, the cook who worked with the Bowens for more than thirty years. Generations of Charlestonians have made the pilgrimage to sit at tables covered with yesterday's newspaper and piled high with today's catch. They come for plump oysters pulled from local waters and served without pretense. Present-day proprietor Robert Barber, a grandson of the Bowens', takes his responsibility seriously; he and his staff serve as guardians of Bowen family tradition and curators of imperiled Carolina folkways. In those roles, they dish the house specialty: clusters of oysters, harvested by hand from the Folly River, steamed on a gas-fired griddle under cover of a burlap sack, heaped by the shovelful onto *Charleston Post* and *Courier* place mats, and washed down with cold beer.

The Bright Star

"You've got to have
good employees to have
a good restaurant. And I
am so proud of these people that
have been here so long."

– JIMMY KOIKOS,
The Bright Star in Bessemer, AL

THE BRIGHT STAR

304 19th Street North
Bessemer, AL
Owners: Jimmy Koikos and Nicky Koikos
2010 AWARD WINNER

See page 16.

CROOK'S CORNER

610 West Franklin Street
Chapel Hill, NC
Owner: Gene Hamer
2011 AWARD WINNER

Hubcaps decorate the flanks of the corner building on the fringe of this college town. A pink fiberglass pig stands atop the roof. The dining room does double-duty as an art gallery. From the bar, you can order a cracker plate, piled with housemade pimento cheese and a block of cream cheese smeared with pepper jelly. Since 1982, when restaurateur Gene Hamer and chef Bill Neal opened the doors, Crook's Corner has carried the torch of regional food culture, employing and inspiring a generation of young culinary talent—including two James Beard Award–winning chefs. Bill Neal was one of the first American chefs to explore the cultural import of the regional food he worked to revive. He brought academic rigor and provincial pride to the professional restaurant kitchens of the region. Since Neal's untimely death in 1991, Gene Hamer has served as the restaurant's steward, while Bill Smith has overseen the kitchen, cooking iconic Crook's dishes like shrimp and grits, hoppin' John, and persimmon pudding. In more recent years, Smith, a two-time James Beard Award finalist, has transformed the menu by way of his own flourishes, including house-corned ham, gumbo z'herbes, and honeysuckle sorbet.

DOE'S EAT PLACE

502 Nelson Street
Greenville, MS
Owners: Signa family
2007 AWARD WINNER

Located in Greenville on Nelson Street, this family-owned and -operated restaurant is an icon of the culinary and cultural landscape of the Mississippi Delta.

Doe's Eat Place tells the complicated story of Italian immigration, Delta foodways, and Mississippi social history. In 1941, the restaurant's founder, Dominick "Doe" Signa, took over his father's grocery store, where he began selling hot tamales (made from a recipe taught to him by a former coworker at the Greenville Air Base) to the neighborhood's largely African American clientele. As word spread, more and more people came calling for Doe's tamales, as well as traditional Italian fare such as spaghetti and meatballs. The restaurant eventually transformed itself into a casual steak joint that served both the African American and white communities in segregated Mississippi. Pivotal during the civil rights era, Doe's Eat Place has become a symbol of the region's multiracial culture. Today, Signa family members remain at the helm of this legendary Delta haunt.
.

HANSEN'S SNO-BLIZ

4801 Tchoupitoulas Street
New Orleans, LA
Owner: Ashley Hansen
2014 AWARD WINNER

The snowball, one of the city's iconic desserts, was practically invented at Hansen's. Made of shaved-to-order ice, a Hansen's snowball—which the family calls a Sno-Bliz—comes doused in housemade syrups that run an extraordinary gamut of flavors. Ernest Hansen built one of the first electric ice-shaving machines, receiving a patent from the U.S. government for his creation in 1934. Along with his wife, Mary Hansen, he opened a small shop in 1939. Their granddaughter, Ashley Hansen, runs that shop today and carefully crafts the family syrup recipes, which include blueberry, satsuma, root beer, and the mysterious "cream of nectar." Like her forebears, Ashley Hansen opens her doors only during the summer. When Hansen's is open, a queue forever spills out its door and snakes back through the stand's small interior, following a painted yellow line known to regulars as the yellow brick road. Eventually that line leads to the counter, where a crew of young workers takes orders, shaves ice, douses cones, and cultivates a diverse community, one treat at a time.

JOE'S STONE CRAB

11 Washington Avenue
Miami Beach, FL
Owner: Jo Ann Weiss
1998 AWARD WINNER

Joe's Stone Crab has been a Miami Beach tradition since 1918. Hungarian-born, New York–bred Joe and Jennie Weiss opened the original Miami Beach restaurant in a side-street bungalow with seven or eight tables on the porch. After World War I, the Beach took off and so did Joe's Restaurant, when, in 1921, Joe Weiss discovered that Biscayne Bay stone crab claws contain memorably delicious, uniquely tender sweet meat. Within a year or two, tourists joined locals waiting in line at this shrine to the claw. They've been there ever since, and the family's third and fourth generations still serve platters of cracked crab claws along with mustard sauce, melted butter, hash browns, coleslaw, and key lime pie.

Joe's Stone Crab

JONES BAR-B-Q DINER

219 West Louisiana Street
Marianna, AR
Owners: James Jones and Betty Jones
2012 AWARD WINNER

Some incarnation of Jones Bar-B-Q Diner, one of the oldest African American–owned restaurants in the country, has been open since at least the 1910s. Walter Jones, the founder and first pitmaster, lived in a dogtrot house perched nearby. From the back porch, he served barbecue on Fridays and Saturdays. Hubert Jones, the son of Walter Jones and father of present-day proprietor James Jones, recalled the family's initial barbecue setup as "a hole in the ground, some iron pipes and a piece of fence wire, and two pieces of tin." Today the still-bare-bones joint remains true to those roots. James Jones tends the pits. His cooking apparatus is still elemental. And the pork shoulder, hacked into savory bits and served on white bread with a spritz of vinegary sauce, is as smoky as ever. In the Delta town of Marianna, not far from the Mississippi River, Jones Bar-B-Q Diner is a beacon of community pride and continuity.

LEXINGTON BARBECUE #1

100 Smokehouse Lane
Lexington, NC
Owner: Wayne Monk
2003 AWARD WINNER

North Carolina has two emblematic styles of barbecue, and one is named after the town of Lexington, which is located in the Piedmont, far to the west, between Winston-Salem and Charlotte. You'll know why when you drive into town; the whole place smells sweetly of wood smoke and roasting pork. At one time, a barbecue historian calculated that Lexington had sixteen barbecue emporia, one for every 982 people. Wayne Monk, the proprietor of Lexington #1, is the king of barbecue in Lexington. He can trace his culinary lineage back to the very beginnings of barbecue in the region. Monk learned from Warner Stamey, who bought the business of a certain Jesse Swicegood, who began cooking under tents pitched on a lot across from the Davidson County courthouse, about the time of World War I. Lexington 'cue is newer than its counterpart, Down East 'cue, and it's a whole different proposition, made from pork shoulder only, daubed with a red sauce that includes sugar, vinegar, hot peppers, and ketchup, and served on a bun with a special coleslaw that includes some of the sauce. Most of the customers order hushpuppies on the side, and they're smart to do so. You'll find no better hushpuppies anywhere. No wonder the parking lot starts to fill up with pickups at 10 A.M.

PHOTO: *The Lee Bros. Southern Cookbook*

Cheerwine, a cherry-flavored
soda native to North Carolina,
is a customer favorite at
Lexington Barbecue #1
(and the official soft drink of the
National Barbecue Association).

MOSCA'S

4137 U.S. 90
Avondale, LA
Owners: Mary Jo Mosca and Lisa Mosca
1999 AWARD WINNER

In 1946 Johnny Mosca's father moved the family from Chicago to swampland fifteen miles out of New Orleans and opened a restaurant serving Johnny's grandmother's Italian home cooking. Her Adriatic coast recipes still dominate the short menu today, but over the intervening decades the Moscas have woven a little Bayou State tradition into their own. Locals love shrimp Italian, crabmeat salad, and oyster pie as well as the famous ravioli and whole roasted chicken. The doors did close in the wake of Hurricane Katrina in 2005, but reopened shortly thereafter without change to the beloved Mosca formula. Owners Mary Mosca Marconi and Johnny Mosca passed away in 2010 and 2011, respectively, but Johnny's wife and daughter, Mary Jo Mosca and Lisa Mosca, have kept the restaurant under family ownership. Don't hurry once you trek to this long-standing favorite. As Johnny Mosca told us in 1999, "It takes time to cook our food, and luckily, people want to wait."

MRS. WILKES DINING ROOM

107 West Jones Street
Savannah, GA
Owner: Ryon Thompson
2000 AWARD WINNER

Lunch at Mrs. Wilkes is one of the great culinary bargains in this land. From your seat at a bountiful table-for-eight, you reach out and help yourself to fried chicken, oven-hot biscuits, and a panoply of magnificently cooked vegetables that all add up to a good précis of Deep South boarding house cuisine. We imagine that when Mrs. Wilkes first started serving meals in this dining room in 1943, there were many similar places in cities throughout the region, where boarders as well as frugal local citizens gathered at communal tables to enjoy the special pleasure of a meal shared with neighbors and strangers. Now, the take-some-and-pass-the-bowl style of the old boarding house is a rarity.

Mrs. Seema Wilkes's establishment in the 1870-vintage red-brick building on West Jones Street is a prized opportunity to indulge in the delicious food—and the cordial foodways—of a culinary tradition that values sociability as much as a good macaroni salad. As ever, there is no sign to indicate you can lunch at Mrs. Wilkes. "It would look so commercial," she once wrote, "not at all like home." Besides, everybody in Savannah knows exactly where it is.

PRINCE'S HOT CHICKEN SHACK

123 Ewing Drive
Nashville, TN
Owner: André Prince Jeffries
2013 AWARD WINNER

See page 14.

SALLY BELL'S KITCHEN

708 West Grace Street
Richmond, VA
Owners: Martha Crowe Jones and Scott Jones
2015 AWARD WINNER

Sarah Cabell Jones met Elizabeth Lee Milton at the Richmond Exchange for Woman's Work. Founded in 1883, the Richmond Exchange sold handmade goods produced by women. Jones and Milton opened Sally Bell's Kitchen (then called Sarah Lee Kitchen) in 1924. By 1985, Martha Crowe Jones, the fourth-generation family proprietor, had taken the reins. Each generation of Jones women has proved a faithful steward of this beacon of female entrepreneurship. Sally Bell's is a take-away operation. Step to the counter and order a chicken salad or egg salad sandwich, among other options. The counterwoman will hand you a white pasteboard box tied with twine. Inside, along with your order, will be a paper cup of potato salad or macaroni salad, a deviled egg wrapped in tissue, a cheese wafer crowned with a pecan, and a cupcake enrobed in glaze. All will taste like someone's grandmother made them. Nine decades after it first opened, Sally Bell's still excels at handmade goods, prepared by industrious women.

THE SKYLIGHT INN

4618 South Lee Street
Ayden, NC
Owners: Bruce Jones and Sam Jones
2003 AWARD WINNER

"Down East," as they say in Carolina, they cook the whole hog, pick the meat off the bone, chop it, and serve it with a thin, hot, vinegar-based sauce. No tomatoes in there, and no ketchup. Never. One of the oldest family traditions in the state is the barbecue business in the little town of Ayden, between Greenville and Kinston, owned and operated by Walter B. "Pete" Jones and his family. Known as the Skylight Inn, it is the lineal descendant of the enterprise started by Pete's great-great-grandfather, Skilton Dennis, in 1830, back when Ayden was known as Otter Town. Skilton Dennis cooked pigs over hardwood coals in a pit in his backyard and took his barbecue to town on a covered wagon. Today, when gas cookers have replaced wood fires in most barbecue joints, the Skylight Inn stands with tradition. "If it's not cooked with wood," said Pete Jones in 2003, "it's not barbecue." In 1979, *National Geographic* magazine proclaimed that "The Skylight Inn has the best barbecue in the nation," and the local folks like it fine too. In 1960, at the age of nine, Pete's son, Bruce, started working in the business and he took over its operation, along with his own son, Samuel, after Pete's death in 2006. The Joneses, who serve their meat with flat cornbread, say they aim to keep the tradition of Down East 'cue alive way past their bicentennial in 2030.

> "I heard my grandfather many times saying that at an early age he knew barbecue was in his blood. Pigs was always his passion, you know, and his restaurant wasn't a job to him. It was a way of life."
>
> —SAMUEL JONES,
> The Skylight Inn in Ayden, NC

VERSAILLES

3555 SW 8th Street
Miami, FL
Owner: Felipe Valls Jr.
2001 AWARD WINNER

In a city that boasts over two hundred Cuban restaurants, how has one establishment with an unlikely French name managed to stay in business for over forty years, serving approximately ten thousand customers week in and week out? Maybe people are drawn to its down-to-earth menu featuring generous plates of authentic home-style classics like *masitas de puerco* (fried pork chunks) with *moros* (black beans and rice) and *plátanos maduros* (fried ripe plantains), or *ropa vieja* (shredded beef in tomato sauce) with white rice and tostones (fried unripened plantains). The restaurant is, and always has been, family-run. Felipe Valls Sr., a Cuban exile, opened the original thirty-five-seat café after earning enough money selling used restaurant equipment to start his own place. Originally he planned to create an upscale Cuban restaurant, and the name Versailles seemed to strike just the right sophisticated note. Cubans knew the name well because the island nation's treaty of independence from Spain was signed at Versailles in 1898. Today, the restaurant has expanded tenfold—it has 350 seats, a separate bakery, and an outdoor coffee stand. It may be bigger, but, happily, its lively energy, irresistible coffee, and true Little Havana spirit remain the same as ever.

WILLIE MAE'S SCOTCH HOUSE

2401 St. Ann Street
New Orleans, LA
Owner: Kerry Seaton
2005 AWARD WINNER

See page 18.

Willie Mae's Scotch House

NORTHEAST

TOTONNO'S

BROOKLYN, NY

2009 AWARD WINNER

A stone's throw from the Cyclone in Coney Island, Totonno's has been serving Neapolitan-style pies for more than ninety years. One of New York's first pizzaiolos, Anthony "Totonno" Pero, left his job making pizzas at Lombardi's in 1924 to open his own pizzeria, and his new enterprise, Totonno's, has been in his family ever since. Fourth-generation owners and siblings Antoinette Balzano, Frank Balzano, and Cookie Ciminieri have had to deal with more than their fair share of hardships in recent years: In 2009 a fire forced the restaurant to close for several months for substantial refurbishment. And in 2012 Hurricane Sandy hit the beloved neighborhood institution with four feet of water, flooding the dining room and kitchen, which had to be completely renovated. Despite weathering these difficulties, today's owners remain as committed to their family business as ever. And throughout it all, the restaurant has stayed true to the original recipe. Each pizza is made with imported Italian tomatoes, locally made mozzarella, yeast, flour, salt, and not much else. The last—and arguably most important—component is the oven. Totonno's original coal-fired oven creates a distinct and flavorful char on the crust that cult pizza lovers crave.

GRANDPA STARTED THIS RESTAURANT. His name was Anthony Pero—"Totonno" was his nickname from Italy. They told us when we were growing up that it meant "Little Anthony." He came to America on a ship in 1903, and he went to work in Lombardi's, a grocery store in Little Italy. Grandpa had been a baker back in Naples, and he started making pizza at Lombardi's. It became the first licensed pizzeria in America—Grandpa was the first pizzaiolo. He opened his restaurant here in 1924. We were celebrating last month—ninety years! Same family, same location.

Grandpa had four children, and one of them was my mother. My mother had three children: my sister, Cookie, my brother, and me. We own the restaurant now. When we were younger, we'd come here every day during the week. My aunt Julia and uncle Jerry would cook—they were great cooks. I was a teacher, but I'd still work at the restaurant from time to time. When I worked here nobody got the right pies, nobody got the right pizzas. People didn't care—they love us. It's delicious.

My sister, Cookie, was at the restaurant all the time, and I just filled in sometimes. I really got involved after we had the fire in 2009. March 14, 2009. My brother, Frankie, and I were in church for the anniversary of my father's death. The phone is ringing off the wall while I'm in church, and it's Cookie. I come running here—ambulances, fire trucks, hoses, no windows. Thankfully nobody was hurt. An ember from the coal got loose and it was a wood floor under the oven, but we didn't know that. The oven's here for I don't know how many years, and never a problem until then. For eleven months we were closed.

We opened back up with a big ceremony. John Kuse and the Excellents singing "Coney Island Baby." I had balloons outside, I had streamers, I had these tables set up with all kinds of food and desserts. The mayor came. He pulls up and I had a band outside singing "New York, New York." The whole neighborhood's there. Mayor Bloomberg came and sliced pizza for us. It was the most wonderful thing.

A year and five months later, we had superstorm Sandy. From what I hear, before that, we never, ever got a drop of water here. The ocean is one, two, three major blocks away. But we have the creek. We got the creek and the ocean, and they met. There was no electricity. Our big radio was down on the floor, everything was floating. We had this black soot. I cleaned and cleaned, I'm telling you, for days and days after and we opened after five months. When you have a fire, you can still get your employees. But after Sandy, you call up and hear, "I'll be there in an hour," then "I'll be there tomorrow," then "I got stuck in the Rockaways." It was challenging. Draining.

But now we're open again, and people keep coming back. I think it's the passion we have. That and consistency. After the fire they wanted to put all these wires in the walls. Cookie would do none of that. She wouldn't change a thing. The ingredients are the best. There's nothing frozen. We throw out the dough at the end of the night if it's left over. If my sister sees a can of tomatoes when they're delivered, if there's this much of a dent, out goes the can. The cheese, if there's one dot of some moisture—that goes back. The passion she puts into it—she watches every pie that goes out. She's working her butt off, and we have to do it because that man, our grandpa, Anthony Pero, came over on a boat in steerage, probably on the bottom of the boat. We're trying to keep that name alive.

—ANTOINETTE BALZANO

- -

"When I worked here nobody got the right pies, nobody got the right pizzas. People didn't care–they love us. It's delicious."

– ANTOINETTE BALZANO,
Totonno's in Brooklyn, NY

- -

BEN'S CHILI BOWL

WASHINGTON, D.C.

2004 AWARD WINNER

HOT DOG
S THE HOUSE THAT QUALITY BUILT

In a city packed with monuments, Ben's Chili Bowl stands as one of Washington's most cherished. What began in 1958 as a place to drop by for conversation and maybe a bite to eat before an evening with Duke Ellington or Cab Calloway on "Black Broadway" has survived race riots, drug wars, subway construction, and now gentrification to become a landmark every bit as important to the nation's capital as what you might find on its Mall. You haven't lived in Washington until you've dipped your spoon into a bowl of spicy chili or bitten into a plump half-smoke (a snappy pork-and-beef sausage) at the iconic eatery. Just ask the many celebrities who drop by whenever they're in town, or the construction workers who show up in the morning, or the hipsters who pack in late at night. Or better yet, ask anyone who aspires to public office here, like avid fan Barack Obama, who has been immortalized in a mural alongside the U Street storefront. Straight and gay, black and white, old and young, rich and poor— everyone is made to feel welcome at this eclectic family reunion. Still furnished with its original booths, counter, and stools, Ben's Chili Bowl has edged past sixty years—an eternity in the fickle restaurant business— but since the 2009 death of owner Ben Ali the D.C. landmark has been run by Ben's wife, Virginia, and his three grown sons. These days Ben's has more room to accommodate their patrons at Ben's Next Door, which serves a completely different menu, and at an outpost at the Washington Nationals stadium. Ben's longtime ad boasted, "Our chili will make your hot dog bark!"—and a local's heart sing, the restaurant's many fans would be quick to add.

MY HUSBAND, BEN, WAS FROM TRINIDAD. He came to this country to matriculate at the University of Nebraska, Lincoln, and he worked his way through school by working in restaurants. He came to Washington, D.C., to attend Howard University's Dental School, but he had a serious injury—he injured his back so severely he wasn't able to complete the program. He worked in restaurants the entire time he was in school, starting with mopping the floors and doing the dishes and so on, and worked himself up to being maître d'. He really learned the restaurant business. When we met and decided to marry, the best thing to go into, to find a way to make a living and raise a family, was to open a restaurant, which we did in 1958.

When we opened, I was to be the cashier, or the dayshift manager, and all that. As the owner of a restaurant, you do everything, from serving to managing to ordering to banking—the whole nine yards.

The 1960s were a very crazy time. When Dr. Martin Luther King Jr. was assassinated, the news spread quite rapidly, as did the anger. This man was a man of peace and nonviolence, and to die so violently . . . I think so many people, especially so many young people, they just didn't know how to handle their frustration. So they began the looting, and the rioting, and burning down buildings, and that kind of thing. Our mayor at the time put a curfew into effect, which meant young folks could not be in the street after 8 o'clock at night or so. We were asked to remain open so that there could be a place for city officials, police officers, and activists to come together to try to find a way to quell the violence. Our night-shift employees were given passes and during those days we were open until 3 o'clock in the morning. It was a very scary time, of course. Tear gas everywhere, the National Guard sitting just outside your door with weapons. It was just a very, very scary time.

But we were able to survive all that, and as I said, we remained open during that period. I think the thing I'm most proud of is that we remained in a community that had supported us so much when we opened, and even supported us in the bad times. After the riots of '68, the middle class moved away. Drugs moved in, a lot of crime moved into the area, but we were never robbed or broken into. I felt like we were very respected by our community. They kind of looked out for us.

We've been blessed with three sons who married three lovely young ladies, and all three sons are currently involved with the business. It's a family affair. One of our employees, we call her Peaches, has been here for thirty-six years. Many have been here fifteen or sixteen years. We're family. Most of them address me as "Mom." I see generation after generation after generation coming. The food is good, and we've always believed that we treat people as we would like to be treated. I think that if you're a provider, if you provide folks with good food, well, there's no reason not to succeed.

—VIRGINIA ALI

Number of different types of fries sold at Ben's Chili Bowl in Washington, D.C.: 5 (French fries, chili fries, cheese fries, chili-cheese fries, and veggie chili-cheese fries).

WATERMAN'S BEACH LOBSTER

SOUTH THOMASTON, ME

2001 AWARD WINNER

For those who believe that lobsters are best consumed within sight of the place where they were harvested, Waterman's Beach Lobster in South Thomaston, Maine, is crustacean nirvana. Founded in the mid-1980s by Anne Cousens, this rustic lobster shack is now run by her daughter, Sandy Manahan, and daughter-in-law, Lorrie Cousens. Out-of-state visitors and locals making the summertime pilgrimage order whole lobsters (steamed, not boiled, for maximum tenderness) that weigh one to four pounds, depending on what Lorrie's husband has caught that day. Some head to the beach to dress picnic tables with tablecloths from home and drink bottles of Sauvignon Blanc or Champagne. Others sit down under the large covered deck, sipping on sweet tea while admiring the gorgeous views of the Penobscot Bay, with the Mussel Ridge Islands in the foreground, while they wait for their trays to be delivered. For lobster roll aficionados, Waterman's serves a winner— large lumps of lobster meat with just enough mayonnaise to hold them together, heaped on a toasted, oversize hamburger bun. Sides include local corn, potato salad, and coleslaw. Impossible to save room for pie? Yes, but go ahead and have some anyway. Blueberry, raspberry (simply berries, sugar, and a marvelously flaky crust), rhubarb, pumpkin, pecan, and lemon sponge appear on a rotating basis, all baked to the "retired" Anne Cousens's exact specifications.

THIS IS OUR TWENTY-EIGHTH SEASON at Waterman's Beach Lobster. My mother-in-law, Anne Cousens, started it and it was just a little, tiny, small place that they decided to turn into a restaurant. Everyone told them what a great view they had! It's right across the street from their house, and they said, "Oh, we might as well try to sell off the dinners." They put out a few picnic tables, and had a really small shack, and Anne was running it mainly by herself. She was getting up at four in the morning and baking her own pies, and then going around and getting all of her supplies and picking up the lobsters, and then running it all day.

Since Sandy and I started, we've made the building a little bigger, and we've added tables, but all in all, my mother-in-law had a great idea from the very start and we've kept it pretty much the same. People say, "Oh, please don't change," and we always say, "We won't." It's working the way it is. People like it. We're happy. We don't plan on changing it.

We provide all the lobsters for the lobster rolls. My husband, David, is a lobsterman, as well as my three sons, so they bring us the lobster. Sandy and I have five sons between us. They are all fishermen. We have nieces and their friends work with us too. It's a close-knit bunch. They've been with us for years. Sandy does the window—she makes people feel welcome. Year after year they're always happy to see her. I do all the cooking and organizing, and make sure every single lobster and clam I cook is perfect. I sometimes have eight different-sized lobsters in eight different pots going at the same time. I honestly could eat lobster for every meal. We probably pick out, I don't know, 100 to 200 pounds some days of lobsters to put into our rolls, and I still love it.

Our restaurant is right on the water. It's beautiful, so we have a lot of tourists. When the tourists come to Maine, the first thing they want is a lobster dinner. All the locals around know that if they have out-of-town guests and they want a lobster dinner, they bring them to us.

People come to us in all different modes of transportation. Yesterday, we had a helicopter land in our field! We had an eighty-six-foot Cabin Cruiser docked out in the harbor here with a captain to shuttle people in. It really is kind of a small, out-of-the-way place, but once people have been here, they definitely tell other people, and they'll go to all lengths to get back.

People will ask us, they'll go, "Oh, so is this sustainable?" The new word is *sustainable*. "Where does this come from?" I can go outside and point out to the water, "See those lobster traps out there? That's where the lobsters come from. See that island out there? That's where the clams are dug. And look up the street at the farm on the water. That's where the rhubarb patch is."

I'm proud that we serve food that's from this region and that it's very healthy. I'm proud to be a part of the family that runs it. We have our kids out in lobster boats right out front, and they stop over. I have Sandy's parents come over, my parents come over. It's a nice feeling of a small community.

—LORRIE COUSENS

Amount of lobster meat picked daily to make the lobster rolls at Waterman's Beach Lobster: 100 to 200 pounds.

Chicken Soup

It's hard to find a more universally comforting dish than chicken soup, a brothy bowl with the power to evoke childhood memories like none other. So many of the cultures that have become a part of America's culinary canvas eat variations of the dish, and consequently, chicken soup lovers can find phenomenal and distinct versions across the country. From the dill-flecked matzoh ball soups of New York City to the green chile–infused stews of New Mexico, chicken soup in all its forms can be found at the center of almost every American table.

Region	Soup	Where to Get It	Words of Wisdom
NORTHEAST	Chicken soup with matzoh balls (page 71)	**2ND AVENUE DELI** New York, NY	Matzoh ball soup is the go-to comfort food of NYC chefs like Andrew Carmellini, and 2nd Avenue Deli makes one of the best versions in the city—and country.
SOUTHEAST	Creole chicken soup	**CROOK'S CORNER** Chapel Hill, NC	Chef Bill Smith adds green peppers, onions, diced tomatoes, garlic, oregano, bay leaves, and a pinch of crushed red pepper to this soup and serves it over a scoop of rice. In the summer okra and corn are thrown in as well; in the winter he'll swap in lima and white beans.
MIDWEST	Chicken noodle soup	**STROUD'S** Kansas City, MO	It's no surprise that a restaurant that specializes in chicken would make a spot-on bowl of good old-fashioned chicken noodle soup. Made with wide, chewy noodles, bright diced carrots, and tender shredded chicken, the hearty, comforting soup has a national following.
SOUTHWEST	Green chile chicken chowder	**THE SHED** Santa Fe, NM	Redolent with roasted New Mexican green chiles, this creamy soup is studded with roast chicken, corn, and carrots and served topped with blue corn tortilla strips.
WEST	Saimin	**HAMURA'S SAIMIN STAND** Lihue, Kauai, HI	A traditional Hawaiian dish, saimin is a soup of thin egg noodles topped with a variety of ingredients—green onions, char siu (Chinese roast pork), Japanese fish cakes, sliced Spam, Portuguese linguiça, and nori—each of which reflect the islands' varied cultural influences. Though the exact recipe at Hamura's Saimin Stand is a closely guarded secret, the owners have shared that the soup's deep broth is made with a combination of chicken stock and dried shrimp.

ITALIAN WEDDING SOUP

JOHN'S ROAST PORK

PHILADELPHIA, PA

Open only from early morning through early afternoon, John's Roast Pork specializes in lunch and has become famous for Philly cheesesteak and its roast pork sandwich, which Andrew Zimmern referred to as "maybe the best sandwich in America." But the shop also makes an excellent Italian wedding soup, a Neapolitan soup made with meat and greens that, as the name implies, "marry" well together. John's Roast Pork's version features a rich chicken broth (using homemade broth will yield a more complex, tastier soup), small, flavorful meatballs, and plenty of spinach. Be careful not to overmix the ground meat mixture, as it will result in tough meatballs.

SERVES 6 TO 8

MEATBALLS

1 pound ground meat (any combination of beef, pork, and veal)

1 large egg

1 large egg yolk

¼ cup plus 2 tablespoons plain dried bread crumbs

¼ cup grated Parmesan cheese

1 large garlic clove, blanched, peeled, and minced

1 teaspoon minced fresh flat-leaf parsley

½ teaspoon salt

½ teaspoon freshly ground black pepper

SOUP

4 cups chicken broth, homemade if possible

1 cup tomato sauce, homemade if possible

1 boneless skinless chicken breast, whole

1 medium carrot, chopped (about ¾ cup)

1 celery rib, chopped

½ medium onion, chopped (about ¾ cup)

1 garlic clove, minced

1 bay leaf

½ teaspoon Italian seasoning, or ¼ teaspoon dried oregano and ¼ teaspoon dried basil

¼ cup uncooked acini di pepe or orzo pasta

½ (10-ounce) package frozen spinach (about 1¼ cups)

2 large eggs

¼ cup grated Parmesan cheese, plus additional for serving

TO MAKE THE MEATBALLS: Preheat the oven to 350°F. Lightly oil a baking sheet.

IN a large bowl, combine the ground meat, whole egg and egg yolk, bread crumbs, cheese, garlic, parsley, salt, and pepper. Stir just to combine (do not overmix).

SHAPE the meat mixture into small meatballs, using about 1 tablespoon for each one (each meatball should be about ¾ inch in diameter), and place on the prepared baking sheet. Bake until the meatballs are lightly browned and firm, about 10 minutes.

TO MAKE THE SOUP: In a large soup pot, combine the broth, 2 cups water, the tomato sauce, chicken breast, carrot, celery, onion, garlic, bay leaf, and Italian seasoning.

Bring to a boil over high heat. Reduce the heat and simmer, partially covered, until the chicken is cooked through, 25 to 30 minutes.

REMOVE the chicken breast from the soup and place on a work surface. Using clean hands or two forks, shred the chicken and return it to the soup.

BRING the soup to a boil and add the meatballs. Reduce the heat and simmer for another 30 minutes. Add the pasta and spinach to the soup and simmer until the pasta is just cooked, 8 to 10 minutes.

IN a medium bowl, whisk together the eggs and cheese. While stirring the soup with a fork, slowly pour the egg mixture into the broth to form thin strands of egg, about 1 minute. Cover the pot and remove from the heat. Serve topped with additional grated Parmesan, if desired.

THAI BUTTERNUT SQUASH SOUP

MOOSEWOOD RESTAURANT

ITHACA, NY

Spicy and a little sweet, this vegan soup from the pioneering vegetarian Moosewood Restaurant is enlivened with Thai red curry paste and creamy coconut milk. At Moosewood, they sometimes swap some of the winter squash for small cubes of sweet potato, which cook quickly as well. In fact, the dish comes together in less than 45 minutes and can be made almost entirely with pantry ingredients, making it an easy meatless supper. If preparing the dish with frozen squash, use 2 (12-ounce) packages frozen cubed squash, reduce the amount of vegetable broth to 2 cups, and decrease the simmer time to 15 to 20 minutes. Kaffir lime leaves can be found in Asian groceries and add a deeply fragrant citrus note to the dish, but if they're not available, additional lime zest can be substituted.

SERVES 4

3 cups vegetable broth

1 cup coconut milk

4 teaspoons sugar, or more to taste

1 teaspoon Thai red curry paste

½ teaspoon salt, or more to taste

1 kaffir lime leaf (optional)

4 cups peeled, seeded, and cubed butternut squash (from an approximately 2½-pound squash)

1 tablespoon soy sauce

8 ounces firm tofu, cut into small cubes

2 teaspoons vegetable oil

1 lime

2 cups fresh baby spinach

Chopped fresh cilantro (optional)

IN a soup pot, whisk together the broth, coconut milk, sugar, ½ teaspoon of the curry paste, and the salt. Add the kaffir lime leaf, if using, and the squash. Cover and bring to a low boil over medium-high heat. Lower the heat to maintain a simmer and cook, covered, until the squash is tender, about 30 minutes. Remove the kaffir lime leaf. Puree the soup, then return it to the stove and bring it back to a simmer.

MEANWHILE, prepare the pan-fried tofu: In a medium bowl, whisk together the soy sauce and the remaining ½ teaspoon curry paste. Add the tofu to the bowl and toss to coat. Heat the oil in a medium skillet over medium-high heat. Add the tofu and cook, stirring occasionally, until the tofu is golden brown and slightly crisped, about 5 minutes. Finely grate the lime zest and juice the lime. Add 1 teaspoon of the zest and 2 tablespoons of the juice to the simmering soup. Stir in the spinach and pan-fried tofu and cook until the spinach wilts, about 5 minutes. Add more sugar and salt to taste, if needed.

SERVE the soup garnished with a light sprinkle of cilantro, if desired.

CHICKEN SOUP WITH MATZOH BALLS

2ND AVENUE DELI

NEW YORK, NY

It's practically illegal to walk into the 2nd Avenue Deli and not order the chicken soup with matzoh balls. The deeply flavored chicken broth and fluffy, perfectly round matzoh balls (floaters, not sinkers) are as good, if not better, than any your *bubbe* has ever made. The secret? The restaurant uses a pound of chicken parts plus a whole chicken to make its golden broth. The recipe also calls for dropping a trussed-up bunch of dill into the soup for a minute before serving, which infuses the soup with just the right amount of the herb's aromatic essence. The matzoh balls, a favorite of chefs around the city, are light yet infused with the rich flavor of schmaltz, or rendered chicken fat. You can find schmaltz in the freezer section of some butcher shops. To make your own, ask your butcher for a pound of raw chicken fat and cook the fat in a small, heavy saucepan over low heat for 45 minutes to an hour until all of the fat has rendered from the skin and the liquid is golden yellow in color.

MAKES 8 CUPS SOUP AND 20 TO 22 MATZOH BALLS; SERVES 6 TO 8

CHICKEN SOUP

1 pound chicken parts

2 celery ribs, including leafy tops, cut into 3-inch pieces

1 whole chicken, thoroughly rinsed

1 tablespoon plus 2 teaspoons salt

1 large onion, unpeeled (find one with a firm, golden brown peel)

1 large carrot, peeled

1 parsnip, peeled

¼ teaspoon freshly ground black pepper

1 bunch fresh dill, cleaned and tied into a bundle with a string

MATZOH BALLS

4 large eggs

⅓ cup schmaltz (rendered chicken fat)

¼ teaspoon plus 1 tablespoon salt

¼ teaspoon freshly ground black pepper

1 tablespoon baking powder

1⅓ cups matzoh meal

TO MAKE THE SOUP: Combine the chicken parts, celery pieces, and 12 cups cold water in a large stockpot and bring to a boil over high heat. Rub the inside of the whole chicken with 1 tablespoon of the salt. When the water comes to a boil, add the whole chicken to the pot. Cover, reduce the heat to low, and simmer until the chicken is tender and fully cooked, about 30 minutes. Transfer the whole chicken to a large platter and let cool.

(continued)

ADD the onion, carrot, parsnip, remaining 2 teaspoons salt, and the pepper to the chicken parts in the broth. Simmer, partially covered, for 1 hour 15 minutes, skimming scum off the surface as necessary.

WHEN the whole chicken is cool enough to handle, remove the skin and bones and cut the meat into bite-size pieces. You can add the meat to the soup just before serving or save it for chicken salad.

STRAIN the broth and discard all the solids except the carrot. Cut the carrot into ¼-inch-thick slices and reserve. Return the broth to the pot. (If making the soup ahead of time, cover and refrigerate the broth and carrot pieces separately. Remove any fat that has congealed on top of the soup before reheating.) When ready to serve, bring the broth to a simmer over medium-high heat.

TO MAKE THE MATZOH BALLS: In a large bowl, whisk the eggs to blend thoroughly. Add the schmaltz, ¼ teaspoon of the salt, the pepper, and the baking powder and whisk to combine. Using a rubber spatula, fold in the matzoh meal, gently mixing until completely blended. Refrigerate the mixture for 30 minutes to 2 hours. (The longer the mixture sits, the denser the matzoh balls will be. For "floaters"—fluffy matzoh balls—chill the mixture for no more than 30 minutes. For "sinkers," the mixture can sit for up to 2 hours.)

FILL a large, wide stockpot three-quarters full with water. Add the remaining 1 tablespoon salt and bring to a rapid boil over high heat.

USING wet hands, quickly shape balls about 1¼ inches in diameter (they will double in size when cooked), making a total of about 22 matzoh balls. Using a slotted spoon, gently place the matzoh balls in the boiling water, then reduce the heat to maintain a simmer. (Be careful not to crowd the pot or the matzoh balls will not cook properly; work in batches or use two pots if necessary.) Cook until the matzoh balls have risen from the bottom of the pot and have puffed up to about twice their original size, about 25 minutes.

(Matzoh balls can be made ahead of time and stored in the broth, but they will get heavier. To freeze the matzoh balls, remove them from the cooking water after the full 25 minutes' cooking time and set on a cookie sheet to cool. Freeze on the cookie sheet, then transfer to a resealable plastic bag. To reheat, place the frozen matzoh balls directly into the cold soup and bring to a gentle boil over medium-high heat. Reduce the heat to maintain a simmer and cook until heated through.)

JUST before serving, add the dill bundle to the simmering broth and cook for 1 minute. Remove the dill bundle and discard. Season the broth with salt and pepper to taste. Add the carrot pieces and the chicken meat, if using.

TO serve, ladle the soup into bowls. Using a slotted spoon, add 2 or 3 matzoh balls to each bowl.

COLD BORSCHT

BARNEY GREENGRASS

NEW YORK, NY

Not counting salt, this recipe has just three ingredients. Three. That's all you need to make the simplest but perhaps most beautiful of peasant foods: a vibrant-hued bowl of beet soup swirled with a dollop of sour cream. The dish, which the restaurant serves in a glass, is rumored to have once been Irving Berlin's regular order (along with a plate of sturgeon). Serve it in summer as an appetizer, or top with diced egg, boiled potatoes, diced radishes, and chopped dill for a heartier main course.

SERVES 4

6 large red beets (from about 2 bunches), scrubbed and trimmed

3 tablespoons sugar

1 tablespoon kosher salt

¾ cup sour cream

PEEL and halve the beets. In a large pot, combine the beets with 8 cups water. Cover and bring to a boil over high heat. Reduce the heat and simmer for 2 hours. Add the sugar and salt and stir to combine.

STRAIN the liquid and discard the beets. Return the broth to the pot, cover, and transfer to the refrigerator. Chill until cold, several hours or overnight.

ADD the sour cream and whisk for about 5 minutes. Chill the soup for an additional 30 minutes, at least, before serving.

CREAMED CHIPPED BEEF

MUSTACHE BILL'S DINER

BARNEGAT LIGHT, NJ

This diner classic is lovingly re-create[d] Mustache Bill's, a Jersey Shore relic th[at] to pack in the crowds. Open daily for b[reakfast and] lunch during the summer and on week[ends only] in the fall, Mustache Bill's offers loyal customers made-from-scratch comfort food like this hearty breakfast dish, a longtime staple at U.S. Army mess halls. "Chipped beef" is thinly sliced dried beef, which can be found in the prepared foods section of most supermarkets. It usually comes in a form that resembles salami. The dish is finished with a creamy white gravy made with a simple roux and a dash of white pepper. It's traditionally served on toast, but can also be spooned over hash browns, grits, or waffles.

SERVES 2

4 cups whole milk	¼ cup (½ stick) unsalted butter	Dash of freshly ground white pepper
8 ounces dried beef, about 2 cups, cut into ½-inch slices	⅓ cup all-purpose flour	2 slices white or rye bread, toasted

SCALD the milk: Pour it into a heavy-bottomed saucepan over low heat. Stir occasionally until the milk is just hot, with steam and small bubbles appearing around the edges. Do not boil.

ADD half the dried beef to the saucepan and stir to combine. Remove the saucepan from the heat and set aside.

HEAT a large, heavy-bottomed skillet over medium-high heat. Add the butter, and when it has melted, add the remaining dried beef. Cook until the beef has been warmed through and has begun to crisp, 2 to 3 minutes. Add the flour and stir. Continue stirring until the flour has been thoroughly combined and coats the beef, 1 to 2 minutes.

ADD the milk mixture to the flour mixture and stir to combine. Lower the heat to medium and cook, stirring frequently, until the mixture has reduced by a third and thickened to the consistency of a thick gravy, 5 to 8 minutes. Do not allow to boil. Add the white pepper and stir. Serve over toast.

BUFFALO WINGS

ANCHOR BAR

BUFFALO, NY

As the legend goes, Anchor Bar's famed chicken wings were created late one night in the 1960s by then owner Teressa Bellissimo, who wanted to cook up something special for hungry regulars. Whether or not buffalo wings had ever been made before is debatable, but it's clear that Anchor Bar was one of the first places to serve this now ubiquitous snack. (Which begs the question: whatever did college students and Super Bowl fans eat before then?) Anchor Bar won't release the recipe for their famous wing sauce, but they sell bottles of it at their four upstate New York and Canadian locations and on their website in flavors ranging from "Mild" to "Suicidal." If Anchor Bar's sauce is unavailable, Frank's Red Hot Original Cayenne Pepper Sauce is a close approximation. This recipe will yield crispy, tangy wings of medium heat. For milder wings, use more butter; for spicier wings, use less. Serve wings with celery sticks and blue cheese dip alongside.

SERVES 6 TO 8

Peanut or canola oil for deep-frying	Salt and freshly ground black pepper	½ cup (1 stick) unsalted butter, melted
5 pounds chicken wings (about 30 whole wings), split into two pieces, wing tips removed	1 cup Anchor Bar Wing Sauce or other hot sauce such as Frank's Red Hot Original Cayenne Pepper Sauce	Celery sticks Blue Cheese Dip (recipe follows)

POUR 2 inches of oil into a Dutch oven or deep, heavy pot and heat to 350°F.

WORKING in batches, immerse the wings in the hot oil, being careful not to crowd the pot, which will cause the temperature to dip. Deep-fry at 350°F for 12 to 15 minutes, or until completely cooked and crispy. (When the chicken is fully cooked, the juices will run clear.) Drain on paper towels. Season with salt and pepper to taste.

WHISK the hot sauce and melted butter in a large bowl. Toss the fried wings in the hot sauce mixture until completely coated. Serve immediately with celery sticks and blue cheese dip.

BLUE CHEESE DIP

MAKES ABOUT 2 CUPS

1 cup mayonnaise

½ cup sour cream

¼ cup crumbled blue cheese

Juice of ½ lemon

1 garlic clove, minced

Salt and freshly ground black pepper

IN a large bowl, mix the mayonnaise, sour cream, cheese, lemon juice, garlic, and salt and pepper until thoroughly combined. Cover and refrigerate for at least 1 hour before serving.

"I don't like gourmet cooking or 'this' cooking or 'that' cooking. I like good cooking."

—JAMES BEARD

CHOPPED LIVER

2ND AVENUE DELI

NEW YORK, NY

Served as an appetizer on a bed of lettuce or piled between two slices of bread and eaten as a sandwich, the 2nd Avenue Deli's smooth, creamy chopped liver is among the best in New York City. The restaurant makes its version of this traditional eastern European Jewish dish with both beef and chicken livers, which gives it a meatier, richer taste. (Additional chicken livers can be substituted for the beef liver for those who prefer it that way. It will have a lighter, somewhat creamier texture.)

MAKES ABOUT 6 CUPS

4 tablespoons corn oil

3 tablespoons schmaltz (rendered chicken fat)

2 large onions, coarsely chopped (about 4 cups)

1½ pounds beef liver

1 pound chicken livers

4 hard-boiled eggs, peeled

2 teaspoons salt

¼ teaspoon freshly ground black pepper

IN a large skillet, heat 2 tablespoons of the corn oil and 2 tablespoons of the schmaltz over medium heat. Add the onions and sauté until well browned, about 30 minutes. Transfer the onions to the refrigerator to chill.

MEANWHILE, preheat the broiler. Rinse the livers thoroughly. Using a small, sharp knife, cut away membranes and visible fat. Cut the beef liver into 1-inch pieces (the chicken livers can remain whole).

PUT the beef and chicken livers in a single layer on a large baking sheet and drizzle with the remaining 2 tablespoons corn oil. Broil for 8 to 10 minutes (keep an eye on it to make sure it doesn't burn). Turn the liver pieces over and broil until the livers are cooked through and lightly browned on both sides, an additional 5 minutes. Transfer the livers to a mixing bowl and place in the refrigerator to chill.

WORKING in two batches, combine the livers, onions, hard-boiled eggs, remaining 1 tablespoon schmaltz, the salt, and the pepper in the bowl of a food processor and blend until smooth. Chill before serving.

> "There's an authenticity there because these guys are just old-school New York waiters, not a musician or an actor. It's not contrived hospitality, it's a 'Honey, you want a bagel with that?' If I could find waiters like that I would love it."
>
> —ANDREW CARMELLINI, JBF Award Winner

WHITE CLAM PIZZA

FRANK PEPE PIZZERIA NAPOLETANA

NEW HAVEN, CT

Pizza lovers drive from all over the Northeast and wait on line for hours for a taste of the crisp-crusted, perfectly charred pies coming out of this New Haven institution's coal-fired oven. The pizzeria's signature dish is its white clam pizza, a mozzarella-free masterpiece dotted with freshly shucked Rhode Island littleneck clams, olive oil, garlic, oregano, and the merest hint of Parmesan. The dish can be made with canned clams, but the effect will not be the same. The secret to making this dish at home is a screaming-hot oven and a preheated pizza stone, if possible. (If you don't have a pizza stone you can use a pizza crisper or a half-sheet pan turned upside down.) Don't skip the cornmeal dusting on the baking peel—it helps the pizza slide off the peel and onto the stone when transferring it into the oven. Make sure to allot 2 to 3 hours for the dough to rise, or make the dough ahead of time; it will keep, wrapped in plastic, in the refrigerator for up to three days or in the freezer for up to two months. Defrost the dough overnight in the fridge before using.

SERVES 2

1 (¼-ounce) packet instant yeast (2 teaspoons)

1 teaspoon sugar

2½ cups all-purpose flour, plus more if necessary

2 teaspoons salt

Cornmeal for dusting

3 tablespoons olive oil

3 large garlic cloves, finely minced

1 dozen just-shucked littleneck clams, juice reserved

1 teaspoon dried oregano

2 tablespoons grated Parmesan cheese

COMBINE the yeast, sugar, and ¼ cup warm water in a small bowl. Stir to dissolve the sugar. Set aside until a bubbly foam starts to form on the surface of the water, about 4 minutes.

IN a large bowl, combine 2 cups of the flour and ¾ cup warm water. Add the yeast mixture and salt and stir with a wooden spoon until a dough begins to form. Turn the dough out onto a lightly floured work surface and let it rest while you oil a large ceramic bowl. Knead the dough vigorously for a full 15 minutes, until silky. If the dough is too sticky, add 1 to 2 tablespoons additional flour.

(continued)

TO make the dough in a stand mixer, combine the flour, ¾ cup water, yeast mixture, and salt in the bowl of the mixer fitted with the dough hook. Turn the mixer to low and mix until the dough starts to form into a ball around the dough hook, then increase the speed slightly and mix for 1 to 2 minutes, until the dough is smooth and elastic. Turn the dough out onto a lightly floured work surface and let it rest while you oil a large ceramic bowl. Knead for 1 to 2 minutes by hand to form a smooth ball.

PLACE the kneaded dough in the oiled ceramic bowl and cover tightly with two layers of plastic wrap. Place the bowl in a warm, dark place to rise until doubled in size, 1½ to 2 hours.

PLACE a pizza stone on the top rack of the oven and preheat the oven to 500°F.

REMOVE the plastic wrap and punch down the dough to compact it to its original size. Turn the dough out onto a lightly floured board and, using the heel of your hand, carefully and methodically flatten the dough and work it into a circle that's about 12 inches in diameter and no more than ¼ inch thick in the center, with a ½-inch-thick ring of slightly thicker dough around the circumference.

SPRINKLE a baker's peel liberally with cornmeal and place the circle of dough on it.

COVER the dough lightly with a sheet of plastic wrap to prevent it from drying out. Set aside to rest for 10 to 12 minutes.

WHILE the dough is resting, put the oil in a small bowl. Mince the garlic and add it to the bowl with the oil. Set aside.

AFTER the dough has rested, remove the plastic wrap and use a pastry brush to brush on the oil and garlic, leaving ½ inch along the circumference untouched. Spread the clams on the pie with a dash of their own juice. Sprinkle the pie with the oregano and Parmesan.

USE the baker's peel to transfer the pie to the preheated pizza stone in the oven. Bake for 10 to 12 minutes, or until the crust is light brown. Remove, slice, and serve.

OYSTER PAN ROAST

GRAND CENTRAL OYSTER BAR & RESTAURANT

NEW YORK, NY

James Beard, a native Oregonian who appreciated a good pan roast, insisted that "the tiny oysters of the Pacific Coast are far better for this dish than the larger ones," but anyone who has been served a creamy, paprika-dusted bowl of the Grand Central Oyster Bar's iconic version—made with plump, briny East Coast oysters—will undoubtedly beg to differ. Chef Sandy Ingber ups the ante with a long-standing recipe that includes a healthy pour of half-and-half added to the poaching liquid after the oysters have been gently cooked and removed. A dash (or three) of chili sauce adds just the right touch of heat to the dish.

SERVES 1

¼ cup clam juice, or ¼ cup water and ¼ teaspoon clam base

1 tablespoon unsalted butter

½ teaspoon Worcestershire sauce

¼ teaspoon celery salt

¼ teaspoon sweet Hungarian paprika, plus more for garnish

6 extra-select or large East Coast oysters (such as Wellfleet, Bluepoint, or Malpeque), shucked, with their liquor (about 1 pound oysters)

2 cups half-and-half

3 tablespoons tomato-based chili sauce

1 slice white bread, toasted, crusts removed

Oyster crackers

IN a medium saucepan, combine the clam juice, butter, Worcestershire sauce, celery salt, and paprika and place over high heat. When the butter melts, add the oysters and their liquor and cook, stirring, until the edges of the oysters begin to ruffle, about 1 minute. Using a slotted spoon, transfer the oysters to a plate and keep warm. Stir the half-and-half and chili sauce into the liquid and cook, stirring often, until the liquid just comes to a boil, 3 to 4 minutes. Return the oysters to the pan and remove from the heat.

PUT the slice of toasted bread in a warmed soup plate and pour in the pan roast. Garnish with a shake of paprika and serve immediately with oyster crackers.

"When I go to the Oyster Bar, I just sit at the bar, order some oysters, and watch them pump out those pan roasts. If you want to get a sense of New York, it's a great place to experience."

—APRIL BLOOMFIELD, JBF Award Winner

MARISCADA IN GREEN SAUCE

SEVILLA
RESTAURANT & BAR

NEW YORK, NY

Native to coastal regions in both Spain and Portugal, this dish features pristine seafood gently cooked with aromatics and finished with a generous splash of white wine. (The "green" in the recipe name comes from a bright burst of parsley.) Serve with crusty bread for dipping in the plentiful, fragrant broth. Mariscada can be made with many different types of shellfish, but at Sevilla each generous serving includes half a lobster. Since the dish continues cooking after the lobster has been added, it's important not to cook the seafood through when initially preparing it. Steaming the live lobster in a small amount of heavily salted water will cook it enough to loosen the meat from the shell, but not so much that it will overcook in the final dish. To do so, bring 1½ inches of water to a rolling boil in a wide, heavy pot with a tight-fitting lid. Add 2 tablespoons kosher salt. Put the lobster in the pot, cover it, and cook just until the shell turns bright red, about 2 minutes. Remove the lid and use tongs to remove the lobster and rinse under cold running water.

SERVES 4

2 tablespoons extra-virgin olive oil	1½ teaspoons all-purpose flour	20 medium shrimp, peeled and deveined
4 garlic cloves, chopped	2 cups Verdejo or other dry white wine	16 fresh, small sea scallops, tough muscle removed
2 tablespoons chopped Spanish onion	½ teaspoon salt	12 littleneck clams
1 tablespoon chopped fresh parsley	1 (1½-pound) fresh lobster, steamed and split in half, still in the shell (see headnote)	12 mussels, scrubbed and debearded

HEAT a large, heavy-bottomed pot over medium heat. Add the oil, garlic, onion, and parsley. Stir to combine and cook for 1 minute. Add the flour and cook, stirring, for 1 minute. Add the wine, ¾ cup water, and the salt. Increase the heat to medium-high and bring to a boil. Lower the heat and simmer for 5 minutes.

ADD the lobster, shrimp, scallops, clams, and mussels and cover the pot. Cook, covered, for 5 minutes. Remove from the heat and serve immediately.

POUSSINS EN COCOTTE "BONNE FEMME"

POUSSINS WITH BACON AND MUSHROOM SAUCE

LE VEAU D'OR

NEW YORK, NY

A staple on the menu at Le Veau d'Or, a traditional French restaurant and former celebrity haunt on New York's Upper East Side, this rustic dish is a cousin of coq au vin: Many of the same ingredients are used, but *poussins en cocotte* is slightly less fussy, yet still elegant. The dish is richly flavored with smoky slab bacon and earthy mushrooms; a wine-based braise infuses the sweet, tender meat. Poussins, or baby chickens, can be found at some specialty butchers or from online purveyors, but if unavailable, Cornish game hens make a good substitute. Cook the dish in a pot or casserole with a tight-fitting lid to keep all the moisture and flavor from evaporating.

SERVES 2

---

3 tablespoons unsalted butter

8 ounces slab bacon, rind discarded, cut into ½-by-1½-inch strips

2 (1-pound) poussins

2 shallots, peeled and minced (about ½ cup)

8 ounces button mushrooms, trimmed and quartered (about 2 cups)

1 cup dry white wine

1 cup beef stock

½ teaspoon salt

Freshly ground black pepper

PREHEAT the oven to 325°F.

IN a large, heavy-bottomed pot or Dutch oven, melt 1 tablespoon of the butter over medium-high heat. Add the bacon and cook until dark brown and crisp, about 6 minutes. Remove the bacon with a slotted spoon or tongs, transfer to a small bowl, and set aside.

PAT the poussins dry and place them in the pot. Sear the poussins, turning them occasionally, until they are deep golden on all sides, about 15 minutes total. Using tongs, carefully transfer the poussins to a plate and set aside.

REDUCE the heat to medium and add the remaining 2 tablespoons butter to the pot. Add the shallots and cook until just softened, 2 to 3 minutes. Add the mushrooms and cook until just softened, about 1 minute. Add the bacon, wine, stock, salt, and pepper to taste; stir to combine. Return the poussins, breast-side up, to the pot. Tightly cover the pot, transfer to the oven, and cook for 30 minutes. Uncover the pot and increase the oven temperature to 375°F. Return the pot to the oven and cook until the sauce has thickened slightly, about 45 minutes more.

REMOVE the pot from the oven. Taste the sauce and adjust the seasonings if necessary. To serve, place each poussin on a plate and top with sauce and mushrooms.

ROAST PRIME RIB OF BEEF WITH THYME JUS

KEENS STEAKHOUSE

NEW YORK, NY

The famous prime rib at Keens is no joke. They start with a full, 7-bone USDA prime-grade rib that weighs between 23 and 25 pounds, but you can have your butcher prepare a smaller 3- or 4-bone rib (estimate serving about two people per rib). When buying the meat, ask your butcher to remove the chine bones and the fat cap covering the rib and to trim the bones if they are longer than 7 to 8 inches so it will fit in the oven. A well-marbled prime rib will be full of flavor and require very little in the way of seasoning, but salt is key to the success of this dish. Properly salting the rib will not only flavor the meat and keep it juicy, but will also yield a crisp, mahogany steakhouse crust. Make the jus while the beef is roasting and reheat just before serving.

SERVES 6 TO 8

1 standing rib roast (3 or 4 ribs), chine bones and fat cap covering the ribs removed

Kosher salt

3 tablespoons vegetable oil

1 tablespoon chopped shallot

2 garlic cloves, chopped, plus 1 garlic clove, sliced

¼ cup white wine

4 cups veal or beef stock, homemade if possible

½ bunch fresh thyme

Freshly ground black pepper

REMOVE the roast from the refrigerator 1 hour before cooking to allow it to come to room temperature.

PREHEAT the oven to 300°F.

USING a small, sharp knife, cut out the meat between the rib bones down to the eye and reserve for the jus. Rub the roast liberally with salt.

IN a large skillet, heat 2 tablespoons of the oil over high heat. Add the roast and sear until browned on all sides, about 12 minutes total. Transfer the roast to a rack set in a roasting pan and place in the oven; cook until the internal temperature reaches 120°F for medium-rare, about 2 hours. (To ensure a perfect doneness, use a meat thermometer to measure the temperature and remove the roast a few minutes before the desired temperature is reached, as the meat will continue to cook once it's out of the oven.)

REMOVE the roast from the oven and transfer to a cutting board. Let it rest at room temperature for 30 minutes before slicing.

WHILE the roast is resting, heat the remaining 1 tablespoon oil over high heat in a medium saucepan. Add the reserved rib meat and cook, stirring occasionally, until browned, about 4 minutes. Reduce the heat to medium-low. Add the shallot and cook until soft, about 2 minutes. Add the chopped garlic and cook, stirring, until slightly browned, about 2 minutes. As soon as the garlic begins to brown, add the wine and increase the heat to medium. Simmer until the wine has reduced by half, about 3 minutes.

ADD the stock to the pan. Increase the heat and bring to a boil. Reduce the heat and simmer for 15 minutes.

ADD the sliced garlic and the thyme and simmer for 5 minutes. Strain the jus through a fine-mesh strainer and season to taste with salt and pepper.

TO serve a king's cut, cut between the bones so each piece is served on the bone. For smaller portions, cut the rib entirely away from the bones and thinly slice the meat. Drizzle each serving with some of the jus.

This Gate Hangs High
And
Hinders None
Pay

Steak House Cuts

Old-school steak houses like Peter Luger's (page 108) and Keens (page 106) don't mess around with thin, bistro steaks like hangar or flank. They serve big, well-marbled cuts of prime beef—a grade of meat most often reserved for restaurants—that have been dry-aged for weeks to intensify the flavor. Here's a guide to the premium steak-house cuts:

Rib-Eye

With its incredible marbling, the bone-in rib-eye is one of the most popular steak house offerings. Streaked with fat, this steak is full of flavor and needs very little in the way of seasoning: just salt, pepper, and a turn in a sizzling hot cast-iron pan (or better yet, on the grill).

Filet Mignon

Filet mignon is the most tender steak—you can cut it with a fork—but it's low in fat and, consequently, doesn't have a particularly rich taste. To round out its flavors, top a grilled filet with a simple, creamy pan sauce or an herb-speckled pat of butter.

New York Strip

Also known as Delmonico steak, Kansas City steak, or shell steak, New York strips are marbled and firm boneless cuts, with a little more chew than a rib-eye. Cook it to medium-rare to keep it tender and juicy.

Porterhouse and T-Bone

Diners at Peter Luger's come for the Porterhouse, which is listed on the menu simply as "Steak for two, three, four." This large, succulent, bone-in cut offers something for everyone: buttery tenderloin (filet mignon) on one side of the bone and the heartier New York strip on the other. A T-bone steak has a smaller piece of filet than a Porterhouse.

KEENS STEAKHOUSE'S MUTTON CHOP

KEENS STEAKHOUSE

NEW YORK, NY

Keens serves incredible prime aged steaks grilled to perfection, but the steak house's most famous cut of meat is not beef—it's the prehistorically sized mutton chop. In one of the restaurant's few nods to modernization, the mutton is now lamb, but you wouldn't know by looking at it: Each 2-inch-thick chop is 26 ounces of well-marbled meat. The saddle chop is sometimes called the double loin or the double rack, as it's really two loin chops attached by the backbone. The cooking technique is as simple as the ingredient list—each chop is very generously salted, seared under the kitchen's scorching-hot broiler, and finished in a hot oven. Diners at Keens used to receive a baked potato alongside their jaw-dropping chop, but these days the dish is served with garlicky sautéed escarole instead.

SERVES 1 EXTREMELY HUNGRY PERSON

1 (26- to 30-ounce) saddle-cut mutton chop, or 2 (16-ounce) lamb chops

Kosher salt

Large-flake sea salt for serving

REMOVE the chop from the refrigerator at least 30 minutes before cooking to allow it to come to room temperature.

PREHEAT the oven to 425°F. If you have a separate broiler, preheat it as well.

PLACE the chop on a large cast-iron skillet. (You can use a baking sheet if need be, but a cast-iron skillet will yield the best results.) Season all sides liberally with kosher salt.

PLACE the chop under the broiler until the top of the chop is nicely browned, 3 to 4 minutes. Turn the chop so the fat cap is facing up and place under the broiler to brown, 3 to 4 minutes. Finally, turn the chop onto the remaining side and place under the broil to brown, 3 to 4 minutes. Transfer the chop to the oven and roast for 11 to 12 minutes for medium-rare or 13 to 14 minutes for medium.

REMOVE the chop from the oven and let it rest for 10 to 15 minutes. Season with sea salt to taste and serve.

Number of mutton chops sold weekly at Keens Steakhouse in NYC: 350.

OATMEAL BREAD

POLLY'S PANCAKE PARLOR

SUGAR HILL, NH

For over seventy-five years, Polly's Pancake Parlor has been serving superlative homemade breakfast and lunch favorites, including fluffy pancakes, golden waffles, and a variety of baked goods, like this oatmeal bread. A soft, sliceable loaf with just a touch of sweetness, the oatmeal bread is made with organic grains that are stone-ground in-house. A handful of oat groats, which need to be softened in hot water before using, adds texture and nutrients. The recipe isn't a quick one—it calls for a double rising—but it's easy and forgiving, even for inexperienced bread bakers. Often used to make the restaurant's French toast, this bread is also fantastic for sandwiches, like the grilled cheese with sharp cheddar, ham, apple slices, and maple mustard that is owner Kathie Coté's favorite.

MAKES 2 LOAVES

¾ cup rolled oats, plus more for sprinkling

½ cup oat groats

½ cup molasses

¼ cup canola oil

2 large eggs, beaten

1 (¼-ounce) packet instant yeast (2 teaspoons)

2 teaspoons salt

5 cups unbleached all-purpose flour, plus more as needed

¼ cup whole-wheat flour

¼ cup cornmeal

1 egg white, beaten

IN a large bowl or the bowl of stand mixer fitted with the dough hook, combine the rolled oats and oat groats with 2 cups hot water and allow to soften, about 5 minutes.

ADD the molasses, oil, whole eggs, yeast, and salt to the bowl and mix thoroughly. Add the all-purpose flour, whole-wheat flour, and cornmeal and mix until the ingredients come together to form a rough dough. Knead until the dough becomes smooth and elastic, about 10 minutes by hand or 5 minutes with the stand mixer. Add 1 tablespoon or more of all-purpose flour if the dough is too sticky.

PLACE the kneaded dough in a lightly greased bowl. Cover and allow to rise at room temperature until doubled in bulk, 1 to 2 hours. Gently punch down the dough and place it on a lightly floured work surface.

FORM 2 loaves and place in 4-by-8-inch loaf pans. Cover the pans and allow the loaves to rise at room temperature until they reach 1 inch above the loaf pan's edge, 1 to 1½ hours.

PREHEAT the oven to 400°F.

BRUSH the loaves with the beaten egg white and sprinkle a few rolled oats over the tops. Bake until the loaves are a rich golden brown and the internal temperature is 190°F, about 30 minutes.

ALLOW the loaves to cool in the pans on a cooling rack. Once cooled, invert the pans to remove the bread. The loaves will keep at room temperature for 2 to 3 days, but they're best within 24 hours of baking. If making ahead of time, wrap in plastic wrap and freeze for up to 3 months.

CHEESE BLINTZES

BARNEY GREENGRASS

NEW YORK, NY

One of New York City's oldest and most enduring purveyors of Jewish appetizing, a food tradition that centers around cured fish and dairy products (think: everything you'd typically eat with bagels), Barney Greengrass is best known for its sable and salmon, but it also serves unbeatable blintzes. Golden brown and delicate, the blintzes are filled with lightly sweetened farmer cheese, a pot cheese with a soft but crumbly consistency that's often used in eastern European cooking. If you can't find farmer cheese in a store, you can make your own by pressing cottage cheese in cheesecloth overnight to remove the moisture. Ricotta or fromage blanc can also be substituted. Both the crêpes and the filled blintzes can be made ahead of time; just cover and chill overnight or freeze for up to one month. If frying the blintzes from frozen, do not thaw before cooking.

MAKES 1 DOZEN BLINTZES

CRÊPES
4 large eggs
1 cup all-purpose flour
½ cup milk
½ teaspoon kosher salt
¼ cup (½ stick) unsalted butter, melted, for frying

FILLING
1 pound farmer cheese
½ cup sugar
1 extra-large egg
2 teaspoons vanilla extract

Sour cream, for serving (optional)

Fruit preserves, for serving (optional)

TO MAKE THE CRÊPES: Combine the eggs, flour, ½ cup water, the milk, and the salt in a medium bowl and whisk until foamy. Cover and transfer to the refrigerator and let rest for 6 hours or overnight. Remove from the fridge 30 minutes before using to bring to room temperature.

HEAT an 8-inch crêpe pan or nonstick skillet over medium-high heat and lightly brush with some of the melted butter. (Reserve the remaining melted butter for frying the blintzes.) Pour ¼ cup of the egg mixture into the pan, swirling it around to coat the bottom evenly and pouring off any excess to leave a thin layer. Cook for 30 to 45 seconds to let the crêpe batter set and begin to brown. Use a spatula to loosen the crêpe from the pan and flip it (you may need to use your fingers to flip the crêpe; take care

(continued)

when doing so to avoid burning yourself). Allow the crêpe to cook on the other side for 15 seconds more. Remove immediately and transfer to a plate. The crêpes should be lightly browned but still soft and pliable. Repeat until all the batter is used, stacking the crêpes as you go and covering the stack of crêpes with a towel to prevent them from drying out. There should be about a dozen crêpes. If not using the crêpes right away, keep wrapped in the refrigerator for up to 2 days.

TO MAKE THE FILLING: In a large bowl, stir together the cheese, sugar, egg, and vanilla.

TO ASSEMBLE THE BLINTZES: Place a crêpe on a work surface. Place a heaping tablespoon of the cheese filling in the center and fold the bottom edge up to cover the filling. Fold each of the sides in toward the center, enclosing the filling, then roll the crêpe up and over, tucking the edges in, to form a blintz, leaving the seam side down. Repeat with the remaining crêpes and filling.

HEAT a large skillet over medium heat. Working in batches, brush the skillet liberally with the remaining melted butter and cook the blintzes until brown on both sides, about 2 minutes per side. Serve with sour cream or fruit preserves.

"Barney Greengrass may not have ruled any kingdoms or written any great symphonies, but he did a monumental job with sturgeon."

– GROUCHO MARX
on Barney Greengrass

FLAN

SEVILLA RESTAURANT & BAR

NEW YORK, NY

There is no more fitting ending to a meal at Sevilla than the restaurant's smooth, creamy flan. The custard base is infused with lemon peel and cinnamon, a subtle enhancement to a classic recipe, and is prepared in a 2-quart porcelain mold for family-style serving. (An 8-inch cake pan can be used instead.) If cooking in individual ramekins, decrease the cooking time to 30 to 40 minutes.

SERVES 6 TO 8

¾ cup plus 2 tablespoons sugar

4¼ cups whole milk

2 (1-inch) strips lemon peel

½ cinnamon stick

5 large eggs, beaten

Fresh mint leaf (optional)

PREHEAT the oven to 390°F. Bring a kettle of water to a boil for the water bath and keep it hot.

TO make caramel, have a 2-quart porcelain flan mold at the ready. Combine ¼ cup of the sugar and 2 tablespoons water in a heavy-bottomed pot or skillet over low heat. Swirl the pan over the heat until the mixture turns a rich golden brown, about 10 minutes; don't stir. Pour the caramel into the porcelain mold and immediately swirl it so the caramel evenly coats the bottom and reaches about ⅛ inch up the sides of the mold. Let it sit at room temperature until it hardens.

TO make the pudding, combine the milk, the remaining ½ cup plus 2 tablespoons sugar, the lemon peel, and the cinnamon in a saucepan over medium heat. Bring to a boil, then immediately remove from the heat; pour into a large bowl and set aside to cool, about 15 minutes.

MAKE sure the milk mixture is barely warm before proceeding with the recipe. Remove the lemon peel and cinnamon stick; discard. Add the beaten eggs to the milk mixture and whisk immediately. Pour the custard base into the flan mold.

TO create the water bath, place the flan mold in the center of a large roasting pan. Carefully pour hot—but not boiling—water from the kettle into the roasting pan until it reaches halfway up the side of the mold. Place the pan in the oven and bake for 50 minutes to 1 hour, until the custard is set and jiggles slightly when gently shaken.

REMOVE the mold from the water bath and set aside to cool, about 30 minutes. The flan can be made up to 1 day ahead of time; keep covered in the refrigerator and let it come to room temperature before serving. When ready to serve, run a thin paring knife around the outside edge of the flan. Flip the mold onto a serving dish and shake lightly until the flan is released. Garnish with the mint leaf, if desired.

MAPLE SUGAR COOKIES

POLLY'S PANCAKE PARLOR

SUGAR HILL, NH

These thin, chewy cookies are baked with maple sugar and sold year-round at the bakery run out of Polly's Pancake Parlor. The restaurant makes its own maple sugar, heating local maple syrup to just the right temperature before cooling and pressing it through a very fine sifter to produce the golden, granulated sweetener. Luckily for less intrepid home cooks, they also sell the sugar online. Similar in texture to tea biscuits, these buttery cookies are perfect for dunking into a cup of milky coffee.

MAKES 36 COOKIES

2 cups granulated maple sugar, plus extra for sprinkling

½ cup (1 stick) unsalted butter, at room temperature

1 large egg

1 teaspoon salt

½ cup whole milk

3 cups unbleached all-purpose flour

PREHEAT the oven to 425°F. Line a cookie sheet with parchment paper.

IN a large bowl or the bowl of a stand mixer, beat together the maple sugar and butter until the mixture is smooth and fluffy. Add the egg and salt to the bowl and stir to combine. Add the milk and stir to combine. Add the flour and stir just until the mixture is thoroughly combined and forms a soft, sticky dough. Cover the bowl of dough with plastic wrap and place in the refrigerator to chill until the dough is firm enough to roll, 2 to 3 hours.

REMOVE half the dough from the bowl; leave the remaining dough in the refrigerator so it stays cold. Place the dough on a well-floured large cutting board and roll out to ¼-inch thickness. Using a cookie cutter, cut out shapes or rounds and place them on the prepared cookie sheet. (If the dough becomes too sticky to cut as it warms up, place the cutting board with the rolled dough back in the refrigerator for 15 minutes to cool, or place the bottom of a well-chilled baking sheet on top of the dough for a few minutes to cool it.) Sprinkle the dough rounds with additional maple sugar. Bake until the cookies are lightly browned, 8 to 10 minutes, rotating the cookie sheet half-way through the baking time. Repeat with the remaining dough.

REMOVE the cookie sheet from the oven. Let the cookies sit on the cookie sheet for 2 minutes before transferring them to a cooling rack to cool completely, 10 to 15 minutes. Store in an airtight container for up to 1 week.

The Award Winners

AL'S FRENCH FRYS

1251 Williston Road
South Burlington, VT
Owners: Bill Bissonette and Lee Bissonette
2010 AWARD WINNER

Founded by Al and Genevieve Rusterholz in the late 1940s, Al's French Frys was originally housed in a small hut, open to the elements. Many Chittenden Countians encountered Al's French Frys stand at the Champlain Valley Fair, where it earned a reputation that has endured for more than half a century. Al's is now owned by the Bissonette family, headed by Bill Bissonette, who revealed part of the restaurant's secret when he told a local paper that he starts with Idaho or California russets and fries them twice in a combination of beef tallow and soybean oil at between 300 and 400°F for a total of about seven minutes. The result is exceptional: The fries boast a dark and crackly exterior, and creamy white potato fluff lurks within. Customers line up day and night to order a pint—or the vastly more popular quart size. Al's also serves burgers, sandwiches, chicken strips, and other main-course fare, but the fries invariably steal the show.

ANCHOR BAR

1047 Main Street
Buffalo, NY
Owner: Ivano Toscano
2003 AWARD WINNER

Few cities or restaurants are as closely associated with a dish as Anchor Bar is with Buffalo chicken wings. The origins might be disputed, but the famous birthplace is, thankfully, intact—down to the thirty seats, the beer signs, and the wall of license plates from customers who moved away. The official story of the birth of the wing: One Friday night in October 1964, Teressa Bellissimo—who had emigrated from Sicily with her husband, Frank, and gone into the restaurant business in 1935—rummaged around the kitchen for a late-night snack for peckish regulars. The cupboard was bare save for some chicken wings for soup. Bellissimo deep-fried the wings, dipped them in butter and hot sauce, and served them with celery sticks and blue cheese dip. The late-night part is integral to the legend: Friday was a no-meat day, so the wings were permissible only past midnight. Of course, there are those who take issue: An African American cook named John Young said he popularized deep-fried wings in the Buffalo area at the same time. But there's no disputing the fact that the no-holds-barred snack took off in bars and restaurants across the U.S., and that they continue to take over the country every Super Bowl Sunday. Today Ivano Toscano, a manager for thirty years working alongside the Bellissimo family, owns and lovingly maintains the Anchor Bar and its winged legend.

AUNT CARRIE'S

1240 Ocean Road
Narragansett, RI
Owner: Elsie Foy
2007 AWARD WINNER

Described as the birthplace of the clam cake (a deep-fried, clam-studded bread dumpling), Aunt Carrie's has been serving up Rhode Island classics since 1920. Named for original owner Carrie Cooper, a Point Judith vacationer who started out selling lemonade, clam cakes, and chowder to hungry fishermen and other campers, the seafood shack is the place to go for a real Rhode Island shore dinner (complete with steamers and a plate of fish and chips) or a warm bowl of Indian pudding topped with a scoop of vanilla ice cream. Patrons sit in the humble dining room or take their meal to nearby picnic tables to enjoy the picturesque view of the shore and cool ocean breezes. Open only during the summer, the Ocean State eatery attracts crowds of hungry, loyal patrons eager for a taste of the fried scallops, clam chowder, and fresh-baked apple pies they've enjoyed there since childhood.

BAGADUCE LUNCH

19 Bridge Road
Brooksville, ME
Owner: Judy Astbury
2008 AWARD WINNER

Bagaduce Lunch, a seafood shack on the Blue Hill Peninsula, overlooking Maine's picturesque Bagaduce Falls, has been a summertime destination since 1946. Inside it looks much the same as it did the day it opened: A white clapboard hutch with red trim is flanked by picnic benches. Local fishermen supply Judy Astbury, daughter of original owner Vangie Peasley, with just-caught seafood for her crab rolls, scallops, shrimp, and belly clams, while sides, like double-dipped onion rings, are the purview of Judy's husband, Mike Astbury. In keeping with the seasonality of the seafood on which Judy Astbury builds her menu, Bagaduce Lunch opens in May and closes shortly after Labor Day.

BARNEY GREENGRASS

541 Amsterdam Avenue
New York, NY
Owner: Gary Greengrass
2006 AWARD WINNER

Since 1908, three generations of Greengrasses have been slicing sturgeon, dispensing free advice, and serving up platters of sable, lox, and whitefish to hundreds of thousands of food lovers who have made the pilgrimage to the ageless storefront on Manhattan's Upper West Side. They come for the delicious comfort food and the friendly abuse heaped upon customers by the perpetually cranky but haimish waitstaff. Their silky sturgeon is a work of art, the smoked salmon and sable beyond reproach, and the homemade borscht, pickled herring, and chopped liver are all first-rate. The signature egg dishes, consisting of the holy trinity of softly scrambled eggs, smoked fish, and caramelized onions, are simultaneously salty, smoky, gooey, and rich. It's not the prettiest plate of food you've ever seen, but it tastes like heaven. And accompanying your eggs or smoked fish–and–cream cheese platter are baskets of fresh bagels and their lighter New York relative, perfectly toasted bialys, which a Barney Greengrass waiter once described to an uninitiated customer as a Jewish English muffin. Barney Greengrass is a classic in

the truest sense of the word; the experience is unchanged and the food is better than ever. Groucho Marx put it most aptly in a letter he wrote to Gary's father, Moe, when Barney passed away: "Barney Greengrass may not have ruled any kingdoms or written any great symphonies, but he did a monumental job with sturgeon."

BEN'S CHILI BOWL

1213 U Street Northwest
Washington, D.C.
Owner: Virginia Ali
2004 AWARD WINNER

See page 62.

C.F. FOLKS

1225 19th Street NW
Washington, D.C.
Owner: Art Carlson
2013 AWARD WINNER

Art Carlson's weekday-only lunch haunt on Dupont Circle, open since 1981, is a six-hundred-square-foot temple of honest cooking and goodwill. (The name combines the initials of Carlson and his business partner, Peggy Fredricksen.) The vibe is loud and scrappy, and the food is delicious. Art Carlson, the ever-present host, is one of the last of a dying breed: a hands-on owner who schmoozes and teases his customers, often at the same time. The place, with its eleven counter stools, is comfortable in its age. Behind the long Formica counter, racks of cookbooks from Julia Child and fellow titans share space with scribbled postcards, a rattletrap stereo system, a collection of old political campaign buttons, and a jumble of knickknacks including a Presidential Barbie and dusty cans of Alpo and Cheez Whiz. The standing menu is mostly sandwiches and salads. But the sheet of daily specials surprises and satisfies: garlicky roast chicken with hand-cut fries; mahi-mahi graced with an herbed cream sauce. Mexico gets its due with pork tacos jump-started with jalapeño-cilantro sauce. So does India, with chicken korma on basmati rice and sassy chutneys. Ditto Maine, by way of a lobster roll, slicked with basil mayonnaise.

CHEF VOLA'S

111 South Albion Place
Atlantic City, NJ
Owners: Louise Esposito, Michael Esposito,
Michael Esposito Jr., and Louis Esposito
2011 AWARD WINNER

Some believe that Chef Vola's—operating in the base-ment of a former boardinghouse since 1921—is hard to get into, that you need to know someone, that Louise Esposito, the woman who answers the once-unlisted telephone number, screens applicants for a table. Urban legend. Fact is, all are welcome. Once here, you're family. A single serving of the peerless veal chop, done Parm-style, feeds about six. The red gravy is revered, as is the veal swathed in prosciutto. Ditto the cannellini–green bean salad crowned by cubes of provolone and salami. Frank Sinatra once said he wanted to be buried with one of Chef Vola's banana cream pies. In 1982 the Esposito family bought the restaurant from the Vola clan. Today, Louise, along with her husband, Michael, and sons Michael Jr. and Louis, work the kitchen and the dining room, an always-humming space in which a Naples-born grandma would feel at home. Customers make pilgrimages to eat at Chef Vola's. They come for the people. They come for the food, for dishes that are representative of an Italian-American culinary tradition that may be more loved in the heart of the mid-Atlantic than anywhere else.

When Frank Sinatra would go to Atlantic City, he always sent someone to Chef Vola's to pick up a banana cream pie for him.

DURGIN PARK

340 Faneuil Hall Marketplace
Boston, MA
Owner: Seana Kelley
1998 AWARD WINNER

With origins dating to 1742, Durgin Park still serves Yankee fare and bears the name of nineteenth-century restaurateurs John Durgin and Eldridge Park, whose offerings fed the workers at Quincy Market. Although part of a larger restaurant conglomerate since 2007, the restaurant continues to specialize in boiled din-ners, chowders, and a cranky waitstaff. The scene at the original restaurant is pleasantly rowdy, but those willing to battle the crowds will be rewarded with traditional New England fare like lobster stew, pot roast, and even Boston baked beans.

FRANK PEPE PIZZERIA NAPOLETANA

157 Wooster Street
New Haven, CT
Owners: Gary Bimonte, Francis Rosselli, and family
1999 AWARD WINNER

This Connecticut institution has been a pizza lovers' haunt for almost ninety years. Still run by descendants of the legendary Mr. Pepe himself, the pizzeria is widely considered to be one of the best in the country. Locals, students, and tourists line up for hours year-round to score a table at its main location on New Haven's Wooster Street, and several recently opened outposts in Connecticut and New York have proved equally popular. Famous for perfectly charred, thin-crust pizza baked in a blazingly hot coal-fueled oven, the pizzeria also claims to have originated the white clam pie, a sauceless pizza topped with freshly shucked Rhode Island littleneck clams, a touch of oregano, plenty of garlic, a sprinkling of Pecorino Romano, and a drizzle of olive oil.

GRAND CENTRAL OYSTER BAR & RESTAURANT

89 East 42nd Street
New York, NY
Owner: Employee Stock Option Ownership Plan
1999 AWARD WINNER

The centerpiece of Grand Central Terminal's dazzling 1998 renovation, the Oyster Bar & Restaurant has actually been in business since the terminal opened in 1913. Originally a hub for commuters that served "continental" food, including its famous oyster stew, the restaurant was reimagined as a seafood restaurant when Jerome Brody took over in the 1970s. With its vaulted, tiled ceilings lined with glittering lights and checkered cloth–dressed tables, the space evokes both the glamour of long-ago train travel as well as the casual, mollusk-slinging feel of a beloved seafood joint. Evening commuters in need of sustenance can sit at the bar and order a plate of cold, briny oysters on the half-shell—the restaurant usually has up to fifteen varieties to choose from—and a bracing, well-mixed drink before catching their train home. Since earning the America's Classics award in 1999. Brody has passed away, but he left the establishment in the competent hands of a group of employees.

> "I don't care how drunk you are, I don't care how in love you are, never give this recipe away."
> – JOHN BUCCI,
> John's Roast Pork

JOHN'S ROAST PORK

14 East Snyder Avenue
Philadelphia, PA
Owners: Bucci family
2006 AWARD WINNER

In Philadelphia, the iconic sandwich is not that often imitated but never equaled hot beef–plus–cheese concoction; it is the roast pork sandwich. And in Philadelphia, there is no place those who pledge eternal brotherly love would rather secure this sandwich than at John's Roast Pork, a gritty cinder-block shack with a surprisingly breathtaking view of the city skyline. Domenico Bucci made the first roast pork sandwich sold under his family's name in 1930. By 1932, Domenico and his juicy pork were cooking on the corner of Snyder Avenue and Weccacoe Street in South Philly, and by the mid-1950s Dom's son John ruled the locals' favorite roost. In the waning months of John's life, he passed his top-secret recipe on to his son, John Bucci Jr., with a plea that he never give away the family formula. "Whatever you do," he implored, as the story goes, "I don't care how drunk you are, I don't care how in love you are, never give this recipe away. This is my family's name. This is what's important to me." John Bucci Jr. obeyed. More than eighty years after his grandfather served that peerless sandwich, John Jr. still follows the now-legendary, still-secret recipe that folks line up for at John's Roast Pork. His mother, Vonda, rings up the orders and disciplines anyone—from her son to customers—caught misbehaving.

KEENS STEAKHOUSE

72 West 36th Street
New York, NY
Owner: George Schwarz
2013 AWARD WINNER

New York City specializes in new restaurants, not old ones, and local interest in them is generally measured in months instead of years. So it's nothing short of astonishing that a 120-something-year-old restaurant has managed to stay both relevant and wildly popular

Keens Steakhouse

in the middle of Manhattan. Albert Keen, a theater producer, opened the restaurant in 1885, when the Herald Square Theatre District thrived. Actors came in for a drink between acts. Today, the walls are decorated with over fifty thousand clay pipes, donated by celebrated customers like Teddy Roosevelt and Albert Einstein, souvenirs from an era when smoke clouded many restaurants. George Schwarz, the current owner, took over in the late 1970s, investing much money and sweat equity in reviving the restaurant. What Keens has always done well is to age and grill meat. It was one of the first restaurants to dry-age beef. It's a terrific place to order a prime T-bone steak, well charred on the outside and juicy within, served with a tangy-sweet house steak sauce. And Keens's most famous cut of meat, the enormous mutton chop, is accompanied by mint jelly (now made in-house), just as it was when James Beard himself ate at the restaurant over sixty years ago. The menu is stocked with classics like shrimp cocktail, iceberg wedge with chunky blue cheese, and extra-thick slices of smoked bacon, served unadorned on a plate. And the bar at Keens is one of the more democratic places in the city. Yes, it is a destination for Wall Streeters, artists, and fashion editors, but it also draws shoppers from nearby Macy's. The bar room is especially welcoming in the winter, when the fireplace roars and regulars nibble complimentary chicken wings or drink their way through the 275-plus selection of single-malt Scotches.

LE VEAU D'OR

129 East 60th Street
New York, NY
Owner: Catherine Tréboux
2011 AWARD WINNER

The diminutive French bistro Le Veau d'Or (the Golden Calf) in Midtown Manhattan is a time capsule. There's the classic French fare, straight out of Escoffier and the formal but clubby décor, all beveled glass and polished mahogany. Le Veau d'Or opened in 1937; Monsieur Tréboux—who ran the restaurant with his daughter Catherine, until his death in 2012—bought it in 1985, after a career's employment in many of the neighborhood's now bygone French restaurants. In its heyday, Le Veau d'Or was a celebrity haunt. Grace Kelly met

Oleg Cassini there, and food critic Craig Claiborne called it the one restaurant he couldn't live without. Although the clientele has changed over the years, the food is as traditional and delicious as ever. The affordable table d'hôte menu, which includes an appetizer, entrée, and dessert, offers such classics as coq au vin, cassoulet, boeuf à la bourguignonne, and céleri rémoulade. And on any day of the week, you can get an excellent trout meunière and a stellar terrine du chef.

MARIO'S

2342 Arthur Avenue
Bronx, NY
Owners: Migliucci family
2000 AWARD WINNER

As we Americans have joyfully discovered the myriad pleasures of Italy's most obscure regional cuisines, Mario's of the Bronx has continued to serve a style of Italian food you won't quite find anywhere in Italy: Italian-American. With their roots in the southern regions of Calabria and Naples, five generations of the Migliucci family have upheld the banner of such now classic (but once exotic) menu items as fettuccine Alfredo, sausage and peppers, and veal or chicken parmigiana. Today their restaurant is the anchor store of legendary Arthur Avenue, the Little Italy of the northern borough where so many good Italian-American groceries are sold. Opened by Scholastica Migliucci and her son Giuseppe, Mario's is now in its ninth decade. Starting as a small bakery serving old-country pizza, Mario's is reputedly the first place to offer individual slices to pedestrians (thus creating what remains one of New York's archetypal street foods). Many customers still come not for the soulful Italian-American dinners, but for Neapolitan-style (thin-crust) pizzas, topped with cheese, sausage, vegetables, and herbs all bought in the markets of a neighborhood that has scarcely changed in the last hundred years.

Mario's

Mario's

MOOSEWOOD RESTAURANT

215 North Cayuga Street
Ithaca, NY
Owners: Moosewood Collective
2000 AWARD WINNER

At the time Moosewood opened in the late 1970s, vegetarian food had a hideous reputation, and rightfully so. It was a bad-joke cuisine made up of mock-meat, bitter twigs, and curdled beverages, generally served in restaurants that had all the charm of a locker room. The Moosewood Collective changed all that at its original restaurant, still in the Dewitt Mall in Ithaca, and in its excellent cookbooks, which have become scripture for meat-frowners. Meals at Moosewood taught us that vegetarian food needn't be a lame substitute for "real" food but that, in fact, no-meat cookery encompasses some of the best dishes in America and the world, from the red lentil soup of Egypt to Erma Mabel's rhubarb cake from West Virginia. Moosewood is a brash, free-spirited enterprise, where dining is informal and inexpensive. Anything dressier than jeans would feel inappropriate, and service is communal, meaning that orders are taken and food is served by whichever member of the staff is available to perform the task at hand. The only thing predictable about eating at this counterculture landmark is that the menu will be different every day, based on what's in season and what the people in the kitchen are in the mood to cook.

- - - - - - - - - - - - - -

Number of people served at Mustache Bill's on a typical summer day: 1,000.

- - - - - - - - - - - - - -

MUSTACHE BILL'S DINER

8th Street and Broadway
Barnegat Light, NJ
Owner: Bill Smith
2009 AWARD WINNER

These days, the food at diners is all too often of poor to middling quality. But not at Mustache Bill's. For more than thirty-five years, owner Bill Smith has made everything on the diner's menu from scratch—refusing to buy anything premade. It's the homemade, straight-from-the-heart cooking that makes Mustache Bill's a must-stop destination on the Jersey Shore for both the fishing community regulars and the summertime beachgoers. Fishermen reward their community diner with dayboat fluke and scallops, which Smith prepares with aplomb. But follow the lead of locals and you'll soon be tucking into platters of roasted-that-day turkey, ham, and beef. And legendary pancakes. It's no surprise that the line is often long at this seasonal spot: Mustache Bill's does a thousand covers on a typical summer day, and it's only open 6:00 A.M. to 3:00 P.M.

PETER LUGER STEAK HOUSE

178 Broadway
Brooklyn, NY
Owners: Marilyn Spiera and Amy Rubinstein
2002 AWARD WINNER

Habitués of Peter Luger Steak House have known for more than a hundred years not to ask for menus. They simply tell their gruff waiter that they want steak for however many are in their party, a tomato and onion salad to start, hash browns, and creamed spinach. Steak at Luger's is porterhouse, which has been hand-selected by the owners during one of their daily visits to the wholesale meat market, and then aged for what tastes like three months (they won't say how long). The meat is then seared in one of the huge broilers in the kitchen, sliced, and returned to the broiler to be finished. The steak is extraordinarily beefy and flavorful, and remarkably tender. The hash browns are crisped to a perfect burnished brown, and the nutmeg-y creamed spinach makes vegetable lovers out of the most devout carnivore. To complete this festival of a meal, a slice of cheesecake, chocolate mousse cake, or apple strudel comes with a bowl of whipped cream big enough to swim in.

POLLY'S PANCAKE PARLOR

672 NH-117
Sugar Hill, NH
Owners: Nancy and Roger Aldrich and
Kathie and Dennis Côté
2006 AWARD WINNER

Polly's Pancake Parlor is one of the restaurants New Englanders long for during the seemingly endless winter: an eatery that shows off the best of the maple syrup "sugar shacks" running through the woods of New England and Canada. Syrup lovers know that the best syrup is not the finest grade, which is pale and pure and relatively bland; good syrup has dark color and rich flavor. Polly's hand-picks the syrup it serves and makes its own maple spread from maple sugar, using machinery and a time-consuming process that the owners developed to give the best and deepest flavor to its pancakes. Breakfast items (served through lunch) come with a choice of maple syrup, sugar, or spread. And what pancakes! Unlike other much-loved, modest family-owned businesses, Polly's has only improved its range and quality with age. In 1938 Polly and Wilfred "Sugar Bill" Dexter converted an 1830s carriage shed into a small tearoom and started serving pancakes, waffles, and French toast to stimulate sales of their maple products; their daughter took over in 1949 and gave the restaurant its current name. Today the restaurant is three times its original size and stays open six months a year rather than the original three. Kathie and Dennis Coté, the third generation, serve several kinds of pancakes and waffles—buckwheat, cornmeal, whole wheat, and oatmeal buttermilk, to name a few—all made from scratch. For New Englanders who care passionately about their syrup and pancakes, an annual pilgrimage to Polly's is a must.

PRIMANTI BROTHERS

46 18th Street
Pittsburgh, PA
Owner: Demetrios Patrinos
2007 AWARD WINNER

The first Primanti Brothers restaurant was opened in 1933 in Pittsburgh's warehouse district. Purchased by Demetrios Patrinos in 1974, the small Italian eatery now has several outposts in Pennsylvania, West Virginia, and Florida, all of which are famous for the super-stuffed Primanti's sandwich, which features a generous serving of meat, a scoop of crunchy coleslaw, and the restaurant's crisp French fries, all piled on top of soft Italian bread. The gargantuan handheld meal is believed to have been created for nighttime workers on the loading docks who needed to eat on the job, but today hungry food lovers enjoy it around the clock.

Primanti Brothers

SEVILLA RESTAURANT & BAR

62 Charles Street
New York, NY
Owners: Jose Lloves and Bienvenido Alvarez
2015 AWARD WINNER

The area in Manhattan around 14th Street and Eighth Avenue was known as Little Spain as early as 1900. In addition to community resources like the Spanish Benevolent Society, the neighborhood was also home to a wealth of Spanish restaurants. Sevilla, which began life as an Irish pub in 1923, opened as a Spanish restaurant in 1941 under the direction of Luis Fernandez and Alfonso Uchupi. In 1962, the chef Jose Lloves bought it. Ten years later his brother Bienvenido Alvarez joined as a partner. At Sevilla, the walls are decorated with bull heads and oil paintings of busty doñas. The deep and discreet booths are lit by glowing lanterns. The cocktail list is a time capsule of stingers, grasshoppers, and brandy Alexanders. Waiters wearing burgundy vests and bow ties serve tableside from covered metal *cazuelas*. And regulars flock for shrimp with green sauce, mariscada with hot garlic sauce, veal chops, and pitchers of sangria.

SHADY GLEN

840 Middle Turnpike East
Manchester, CT
Owners: William Hoch and Annette Hoch
2012 AWARD WINNER

Since 1948, families in the fertile dairy country of central Connecticut have made pilgrimages to the sandwich counter, soda fountain, and booths of Shady Glen. Decorated with children's-book murals, the restaurant still makes its dozens of flavors of ice cream using local milk. In addition to great ice cream and house-mixed sodas, Shady Glen serves a singular cheeseburger. Here's how they do it: The custom-ground patty is laid on the griddle and topped with three or four overlapping squares of American cheese. The protruding edges, grilled to Le Corbusier curls, gloriously soar outside the bun. Diners either break off the crisped pieces, or take off the bun top and fold them over the burger. John Rieg, son of German immigrants, learned to make ice cream from University of Connecticut professors. Bernice, his wife, conceived the cheeseburger. Today William Hoch Sr., his wife, Annette, and William Hoch Jr. operate Shady Glen's two locations and stubbornly stick with tradition. "We don't want to be millionaires," William Jr. says. "We're more than happy to see a smile on people's faces."

2ND AVENUE DELI

162 East 33rd Street
New York, NY
Owner: Jeremy Lebewohl
1998 AWARD WINNER

One of the last remaining certified-kosher delicatessens in New York City, the 2nd Avenue Deli has been a mecca for corned beef lovers since it opened in 1954 on the southeast corner of Second Avenue and East 10th Street, in the heart of what had once been the Yiddish Theater District. Since the notorious murder of founder and Holocaust survivor Abe Lebewohl in 1996, the 2nd Avenue Deli has moved and expanded. In 2006, rent disputes led to a closure and a subsequent reopening in Murray Hill. Another location opened in 2011 on the Upper East Side; both have retained the restaurant's charm and iconic menu. Loyal customers return over and over again for favorites like chicken soup with matzoh balls, chopped liver, hot corned beef, or a dish called the "Instant Heart Attack": a hefty helping of meat sandwiched between two large potato pancakes.

TOTONNO'S

1524 Neptune Avenue
Brooklyn, NY
Owners: Louise F. Ciminieri, Frank L. Balzano,
and Antoinette J. Balzano
2009 AWARD WINNER

See page 60.

WATERMAN'S BEACH LOBSTER

343 Waterman Beach Road
South Thomaston, ME
Owners: Sandy Manahan and Lorrie Cousens
2001 AWARD WINNER

See page 64.

WHITE HOUSE SUB SHOP

2301 Arctic Avenue
Atlantic City, NJ
Owner: Basile and Sacco-Conley families
2000 AWARD WINNER

One can find a submarine-style sandwich almost everywhere in the U.S. In some places it will be a very good one—in New Orleans a po-boy, in Miami a Cuban sandwich, in Chicago an Italian beef. The Delaware Valley in general is sub-sandwich central, and includes such sub-genres as the cheesesteak and the hoagie. But if you want the very best, dished out with sass and attitude at no extra charge, there is only one place to go—the White House Sub Shop of Atlantic City. Built on loaves of superb bread that are secured fresh by the kitchen throughout the day, these are true heroes, ranging from the "White House Special," which is a stack of cold cuts tightly packed and drizzled with olive oil, to hot meatball subs that inevitably squish and ooze as soon as you hoist them toward your mouth. Since Tony Basile opened it in 1946, the White House has established and maintained the fundamental rule of good sub-shop décor, which is to cover the walls with pictures of celebrity clientele (Sinatra, Joe Frazier, Jerry Lewis, et al.). For all the stardust, it remains a humble naugahyde-and-neon eat-place with paper napkins, harsh lighting, and brusque service. It would be wrong to serve a great sub sandwich any other way.

MIDWEST

AL'S BREAKFAST

MINNEAPOLIS, MN

2004 AWARD WINNER

In 1950, Al Bergstrom opened Al's Cafe in the former home of the Hunky Dory burger stand in the Dinkytown section of Minneapolis. He started serving three meals a day, seven days a week, largely to students attending the nearby University of Minnesota. After a year, Bergstrom cut back the restaurant's hours. The three-meal days were wearing him down. Plus, he'd noticed that his breakfast menu was so popular that people were ordering from it all day long. So the American-born son of Swedish immigrants began opening at the crack of dawn and closing at 1 P.M. He rechristened the restaurant Al's Breakfast, which today still plays to the strengths Bergstrom recognized early on. Al's has never grown out of its pocket-size, fourteen-seat space, where customers ranging from prominent local politicians and celebrities to multiple generations of university students stream in from the cold to wait against a wall for a seat at the counter. The restaurant is an icon in an area where breakfast is taken almost as seriously as hockey. When Al Bergstrom passed away at the age of ninety-seven in June 2003, it was a front-page story in the Minneapolis Star Tribune.

AL BERGSTROM HAD BEEN WORKING AS A CHEF for a restaurant that he thought he had ownership in. He found out at Christmas that he didn't. He was so upset that he walked across the street, where a guy owned a little, tiny café. Al offered him $500 for his restaurant, and the guy took it. Al opened up Al's Breakfast in 1950. He retired in 1974 and sold it to his nephew. I came on in 1977 and after a couple of months I bought out Al's nephew.

People's tastes have changed. When I first started here we went through about a 12-ounce bottle of salsa a week. We now go through four and a half gallons of our homemade salsa. People eat more potatoes and fewer eggs than they used to. A lot more of our clientele are foreign, tourists, or visitors. We're close to the University of Minnesota, and the number of students has slowly increased over the years. Students didn't have the money to eat out forty years ago. They didn't move into apartments where for $900 apiece they had a bed and a granite countertop, which is what they're doing now. Before, you had to find the money and you had to struggle a bit and you lived on nothing. That doesn't happen so much anymore. Everybody lives on debt now.

People are more willing to spend money than they were thirty years ago. Al set his pricing so customers could buy a basic egg and basic pancakes very inexpensively, which we still do, but now there are a lot fewer takers. Not as often do you see somebody coming in and having two plain pancakes and two eggs.

I have one partner, Jim Brandes, and we're here every day working it. We both operate as the guy out front who's yelling and screaming at everybody and also the guy behind the scenes doing things to keep the restaurant going. Al's is set up differently from the way most restaurants run. When people are hired here we have a sequence they go through to learn the restaurant. You start as a dishwasher, then after maybe four shifts you start learning the counter. After you've done the counter you learn how to cook in back, and anyone who is willing to take the pressure of cooking up front is taught how to work the grill. Everybody learns everything and then when they get there in the mornings they decide what they want to do. They all share the same tips and the same pay. What that does—surprisingly—is make dishwashing incredibly attractive because they don't have to talk to anybody. I'm proud that the people who work here like working here. People like staying here because we're like a honey trap.

Because of our popularity we never tried to see how much we could charge, and so when times get hard we're always a good option. I actually feel that some of our better years have been during economic downturns because people will stop going to more expensive restaurants and start coming to Al's. Keeping our price range low has been good for our longevity. Another thing about us is that everybody who comes here has fun just watching us work and watching all the shenanigans that are going on. We make the experience more than just coming and having breakfast—it's a show as well.

—DOUG GRINA

Al's Breakfast can seat only fourteen people at a time. The restaurant is located in a Minneapolis neighborhood referred to as "Dinkytown."

THE BERGHOFF

CHICAGO, IL

1999 AWARD WINNER

THE STORY
*

The Berghoff first opened in 1898 as a men-only saloon whose sole menu items were the corned beef sandwiches served free with the purchase of a stein of the German-born owners' proprietary beer. Over the years the spot evolved into a beloved full-service restaurant famous for traditional German fare like wiener schnitzel, knockwürst, spaetzle, and creamed herring. The Berghoff was briefly closed in 2005 by its third-generation owners, but the restaurant's basement café resumed business shortly thereafter, and in 2007 the entire restaurant again opened its doors and revealed a new menu that features several less iconically Bavarian items. Although some of the dishes might be lighter, the restaurant still sells its famous Berghoff Root Beer and has an annual Oktoberfest. Berghorff also opened a café at O'Hare, serving sandwiches and beers.

MY GREAT-GRANDFATHER, HERMAN JOSEPH BERGHOFF, emigrated from Germany to the United States in 1870 when he was seventeen years old. He traveled around the country—he worked on ships, he worked with Buffalo Bill—and one day he was on the train and he got off in Fort Wayne, Indiana, to buy a pretzel. The grocer offered to sponsor him to become an American citizen, and got him a job. So he got off the train to work for the grocer. Back in the 1800s grocers were so different because the only way food was transported was through the rail system. So the grocery stores were tied to the rail system and to train stations. Eventually my grandfather opened a brewery in Fort Wayne, and after selling his beer all over Indiana and the Midwest, he decided he wanted to try Chicago.

So he came to Chicago hoping to open a booth in the Columbian Exhibition, the World's Fair, and the World's Fair committee said that they had enough beer, and, "No thank you, Mr. Berghoff," and Mr. Berghoff said, "Okay, well, I'm going to make my stuff known anyway." He set up a booth just outside the gates of the World's Fair and gave customers a corned beef sandwich when they bought a beer. He did that for a year until the World's Fair was over, and then he opened a saloon at the corner of Adams and State Streets. When Prohibition hit, he came up with a solution to continue to employ people and pay the bills: He started brewing root beer and orange soda, and he created a soda for upset stomachs.

Over that period—because Prohibition went on forever—my grandfather Louis and my uncle Clem came in and the saloon became a restaurant. That's when they really started with the food. Then the third generation came in, which was my mom and dad, and now there's me.

People like tradition and things that don't change too much. But obviously, we've had to change over each generation. I mean, I can remember two years ago, when the breading company that made the bread crumbs—the special bread crumbs for the schnitzel—went out of business, just closed their doors. I remember the trauma that we went through to find something as similar in order to keep the schnitzel as consistent as it had been for years, and how many different breadings we tasted, and how many different ways we tried to cook the breadings, hoping to get the same result as what we had before. It was really hard, and we held our breath through the transition of the new product. You don't always have control of what your vendors do.

I think that whenever people are facing economic challenges, the Berghoff has always been one of those places that's a sure thing: a sure thing in its value and a sure thing in its products. Everything's homemade from scratch. We feed thousands of people during the winter season. These are all people fulfilling their family traditions. Whenever we turn around it's, "Oh, we have twenty-two in our group, we have twenty-four in our group." They'll have four generations at a table. I love hearing the stories. I love hearing how people met their husbands or their wives there, or how they were one of the first people to dine in the bar after women were allowed. All walks of life have introduced themselves to me over the last eight and a half years, and shared their stories. It's a place that holds a lot of memories.

—CARLYN BERGHOFF

THREE BROTHERS RESTAURANT

MILWAUKEE, WI

2002 AWARD WINNER

Three Brothers Restaurant is a monument to the immigrant work ethic and family values so intrinsic to American culture. Its story began in eastern Europe during World War II when the patriarch of the Serbian Radicevic family was sent to a concentration camp, shattering the family. The father survived, came to America after the war, and opened a restaurant, which he named Three Brothers as a tribute to his children, whose whereabouts remained unknown for years. Today the restaurant is run by the founder's grandchildren, but the vintage dining room is virtually unchanged from the '50s. A glance into the kitchen will reveal a hill of freshly chopped onions destined to appear in Serbian salad or the irresistible phyllo pillows called burek or the creamy sauce for chicken paprikash. The food is rich and abundant and full of flavor—family food gone public.

THREE BROTHERS RESTAURANT WAS STARTED BY MY GRANDFATHER. He and my grandmother were from Yugoslavia, where they had several restaurants. They also had a winery and a soda bottle company, but they lost everything in the war.

During World War II my family was separated, a separation that ended up lasting fifteen years. My grandfather was in a German concentration camp and he was part of a group that escaped, a group of French underground nationalists. As they were escaping they actually ended up saving a French platoon, and my grandfather was awarded the French Legion of Honor. Through his connections there he ended up in England, and in the early 1950s he received sponsorship and came to Milwaukee. That's when he opened Three Brothers as a bar and tavern; he named it after his three sons.

At that time, he was trying to find out where my father and uncles were. Because of their involvement as freedom fighters, it wasn't easy for them to get the papers they needed. They kept getting denied. Finally my grandmother arrived in Milwaukee and Three Brothers became more of a restaurant. My grandfather's dream was to have his three sons with him, to bring the family back together and to do it here, in Milwaukee. They were all separated for so many years until finally my two uncles and my father escaped Yugoslavia. My uncles arrived first, and my father arrived in Milwaukee in 1959.

The restaurant was small, and everyone lived upstairs. We served Serbian food, and I don't even know if people knew what Serbian was at the time. When my grandparents were ready to retire they asked my father, Branko, the oldest child, who was working at a bank, and my mother, who is of Irish-Lithuanian descent, to take over the restaurant. My grandmother worked to teach my mother the recipes, even though my mother spoke no Serbian and my grandmother spoke very little English. All of the recipes that are on our menu are my grandmother's re-creation of Serbian dishes, and my mother not only mastered the recipes, but she also captured the feel of them and what all of this meant to my grandparents and my father. She carried the sentiment of family and of our tradition forward.

My brother, Branko, and I are running the restaurant now. I always tell people it's in our blood. I've been working here since I was little. We were taught from a very young age how to clean a table, how to wash a dish, how to make a cup of coffee—it was always with the notion that every skill, everything that you know, will enrich your life someday.

I think the restaurant has such longevity in part because of the love that my family had for everything America gave them. My grand-father loved that the country welcomed him and gave him another start. We want the restaurant to let people know that we hope you become part of our family. There's a sense of continuity, a message that says, "Welcome, sit down. Have a meal with us. Share a glass of wine with us." There's just a warmth. My family has taken such great pride in becoming part of America's food landscape, and continuing the tradi-tion of providing home-cooked meals.

—MILUNKA RADICEVIC

- - - - - - - - - - - - - - - - -

"Take short cuts?
Our mother never did that.
We never do that."
— BRANKO RADICEVIC,
Three Brothers in Milwaukee, WI

- - - - - - - - - - - - - - - - -

Pie

"We Americans undoubtedly eat more kinds of pie than any other country," wrote James Beard in *The Armchair James Beard*. His observation seems apt. Early American settlers baked sweet and savory pies in round, shallow pans as a way to stretch basic ingredients; the dish was such a staple that most colonists ate it at every meal. These days, however, a perfectly baked pie—with a flaky, golden crust, a warm, sweet filling, and just the right balance of fruit and pastry—is a rare treat. Pie making is more of a tradition than a technique, a ritual passed down in families, a dish learned through repetition and feel and generations of practice. Each region of the country claims its own pie specialty—a flavor so intrinsic to local identity that its provenance is obvious—and each expert pie maker boasts her own style and secrets. Here's where to find some of the most memorable slices the country has to offer.

Region	Pie	Where to Get It	Words of Wisdom
MIDWEST	Strawberry pie	**BREITBACH'S COUNTRY DINING** Sherrill, IA	Breitbach's is known for their homemade pies, which are listed year-round on the menu. During the summer, owner and resident baker Cindy Breitbach incorporates fresh local strawberries into a gorgeous open-faced pie with a distinctly Midwestern twist: the filling is made with strawberry Jell-O.
SOUTHEAST	Atlantic Beach Pie (page 48)	**CROOK'S CORNER** Chapel Hill, NC	Made with a saltine cracker crust and a creamy citrus filling, this pie is a popular meal-ender in North Carolina seafood restaurants. Chef Bill Smith at Crook's Corner tops his with whipped cream instead of the more commonly found meringue topping.
NORTHEAST	Blueberry pie	**WATERMAN'S BEACH LOBSTER** South Thomaston, ME	Waterman's lobster dinners aren't complete without a generous, overfilled slice of one of their famous pies. Served with a dollop of freshly whipped cream, the blueberry pie offers a quintessential taste of Maine.
SOUTHWEST	Peanut butter pie	**EL CHORRO LODGE** Paradise Valley, AZ	El Chorro Lodge wins raves for its complimentary sticky buns, but the Arizona stalwart's pies are also out of this world. Though it may not be a specifically southwestern specialty, El Chorro's peanut butter pie, made with caramel and chocolate and topped with a dollop of whipped cream, is a customer favorite.
WEST	Olallieberry pie	**DUARTE'S TAVERN** Pescadero, CA	Pascale Le Draoulec, author of *American Pie: Slices of Life (and Pie) from America's Back Roads*, wrote this of the olallieberry pie at Duarte's Tavern in Pescadero, California: "A slice of this pie after a bowl of their famous artichoke soup, and you're a changed person."

FRIED CALAMARI

TUFANO'S VERNON PARK TAP

CHICAGO, IL

Set in the heart of Chicago's Little Italy, Tufano's Vernon Tap is the red-sauce restaurant against which all red-sauce restaurants are judged. Regulars know to start their meal of Italian-American classics with a mound of this crispy fried calamari, served with tangy marinara for dipping. Be careful not to crowd the pan or the squid will soak up too much oil. The calamari cooks quickly; when done it will be golden and tender.

SERVES 6 TO 8 AS AN APPETIZER

Vegetable oil for deep-frying

3 large eggs

¾ cup milk

½ teaspoon salt

¼ teaspoon freshly ground black pepper

1 pound squid with tentacles, cleaned and drained, with bodies cut into ⅓- to ½-inch rings

2 cups all-purpose flour

Lemon wedges

"Tufano's is an amazing neighborhood place, and Joey DiBuono [grandson of the original owners] is such an incredible host. He knows everybody's names—whether it's a politician or a regular who always eats there before a Bulls game. He not only knows their names; he also knows their kids' names, and at which table they want to sit."

— DONNIE MADIA,
JBF Award Winner

POUR 3 inches of oil into a large, heavy saucepan and heat over medium heat to 350°F.

IN a large bowl, whisk the eggs, milk, salt, and pepper until thoroughly combined. Add the squid to the bowl, stir to cover, and set aside for 5 minutes.

PUT the flour in a medium bowl. Line a plate with paper towels.

USING a slotted spoon and working in batches, transfer the squid to the bowl of flour; toss gently to coat evenly and shake off excess. Carefully add the squid to the hot oil and fry until crisp and golden, 1 to 2 minutes per batch. Using tongs or a slotted spoon, transfer the fried calamari to the paper towel–lined plate to drain. Serve immediately, with lemon wedges.

HAM SALAD

LAGOMARCINO'S

MOLINE, IL

This small-town soda shop is know[n] [for its con]fections, but savory offerings like [its] beloved ham salad are also longtim[e favorites.] The proprietors bake bone-in ham [and the] meat closest to the bone is used to [make this] lunchtime staple, which is served as a sand-wich on homemade Swedish rye bread. Ask your butcher to grind cooked ham for you, or use a food processor with the grinder attachment to grind leftover ham at home.

MAKES 2 CUPS, ENOUGH FOR ABOUT 4 SANDWICHES

1½ cups ground cooked ham

1 celery rib, finely chopped (about ¼ cup)

¼ cup sweet pickle relish

½ cup mayonnaise, or more if needed

Salt and freshly ground black pepper

IN a medium bowl, combine the ham, celery, and relish. Stir to combine. (This step can be done up to 2 hours ahead of time.)

RIGHT before serving, add the mayonnaise and mix thoroughly. Season to taste with salt and pepper, adding more mayonnaise if desired.

KING CRAB MAC AND CHEESE

ST. ELMO STEAK HOUSE

INDIANAPOLIS, IN

No one will ever go hungry at St. Elmo Steak House. Every meal begins with the choice of a cup of navy bean soup or a glass of tomato juice, and the steaks and other hearty entrées are served with a choice of green beans or potatoes (fried, baked, or mashed). But customers still make room for this indulgent side: a rich, oven-baked macaroni and cheese topped with a generous mound of lump crabmeat. The subtle smokiness from the Gouda makes this creamy pasta an unexpectedly delicious counterpoint to the sweet, unadorned crabmeat.

SERVES 6 TO 8

Salt

1 pound ditalini or other small pasta

8 tablespoons (1 stick) unsalted butter

⅓ cup all-purpose flour

4 cups (1 quart) half-and-half

1 cup heavy cream

1 teaspoon ground white pepper

½ teaspoon coarsely ground black pepper

½ teaspoon freshly grated nutmeg

¼ teaspoon ground cayenne pepper

1 pound smoked Gouda cheese, shredded (about 4 cups)

¾ cup coarse bread crumbs or panko

8 ounces chopped lump king crab crabmeat

PREHEAT the oven to 350°F.

BRING a large pot of salted water to a boil. Add the pasta and cook, stirring occasionally, until 2 minutes before al dente. (You want to slightly undercook the pasta as it will continue cooking while in the oven.) Drain and rinse until cool. Set aside.

IN a large saucepan over medium heat, melt 6 tablespoons of the butter. When the butter is melted, remove the pan from the heat and stir in the flour. Place the pan back on the heat and cook for 1 to 2 minutes, whisking constantly. Add the half-and-half, cream, 1 tablespoon of salt, the white pepper, black pepper, nutmeg, and cayenne pepper. Continue to cook, whisking constantly, until thickened and smooth. Add 2 cups of the cheese and stir until the mixture is thoroughly blended and the cheese has melted, about 3 minutes. Set aside.

IN a separate bowl, mix together the bread crumbs and remaining cheese. Stir to combine.

(continued)

"You've got to come to Indianapolis to find out why the St. Elmo's shrimp cocktail is so unique, but I'll give you a hint: There's tons of fresh horseradish in it."

— CRAIG HUSE,
St. Elmo Steak House
in Indianapolis, IN

TO assemble the dish, return the pasta to the cooking pot. Add the cream sauce and stir well to combine. Use 1 tablespoon of butter to grease a 2-quart baking dish. Spoon the pasta into the baking dish and top with the bread crumb mixture. Place in the oven and bake until the top is golden brown, the bread crumbs are toasted, and the sauce is bubbling, about 40 minutes.

MEANWHILE, gently heat the remaining 1 tablespoon butter in a large skillet. Add the crabmeat, season with a pinch of salt, and sauté just until heated through, about 2 minutes. Remove from the heat and set aside.

WHEN the macaroni and cheese is done, remove from the oven and let stand for 2 minutes. Top with the warm crabmeat and serve.

CORN FRITTERS

ARCHIE'S WAESIDE

LE MARS, IA

At Archie's Waeside, where they've been cutting and aging their beef in-house for more than sixty years, the fat, juicy steaks are the main attraction. But these addictive corn fritters have a fan club all their own. Light and airy, with just the right amount of corn flavor, the golden fritters have been on the menu at the Iowa steakhouse since 1949 and are served with honey. Mix the slightly sweetened batter by hand to keep the fritters light and airy. The fritters are best served right away, but they can be kept warm in a 250°F oven for up to 30 minutes, or until ready to serve.

MAKES ABOUT 2 DOZEN CORN FRITTERS

Vegetable oil for deep-frying

1 large egg

⅓ cup sugar

½ teaspoon salt

¾ cup plus 2 tablespoons canned creamed corn

½ cup plus 2 tablespoons 2% milk

2 cups all-purpose flour

1 teaspoon baking powder

POUR 2 inches of oil into a Dutch oven, or use a deep-fryer. Heat the oil to 325°F over medium-high heat.

IN a large bowl, beat the egg. Add the sugar and salt and mix well. Add the creamed corn and the milk and stir to combine. Add the flour and baking powder and mix until just blended. (Don't overmix after adding the flour or the dough will be stiff.)

WORKING in batches and being careful not to crowd the fryer, drop the dough by rounded tablespoons into the hot oil and cook for 4 to 6 minutes, until the fritter is brown on all sides and a fork inserted into the dough comes out clean. Drain on paper towels and serve hot.

PIEROGI

SOKOLOWSKI'S UNIVERSITY INN

CLEVELAND, OH

Sokolowski's University Inn serves its famous, butter-browned pierogi smothered in sautéed onions alongside a dollop of sour cream. The dough is enriched with sour cream or cream cheese and the dumplings can be stuffed with a variety of fillings: potatoes and cheese, mushrooms, even sauerkraut. Make the filling first so it has time to cool to room temperature before forming the dumplings. Pierogis freeze beautifully, so make a big batch to have on hand for busy nights. No need to thaw before cooking; they can be cooked straight from the freezer. Serve topped with sautéed onions and a sprinkle of chopped chives or fresh dill if desired.

MAKES ABOUT 3 DOZEN DUMPLINGS

1 egg yolk

1½ teaspoons canola oil

2 cups all-purpose flour, plus more for kneading

2 teaspoons salt, plus more for cooking

2 tablespoons sour cream or cream cheese

Potato and Cheese Filling (recipe follows), cooled

4 tablespoons (½ stick) unsalted butter

IN a medium bowl, beat together the egg yolk and oil with ½ cup cold water. Set aside.

IN a large bowl or the bowl of stand mixer fitted with the dough hook, combine the flour and salt and mix for about 30 seconds. Add the sour cream, 2 tablespoons cold water, and the egg mixture to the flour. Mix until the ingredients are thoroughly combined and the dough is creamy and pliable, about 15 minutes. The dough should not be too sticky; if it is, add a little flour and continue mixing. When the dough is silky and elastic, remove from the bowl and place on a floured surface. Cover and let it sit for 30 minutes.

ON a lightly floured surface, roll the dough out to ⅛ inch thick using a rolling pin. Use a 4-inch round cutter to cut out circles of dough.

TO make the pierogis, stretch a dough circle slightly with your fingertips and place about 1½ tablespoons of the filling onto the center of the dough. Bring the edges of the circles together to form a half-circle. Using your thumbs, crimp the edges to form a tight seal. (If the dough won't seal, moisten the edges with cold water.) Place on a lightly floured baking sheet. Repeat with the remaining circles of dough. If making ahead of time, the uncooked pierogi can be frozen on a waxed paper–lined baking sheet. Once frozen, transfer to resealable plastic bags and freeze for up to 3 months.

TO cook, bring a large pot of salted water to a low boil. Place the dumplings in the boiling water and cook until they float, 2 to 3 minutes. Remove with a slotted spoon and place in a colander to drain.

IN a large, heavy-bottomed skillet, melt 2 tablespoons of the butter. Working in batches, cook the pierogi over medium-high heat until lightly browned, 5 to 7 minutes, adding more butter to the pan as needed. Serve immediately.

POTATO AND CHEESE FILLING
MAKES ENOUGH FILLING FOR ABOUT 3 DOZEN DUMPLINGS

2 baking potatoes, peeled and cut into 3-inch pieces
4 tablespoons (½ stick) unsalted butter
4 ounces sharp cheddar cheese, cubed (about 1¼ cups)
1 teaspoon salt
¼ teaspoon freshly ground black pepper

BRING a medium pot of water to a steady boil. Add the potatoes and cook until fork-tender, 15 to 20 minutes. Drain and put the hot cooked potatoes in a large bowl with the butter; beat with a hand-held mixer or a potato masher until the potatoes are mashed. Add the cheese and let stand for a few minutes until the cheese melts. Add the salt and pepper and mix until smooth. Set aside to cool completely.

The president of Poland has been to Sokolowski's University Inn. As has Kevin Bacon.

SMOKED WHITEFISH PICATTA

THE PICKWICK

DULUTH, MN

Made with smoked Lake Superior whitefish, which the restaurant also serves as an appetizer on rye crackers with all the fixings, this decadent pasta was inspired by the buttery, briny flavors of a classic picatta. The dish comes together very quickly, so make sure to have all the ingredients prepped and ready to go before starting to cook. Add the whitefish at the end so the pieces don't break apart.

SERVES 4

¼ cup olive oil

2 medium zucchini or summer squash, diced (about 2 cups)

2 shallots, finely minced

3 tablespoons capers, drained and rinsed

2 garlic cloves, minced

2 tablespoons unsalted butter

½ cup chicken stock

Juice of 2 lemons

½ cup heavy cream

Pinch of red pepper flakes

1 pound spaghetti or other thin pasta, cooked

8 ounces smoked whitefish, in large pieces (scant 2 cups)

¼ cup grated Parmesan cheese, or more to taste

¼ cup minced fresh flat-leaf parsley

Salt and freshly ground black pepper

HEAT the oil in a very large sauté pan over medium-high heat. Add the zucchini, shallots, capers, garlic, and butter; cook for 1 minute. Add the stock and lemon juice and stir. Add the cream and red pepper flakes. Bring to a gentle boil, lower the heat, and simmer for 1 to 2 minutes, until the sauce has thickened and reduced by one quarter. Add the cooked pasta, smoked whitefish, cheese, and parsley. Toss gently and cook for 1 minute, so the pasta soaks up some of the sauce. Remove from the heat and season with salt and black pepper to taste before serving.

"The Pickwick is located on the shore of Lake Superior. It's kind of funny sometimes because we'll get people who walk in and they want to see the whales migrate and I have to tell them that we're on an inland lake."

— CHRIS WISOCKI,
The Pickwick in Duluth, MN

LEMON CHICKEN

TUFANO'S VERNON PARK TAP

CHICAGO, IL

Regulars speak of the lemon chicken at Tufano's Vernon Park Tap with deep reverence. Crisp, charred, and redolent of garlic and lemon, this dish is one of Tufano's standbys; the kind of dish you order every time you go no matter what. At the restaurant the chicken is served topped with fried rounds of potatoes, some of which fall to the bottom of the plate and soak up the rich, lemony sauce, but it could also be paired with roasted potatoes, rice, or slices of hearty bread for mopping up your plate.

SERVES 4 TO 6

1 small (3-pound) chicken, cut into 8 pieces

4 garlic cloves, minced

1 teaspoon dried oregano

½ teaspoon salt

½ teaspoon freshly ground black pepper

¼ cup olive oil

¼ cup vegetable oil

1 whole lemon, cut in half

PREHEAT the broiler to high. Place the rack 3 to 4 inches from the heat source.

PAT the chicken pieces dry and put them in a medium bowl. Add the garlic, oregano, salt, and pepper and toss to combine. Place the chicken pieces skin-side down in a broiler pan and drizzle with the olive oil and vegetable oil. Squeeze the juice from both lemon halves over the chicken. Place the lemon halves in the pan with the chicken.

PUT the pan under the broiler and cook the chicken on one side for 20 to 25 minutes. Turn the pieces over and cook until the other side is golden and crisp, about 10 minutes. Do not overcook. Discard the lemon halves. Transfer the chicken to a platter and top with sauce from the broiler pan.

WIENER SCHNITZEL

THE BERGHOFF

CHICAGO, IL

Tender, lightly breaded veal pan-fried until golden brown, wiener schnitzel has long been the most popular entrée at the Berghoff, a former men's-only saloon founded by German-born brewers. To make sure the dish is crisp on the outside and tender and juicy within, chill the breaded cutlets before frying. The Berghoff still presents this customer favorite as it always has: alongside lemon wedges to squeeze over the cutlets and dill pickles for crunching on between bites. Serve with fries, mashed potatoes, or warm German potato salad.

SERVES 4

1 cup all-purpose flour

1 teaspoon salt

Freshly ground white pepper

2 large eggs, lightly beaten

2 tablespoons milk

1 cup cracker meal or fine unseasoned bread crumbs

4 (5-ounce) veal cutlets, pounded thin and chilled

Vegetable oil for pan-frying

Lemon wedges

Kosher dill pickle spears

LINE a baking sheet with waxed paper.

IN a medium bowl, combine the flour, salt, and white pepper. In a shallow container, whisk the eggs and milk together. Put the cracker meal in a separate medium bowl. Entirely coat each cutlet with the flour, then the egg mixture, and finally the cracker meal, patting the cutlets with the meal to ensure they are completely coated. Place the cutlets in one layer on the prepared baking sheet, cover, and refrigerate for at least 30 minutes.

LINE a plate with paper towels and set aside. Heat ¼ inch of oil in a large skillet over medium-high heat. When the oil is hot but not smoking, gently add the cutlets, working in batches if necessary to avoid crowding the pan. Cook until golden brown on both sides, 1 to 2 minutes per side. Transfer to the paper towel–lined plate and keep warm until ready to serve.

CINCINNATI CHILI

CAMP WASHINGTON CHILI

CINCINNATI, OH

The owners of Camp Washington Chili were reluctant to part with the secret family recipe for their signature dish, but they happily provided us with this version, a slight variation on the original. Rich with spices, this chili has a deep, beefy flavor and a nice kick. It'll be thicker and tastier if cooked a day ahead of time, chilled overnight, and then reheated before serving. To serve it "five-way"—the most popular order at the restaurant—ladle the chili over a bed of spaghetti and top with red kidney beans, diced white onions, and a heaping mound of shredded Wisconsin cheddar cheese. Serve with oyster crackers and hot sauce.

SERVES 6 TO 8

1 tablespoon hot chili powder

1 teaspoon ground cumin

1 teaspoon dried oregano

½ teaspoon dry mustard

¼ teaspoon ground cinnamon

¼ teaspoon ground cloves

¼ teaspoon ground ginger

⅛ teaspoon freshly grated nutmeg

2 tablespoons olive oil

3 yellow onions, finely chopped (about 3 cups)

6 garlic cloves, minced (about 2 tablespoons)

1 tablespoon coarse salt, or more to taste

2 pounds lean ground beef

2 (28-ounce) cans crushed tomatoes

2 beef bouillon cubes, or ¼ cup beef demi-glace

IN a small bowl, stir together the chili powder, cumin, oregano, dry mustard, cinnamon, cloves, ginger, and nutmeg. Set aside.

HEAT the oil over medium heat in a large pot. Sauté the onions and garlic until soft, 3 to 5 minutes. Add the spice mixture and salt and stir until fragrant, 1 to 2 minutes. Add the beef and stir thoroughly to combine. Continue stirring until the beef is lightly browned, 7 to 10 minutes. Add the tomatoes and bring the mixture to a gentle simmer. Add the bouillon cubes and stir. Simmer, covered, for 2 to 3 hours, until the chili is very thick and fragrant. Season with additional salt and spices if desired.

HEARTY HOLUBETS
STUFFED CABBAGE ROLLS

KRAMARCZUK'S

MINNEAPOLIS, MN

Filled with a meaty pork-and-rice mixture or oniony roasted kasha, these savory stuffed cabbage rolls (or *holubets* in Ukrainian) truly live up to their name. The key to rolling up the cabbage leaves is to remove the thick rib from the base of each one, and to use two leaves for each roll. Kramarczuk's serves their cabbage rolls alongside ham-strewn sauerkraut and a pickle, but to round out the meal, add a mound of mashed potatoes and an ice-cold lager.

MAKES ABOUT 12 STUFFED CABBAGE ROLLS; SERVES 6 TO 8

Salt

1 medium to large head green cabbage (2 to 3 pounds)

¼ cup white vinegar

¼ cup (½ stick) unsalted butter, cold, cut into thin slices

1 (15-ounce) can tomato sauce

2 cups chicken stock

Savory Pork and Rice Filling or Kasha Filling (recipes follow)

Tomato-Cream Sauce (recipe follows)

TO prepare the cabbage leaves, bring a large stockpot of salted water to a boil. Using a small paring knife, remove the entire core from each cabbage. Place the heads of cabbage in the boiling water, making sure they are fully submerged. Add the vinegar. Boil the cabbage until the leaves fall freely from the heads with the poke of a fork, 45 minutes to 1 hour. Remove the cabbage head and allow it to cool. Carefully peel off each leaf one by one and place on a paper towel–lined baking sheet to dry. Set the outer leaves aside; keep these separate from the rest of the cabbage leaves.

PREHEAT the oven to 350°F.

TO make the cabbage rolls, line the bottom of a deep 9-by-13-inch baking pan with the outer cabbage leaves. Using a small paring knife, remove the large, triangular rib from the base of each inner cabbage leaf. Stack two leaves together, one on top of the other, so their stems align. Place ⅓ cup of filling in an oval shape horizontally across the bottom third of the cabbage leaves. Roll it up once, then tuck in both sides of the leaves and continue to roll until you form a cabbage roll. Place in the baking pan. Repeat until the pan has been filled, placing the rolls side by side.

PLACE the butter slices and spoonfuls of the canned tomato sauce evenly between the cabbage rolls. Pour chicken stock over the rolls until they're submerged. Cover the rolls with any remaining cabbage leaves or aluminum foil. Bake for 40 minutes or until the liquid is boiling. Lower the oven temperature to 300°F and bake for 1 hour. Serve topped with tomato-cream sauce or with the sauce on the side.

(continued)

SAVORY PORK AND RICE FILLING

MAKES ENOUGH FOR 12 CABBAGE ROLLS

½ cup white rice

1 tablespoon unsalted butter

½ large onion, diced

8 ounces ground pork

Salt and freshly ground black pepper

COOK the rice according to the package directions and allow it to cool. In a large, heavy-bottomed skillet, heat the butter over medium heat. Add the onion and cook until lightly golden, about 10 minutes. Increase the heat to medium-high and add the pork, cooking until the pork is lightly browned, about 12 minutes. Allow the mixture to cool and combine with the cooked rice. Season to taste with salt and pepper.

KASHA FILLING (VEGETARIAN)

MAKES ENOUGH FOR 12 CABBAGE ROLLS

Salt

1 cup kasha (sometimes labeled as "roasted buckwheat groats")

3½ tablespoons unsalted butter

1 egg yolk, lightly beaten

½ onion, chopped

½ potato, peeled and grated

Freshly ground black pepper

PREHEAT the oven to 350°F.

BRING 2 cups salted water to a boil. Add the kasha and bring the water back to a boil. Lower the heat to a simmer and cover; cook for 12 to 15 minutes, until the liquid is absorbed. Fluff with a fork.

MELT 2½ tablespoons of the butter. In a medium bowl, combine 1 cup of the cooked kasha with the egg yolk and the melted butter and stir well. (Reserve the remaining kasha for another use.) Spread the kasha mixture on a baking sheet. Bake for 30 minutes or until browned, stirring the mixture every 10 minutes.

MEANWHILE, heat the remaining 1 tablespoon butter over medium heat in a large, heavy-bottomed skillet. Add the onion and cook until lightly golden, about 10 minutes. Set aside.

REMOVE the kasha from the oven and add the grated potato and fried onions. Stir well to combine. Return the baking sheet to the oven and cook for an additional 10 minutes. Remove from the oven and allow to cool. Season with salt and pepper to taste.

TOMATO CREAM SAUCE

MAKES 2 CUPS

3 tablespoons unsalted butter

½ onion, chopped (about ¾ cup)

¼ cup all-purpose flour

1 teaspoon sugar

½ teaspoon salt, plus more as needed

¼ teaspoon freshly ground black pepper, plus more as needed

1 (15-ounce) can tomato sauce

1½ cups chicken stock

¼ cup heavy cream

IN a small saucepan, melt 1 tablespoon of the butter over medium heat. Add the onion and cook until tender, about 7 minutes.

IN a separate pot, melt the remaining 2 tablespoons butter over medium heat and add the flour. Cook, stirring constantly, until the flour begins to color, about 2 minutes. Add the cooked onion, sugar, salt, and pepper while continuing to stir. Gradually add the tomato sauce about ½ cup at a time, stirring until smooth after each addition. Add the stock and bring to a simmer over medium heat. Simmer until the sauce is thick enough to coat the back of a spoon, about 15 minutes.

REMOVE the sauce from the heat and add the cream. Stir to combine and taste for seasoning, adding additional salt and pepper to taste if necessary.

SBURY STEAK

SOKOLOWSKI'S UNIVERSITY INN

CLEVELAND, OH

"Our Salisbury steak is probably the most important dish that we serve," says Sokolowski's co-owner Michael Sokolowski. Made with ground beef, eggs, and bread crumbs, Salisbury steak is not actually a steak: It's more of a cross between a burger and meat loaf. Named after the Civil War–era doctor who expounded on the nutritive benefits of minced meat, the destined-for-TV-dinners dish was originally considered a health food. At Sokolowski's, the oblong patties are topped with a generous pour of gravy and accompanied by grilled Spanish onions. The rich gravy takes a bit of elbow grease—be ready to stir—but it's well worth it. Sokolowski's customers certainly agree. "My mom always said, 'This is what put you kids through college!'" says Michael's sister, Mary Balbier, of this longtime favorite. Serve these gravy-doused patties with mashed potatoes or buttered egg noodles.

SERVES 6 TO 8

2 pounds lean ground beef

4 large eggs

1 cup plain unseasoned bread crumbs

1 (10.75-ounce) can condensed cream of mushroom soup

1 tablespoon salt

1 tablespoon garlic powder

¾ teaspoon freshly ground black pepper

½ cup (1 stick) unsalted butter

2 tablespoons beef base, 2 beef bouillon cubes, or 4 cups rich beef stock

½ cup all-purpose flour

PREHEAT the oven to 350°F.

IN a medium bowl, combine the beef, eggs, bread crumbs, mushroom soup, salt, garlic powder, and pepper. Mix well. Form 6 to 8 thick patties (about 1½ inches thick and 4 inches in diameter) and set aside.

IN a large, heavy skillet over medium-high heat, melt the butter. (It may seem like a lot of butter, but it will be incorporated into the gravy after the patties are cooked.) Working in two batches, place 3 or 4 patties in the pan and cook until browned, about 4 minutes per side. Remove the patties from the skillet and place in a 9-by-13-inch baking pan or dish large enough to hold all of the patties in one layer. Repeat with the remaining patties.

TO make the gravy, combine the beef base with 4 cups water and set aside. (If using beef stock, skip this step.) Keeping the skillet with the drippings over medium-high heat, add the flour, stirring constantly. Slowly pour the bouillon mixture or stock into the pan, adding about ½ cup at a time and stirring until smooth after each addition. Once all the liquid has been added, stir vigorously until the gravy begins to bubble, about 5 minutes. Pour the gravy over the beef patties and bake until the gravy is bubbling and the patties are no longer pink inside, 45 to 50 minutes. Serve.

"How would you like to work with your brothers 360 days a year? And not only that, but listen to polkas in the background? That would drive anyone crazy."

— MARY BALBIER,
Sokolowski's University
Inn in Cleveland, OH

Eastern European Sausage Glossary

There's probably no hot dog in the world more famous than a Chicago-style dog, which is served on a poppyseed bun and loaded with diced onions, tomato wedges, sweet relish, yellow mustard, a dill pickle spear, pickled hot peppers ("sport" peppers), and a dash of celery salt. (Never ketchup. Never.) Legend has it that the Windy City wiener was invented during the Great Depression by an enterprising young man looking to make a few nickels. But the Midwest's sausage history significantly predates this era; German and other eastern European immigrants had been replicating the bratwursts, knockwursts, kielbasy, and other sausages of their native countries since settling in the area in the nineteenth century. Today, restaurants like the Berghoff in Chicago, Kramarczuk's in Minneapolis, and Sokolowski's in Cleveland carry on the tradition.

Bratwurst

In Germany, each region is known for its own version of bratwurst (long/fat/thin/pork/veal), but most "brats" found in the United States are made with pork and seasoned with nutmeg. This sausage gets its rich, juicy flavor from the addition of heavy cream and cold eggs to the grind.

Frankfurters or Wieners

The ancestor of the modern-day American hot dog, frankfurters (often called "wieners" in the Midwest) are long, thinner sausages made with beef or a combination of beef and pork. The twice-ground meat is flavored with garlic, beef fat, and paprika, and well seasoned with salt before being hot-smoked.

Kielbasa

Kielbasa's smoky flavor sets this Polish sausage apart. Usually made with pork (though occasionally beef or veal are used instead), kielbasa is liberally seasoned with garlic and hot-smoked, traditionally over juniper wood. The sausages can be served sliced and eaten like a cold cut or heated and paired with sauerkraut.

Knackwurst

Plump and garlicky, knackwurst are a hot-smoked fresh sausage made with veal as well as pork. The best knackwurst should snap when you bite into it, releasing its juices with a satisfying crack. (*Knacken* means "to crack" in German.) Paprika and black pepper give it a touch of heat, and oak wood–smoking rounds out the flavor.

Weisswurst

A traditional Bavarian sausage, Weisswurst is lighter and more delicate than many of its encased counterparts. Often called "morning sausages" because they wouldn't keep past lunchtime in the days before refrigeration, Weisswurst gets its name from its stark white color. Made with lean veal and pork fat and flavored with lemon, fresh parsley, and mace, these finely textured sausages are cooked gently in water and served with sweet mustard and soft pretzels.

NORDEAST BEER BRATS

KRAMARCZUK'S

MINNEAPOLIS, MN

A mild German sausage made with pork and veal, bratwurst (see Sausage Glossary, page 140) benefits from a flavor-boosting beer braise before grilling or pan-frying. Named after Minneapolis lager Grain Belt Nordeast, these brats are a perpetual best-seller at Kramarczuk's. The owners like to cook with local brews, but any good lager or brown ale will do. Top with whole-grain mustard, sauerkraut, and fried cubes of slab bacon. **SERVES 4**

1 tablespoon unsalted butter

1 medium onion, thinly sliced

4 cups (32 ounces) lager or brown ale

1 pound raw bratwurst links (cooked brats can be used but won't yield the same flavor)

IN a large, heavy skillet, melt the butter over medium heat. Add the onion and lower the heat. Gently cook until they're transparent and beginning to turn golden brown, about 20 minutes.

POUR the beer into a large, heavy-bottomed pot or Dutch oven and bring to a boil over medium-high heat. Add the cooked onion and the bratwurst. Let the mixture come back up to a boil, then lower the heat and simmer until the brats are firm and cooked through, about 15 minutes. (If using cooked bratwurst, add the sausages during the last 5 minutes of cooking time to heat through.) Remove the brats from the pot.

PREPARE a charcoal grill or heat a large, heavy skillet over medium-high heat. Transfer the brats to the grill or skillet and cook until skin is deep brown, about 3 minutes per side. Serve with the beer-braised onions.

After emigrating to America, the founders of Kramarczuk's spent six months working in Louisiana as sharecroppers before moving to Minneapolis and opening their own business.

CREAMED CORN

BROOKVILLE HOTEL

ABILENE, KS

The Brookville Hotel's famous family-style chicken dinners are always served with the same accompaniments: biscuits, mashed potatoes, gravy, and a bowl of sweet creamed corn. Food writer Michael Baeur of the *San Francisco Chronicle* once remarked—reverently—that this dish "would be considered dessert in any other place than the Midwest."

SERVES 8 AS A SIDE DISH

1 teaspoon cornstarch

⅓ cup plus 1 tablespoon heavy or whipping cream

2 (10-ounce) packages frozen corn, or 2½ cups fresh corn kernels (about 4 ears)

1½ teaspoons sugar

½ teaspoon salt

TO make a cornstarch slurry, whisk the cornstarch and 1 tablespoon of the cream in a small bowl until well combined.

HEAT the corn over medium-low heat with 2 to 3 tablespoons water in a medium saucepan. Add the remaining ⅓ cup cream, the sugar, and salt. Bring to a boil and immediately add the cornstarch slurry while stirring. Cook until the sauce has thickened, about 2 minutes. Remove from the heat and serve.

BLUEBERRY AND WALNUT PANCAKES

AL'S BREAKFAST

MINNEAPOLIS, MN

Everything on the menu of Al's Breakfast is made from scratch. The recipes for the waffle batter and hollandaise are as old as the restaurant itself, and the corned beef is house-cured. The famous hash browns are built from shredded potatoes browned to a crisp, and in true Twin Cities fashion, they're available as a side item or as the foundation to a variety of dishes involving a topping of farm-fresh eggs, preferably soft-poached. The secret to these fluffy, ever-popular pancakes? A generous pour of buttermilk and a drizzle of melted butter in the batter.

MAKES ABOUT 12 PANCAKES

2 cups buttermilk

1 large egg, beaten

1¾ cups all-purpose flour

1½ teaspoons baking powder

1 teaspoon baking soda

1 teaspoon sugar

½ teaspoon salt

3 tablespoons unsalted butter, melted, plus extra for cooking and serving

½ cup frozen blueberries

⅓ cup chopped walnuts

Maple syrup

IN a medium bowl, combine the buttermilk and beaten egg. In a separate large bowl, combine the flour, baking powder, baking soda, sugar, and salt. Add the buttermilk mixture to the flour mixture and stir to combine. Stir in the melted butter. Allow the mixture to sit for at least 15 minutes, or overnight in the refrigerator.

HEAT 1 tablespoon of the butter over medium heat in a heavy skillet or griddle. When the butter is sizzling, pour about ¼ cup of the batter per pancake onto the skillet, leaving space between the pancakes. (Depending on the size of your griddle, it'll take 3 or 4 batches to make all the pancakes. Be sure to add more butter to the griddle between each batch.) Turn the heat to low and immediately place 5 or 6 frozen blueberries and 3 or 4 walnut pieces on each pancake. Cook until lightly brown, turning once with a spatula, about 4 minutes per side. Repeat with the remaining batter. Serve topped with a pat of butter and a drizzle of maple syrup.

APPLE STRUDEL

THE BERGHOFF

CHICAGO, IL

A bowl of warm, freshly baked apple strudel adorned with a scoop of vanilla ice cream is the dessert of choice for most diners at The Berghoff, which serves an exceptional version of the classic German pastry. The secret is in the filling: The restaurant substitutes dried cake crumbs for bread crumbs, using the cake scraps made when leveling the tops of baked cakes before frosting. (If you don't cook cakes regularly, the crumbs can be frozen in sealable plastic bags for up to 3 months before using, or you can substitute coarse white unseasoned bread crumbs.) Frozen phyllo dough works well in the dish, but be sure to thaw it the night before and keep it chilled before using. For best results, serve the strudel the same day it is baked, and accompany with a scoop of vanilla ice cream.

SERVES 8 TO 10

1¼ cups apple juice	½ cup dark seedless raisins	⅓ cup (5⅓ tablespoons) unsalted butter, melted
2 tablespoons cornstarch	3 tablespoons granulated sugar	3 tablespoons dry cake crumbs or coarse white bread crumbs
5 to 6 medium Granny Smith apples, peeled, cored, and cut into ¼-inch-thick slices (about 5 cups)	1 teaspoon ground cinnamon	Confectioners' sugar
	⅓ cup chopped pecans	Vanilla ice cream
	4 sheets phyllo dough	

IN a small bowl, create a slurry by combining ¼ cup of the apple juice with the cornstarch; mix until smooth and set aside.

> "Home to the best corned beef Reuben and apple strudel in Chicago—and amazing schnitzel, too!"
> – EMERIL LAGASSE on The Berghoff in Chicago, IL

IN a large saucepan over medium heat, cook the apples with the remaining 1 cup apple juice, the raisins, sugar, and cinnamon until the apples are tender, 8 to 10 minutes. Stir the cornstarch slurry and add it to the apple mixture, mixing well. Simmer for 1 minute, stirring constantly, until the sauce is thick. Remove from the heat and let cool to room temperature. Stir in the pecans, cover, and chill in the refrigerator until cold.

PREHEAT the oven to 450°F. Line a baking sheet with parchment paper.

LAY out one sheet of phyllo dough on a clean, flat, lightly floured surface. Brush with melted butter and sprinkle with 1 tablespoon of the cake crumbs. Top with another layer of phyllo, butter, and crumbs and repeat this procedure one more time. Top with the fourth sheet of phyllo. Spread the apple filling evenly onto the phyllo surface, leaving a ½-inch clean edge on all sides. Roll into a log, folding ragged edges at each end beneath the log. Carefully place the strudel on the prepared baking sheet, seam side down. Brush with melted butter. Bake the strudel for 18 to 20 minutes, or until deep golden brown.

REMOVE from the oven and let cool for 15 minutes. Cut crosswise into 2-inch slices and sprinkle with confectioners' sugar just before serving with ice cream.

SCONES WITH WINE

WATTS TEA SHOP

MILWAUKEE, WI

Located on the second floor of a beloved and long-standing fine home goods store, Watts Tea Shop serves breakfast, lunch, and high tea, at which these spectacular scones play a starring role. The kitchen makes them with a splash of white wine, preferably Chardonnay or Riesling. The recipe is versatile: Try substituting dried cherries or fresh blueberries for the cranberries, or making the scones with lemon zest instead of orange. The restaurant uses a mixture of cake and bread flour, but 3 cups all-purpose flour can be used instead.

For light, tender scones, make sure your butter is very cold and be careful not to overmix the dough; use your hands rather than a food processor to work in the ingredients.

MAKES 16 LARGE SCONES

2 cups cake flour

1 cup bread flour

¾ cup sugar

1 tablespoon baking powder

1 teaspoon salt

¾ cup (1½ sticks) unsalted butter, chilled and cut into cubes

1 cup dried cranberries

2 tablespoons orange zest

1 cup heavy cream

½ cup white wine

3 to 4 tablespoons melted butter to top scones

PREHEAT the oven to 350°F. Line a baking sheet with parchment paper.

IN a large bowl, combine the flours, ¼ cup of the sugar, the baking powder, and the salt. Using clean hands, add the butter and gently work it into the flour mixture, just until the mixture looks like it has pebbles in it. Add the cranberries and orange zest and combine.

MAKE a well in the middle of the flour mixture. Pour the cream and wine into the well and stir just until the dough starts to hold together. Do not overmix.

FORM the dough into a 10-inch round and set on the parchment-lined baking sheet. Brush melted butter on top of the dough and sprinkle with the remaining ½ cup sugar. The sugar will provide a layer of crunch after it is baked.

BAKE until the dough is lightly brown on the edges and pale in the middle and a cake tester inserted into the middle comes out clean, 30 to 35 minutes.

REMOVE from the oven and transfer to a wire rack; allow to cool for 5 to 10 minutes. Cut into 16 wedges and serve immediately.

DOUBLE CHOCOLATE PECAN WHIP BANANA SPLIT

LAGOMARCINO'S

MOLINE, IL

Forget about Hershey's: Lagomarcino's makes their chocolate syrup in-house. The soda fountain adds the syrup to sodas and shakes and drizzles it over sundaes. In this dish, one of the restaurant's most popular, the basic banana split is elevated with two scoops of housemade chocolate ice cream (though store-bought will work just fine), a handful of pecans, chocolate syrup, whipped cream, and a cherry.

MAKES 1 BANANA SPLIT

1 ripe banana, cut in half, each half sliced lengthwise into 4 pieces

2 scoops rich chocolate ice cream

Chocolate Syrup (recipe follows)

1 tablespoon chopped pecans

Whipped cream

Maraschino cherry

PLACE the banana slices in a star pattern in a shallow bowl, so that each slice juts out past the edge of the bowl. Top with the ice cream. Drizzle with 2 to 3 tablespoons chocolate syrup and sprinkle with the pecans. Top with a dollop of whipped cream and a maraschino cherry.

> "In this fast-paced world, people need something that doesn't change. That's what we represent."
>
> — BETH LAGOMARCINO, Lagomarcino's in Moline, IL

CHOCOLATE SYRUP

MAKES 1¾ CUPS

¾ cup sugar

Scant ⅓ cup cocoa powder

3 tablespoons light corn syrup

1½ teaspoons vanilla extract

COMBINE the sugar, cocoa powder, corn syrup, and 1 cup water in a medium saucepan. Bring to a full boil over medium-high heat. Stir constantly until the temperature reaches 215°F on a candy thermometer. Immediately remove from the heat and transfer to a heatproof bowl. Add the vanilla and stir to combine. Leave uncovered to cool completely. Store in a glass jar in the refrigerator for 2 to 3 months.

SUNSHINE CAKE

WATTS TEA SHOP

MILWAUKEE, WI

The star of the show at Watts Tea Shop is this cake, a spectacular three-layer chiffon extravagance that's filled with French vanilla custard, slathered in a thick seven-minute icing, and garnished with an edible flower. The cake has been served since the tea shop opened on the second floor of the George Watts & Son store building in the mid-1920s. Many third- and fourth-generation customers bring their children and grandchildren to the restaurant specifically for this stunning dessert, which they remember from their own childhood.

SERVES 8 TO 10

CAKE

9 large eggs, separated

1 cup granulated sugar

1 cup cake flour, sifted

1 teaspoon vanilla extract

¼ teaspoon cream of tartar

¼ teaspoon salt

CUSTARD FILLING

¾ cup confectioners' sugar, sifted

¾ cup whole milk

4 large egg yolks, beaten

1 teaspoon vanilla extract

1 cup (2 sticks) unsalted butter, at room temperature

FROSTING

3 large egg whites (from pasteurized eggs)

Pinch of salt

1⅓ cups granulated sugar

1 teaspoon vanilla extract

Grated zest of 2 large oranges, for garnish

TO MAKE THE CAKE: Preheat the oven to 350°F.

IN a large bowl or the bowl of a stand mixer fitted with the paddle attachment, combine the egg yolks, ½ cup of the granulated sugar, and ¼ cup water and beat until light and fluffy. Add the flour gradually, beating well after each addition. Add the vanilla and stir to combine.

IN a large metal bowl, whisk the egg whites with the cream of tartar and salt until the whites are stiff. Add the remaining ½ cup granulated sugar and whisk just until peaks begin to form. Use a rubber spatula to fold the egg white mixture into the batter. Pour the batter into an ungreased 10-inch tube pan. Bake until the cake is light brown and a toothpick inserted into the center comes out clean, about 45 minutes. Remove from the oven and let cool completely on a wire rack.

TO MAKE THE CUSTARD FILLING: Combine the confectioners' sugar, milk, and egg yolks in the top of a double boiler or in a metal bowl placed over a pot of simmering water.

(continued)

Cook over medium heat, stirring constantly, until the mixture thickens and coats the back of a spoon, 4 to 5 minutes. Remove from the heat and let cool to room temperature. Add the vanilla and stir to combine. In a medium bowl or the bowl of a stand mixer fitted with the paddle attachment, beat the butter until light and fluffy. Slowly add the cooled custard mixture to the butter, beating well. Set aside.

TO MAKE THE FROSTING: Beat the egg whites and salt in a large metal bowl or the bowl of a stand mixer fitted with the whisk attachment until soft peaks form. (It will take longer to whip the whites of pasteurized eggs than those of nonpasteurized eggs.) Set aside.

COMBINE the granulated sugar and ½ cup water in a medium saucepan and bring to a boil over medium-high heat. Boil just until the syrup spins a thread (it should reach 220°F on a candy thermometer).

VERY slowly drizzle the hot sugar syrup into the beaten egg whites with the stand mixer on medium speed. Beat constantly until the frosting stands in stiff peaks and is spreadable. Add the vanilla and beat well.

TO assemble, carefully cut the cooled cake horizontally into three layers. On top of the first cake layer spread a layer of French custard filling. Top with the middle cake layer and repeat. Top with the final cake layer and frost the top and sides of the cake with the frosting. Sprinkle grated orange rind over the top of the cake before serving.

The Award Winners

AL'S BREAKFAST

413 14th Avenue SE
Minneapolis, MN
Owners: Doug Grina and Jim Brandes
2004 AWARD WINNER

See page 114.

ARCHIE'S WAESIDE

224 4th Avenue Northeast
Le Mars, IA
Owner: Robert Rand
2015 AWARD WINNER

Set in what was once a roadhouse bar, Archie's Waeside is a citadel of American beef cookery. Seated in commodious booths, in a dining room accented with Christmas tchotchkes, regulars drink perfect Manhattans, snack on house-corned beef and a well-curated relish tray, and eat porterhouses, dry-aged in-house for four weeks. Archie Jackson, who escaped Russia during the Bolshevik Revolution, learned to cut and dry-age beef in packinghouses in Sioux City in the 1930s and Chicago in the 1940s. He opened the Waeside in 1949. Valerie Rand, his daughter, grew the business in the 1960s and '70s. Her youngest child, Robert Rand, is now the owner, presiding over a menu that features twelve cuts of dry-aged beef, sourced from farms in northwest Iowa and northeast Nebraska; a large selection of seafood including regional freshwater fish like walleye; and a deep cellar of red wines.

THE BERGHOFF

17 West Adams Street
Chicago, IL
Owner: Carolyn Berghoff
1999 AWARD WINNER

See page 116.

BREITBACH'S COUNTRY DINING

563 Balltown Road
Sherrill, IA
Owner: Mike Breitbach
2009 AWARD WINNER

In business since 1852 and touted as Iowa's oldest bar and restaurant, Breitbach's Country Dining has been owned and operated by the same family for five generations. Love for Breitbach's goes well beyond devotion to the restaurant's fried chicken, bacon-wrapped pork chops, and pies. This adoration was put to the test on Christmas Eve 2007, when a fire destroyed the eatery's original building. As Mike Breitbach faced the daunting task of starting over, the community rallied, and a slew of volunteers pitched in to rebuild the restaurant, completing the work in a stunning sixty-nine days. Unbelievably, less than six months later the restaurant burned to the ground again. Spirit unbroken, Breitbach's rebuilt once more, and is once again serving its long-standing dishes to clamoring regulars.

"If we can be a plus, and make
a mark in somebody's life—
'Oh my god, you can't believe this
place we just stopped into
in the middle of nowhere!'—
then it's worth it."

— CINDY BREITBACH,
Breitbach's Country Dining
in Sherrill, IA

CALUMET FISHERIES INC.
95TH AT THE BRIDGE
FINEST FRENCH FRIED
ShRIMP SMELT FISH CHIPS OYSTERS CATFISH
SMOKED FISH CHUBS SALMON
STURGEON TROUT SABLE EEL

OPEN

PLEASE PLACE ORDERS BY ½ OR FULL ORDER - THANK YOU
SEAFOOD WEIGHED BEFORE FRYING
FRIED WEIGHT MIN. ½ ORDER 6 OZ — FULL ORDER 12 OZ
SERVED WITH ALL DINNERS

	HALF ORDER	FULL ORDER		
FRIED SHRIMP	6 59	12 79	FISH DINNER	6 45
FISH CHIPS (NO FRIES)	4 25	7 99	CATFISH DINNER	7 55
CATFISH	5 35	10 29	SCALLOP DINNER	9 35
SCALLOPS	7 15	13 59	SHRIMP DINNER	8 79
FROG LEGS	6 65	12 50	SALADS	1 49 ½ LB 2 49 LB
OYSTERS	5 99	11 69	ONION RINGS	2 59
STUFFED SHRIMP	6 99	13 89	CUP OF SLAW	.49 ¢
SMELTS ORDER ONLY		6 25	CRACKERS ¼ LB.	.49 ¢
FRENCH FRIES	1 99	3 25		

SAUCE, FRIES, SLAW, CRACKERS, FORK, SALT & PEPPER

"TRY OUR NEW
SMOKED SHRIMP
DINNER
$8.79

CHEESE
STICKS
$3.99 order

Calumet Fisheries

BROOKVILLE HOTEL

105 East Lafayette Avenue
Abilene, KS
Owners: Connie Martin and Mark Martin
2007 AWARD WINNER

Originally known as the Cowtown Café, the Brookville Hotel has been owned by the same family since 1894. Though the hotel was moved a few years ago from small-town Brookville, Kansas, to Abilene, the fourth-generation owners, Connie and Mark Martin, re-created its original façade and Victorian dining room. They even duplicated four rooms upstairs, which aren't rented out, but are furnished so people can take a step back in time.Thankfully, they also left intact the restaurant's one, beloved offering: family-style chicken dinners. The fixed-price meal begins with relishes: cottage cheese, bread-and-butter pickles, spiced apple rings and peaches. Then the waitresses in baby blue uniforms with white collars and starched aprons bring the platters of skillet-fried chicken, airy baking powder biscuits, mashed potatoes, gravy, and the Brookville's famous creamed corn. Ice cream is the included dessert. The food is served on Blue Willow Ware in a Victorian room with heavy swagged draperies at the windows and a classic tin ceiling.

CALUMET FISHERIES

3259 East 95th Street
Chicago, IL
Owners: Kotlick and Toll families
2010 AWARD WINNER

Chicago's 95th Street Bridge, which spans the Calumet River on the city's South Side, is known for two things. One, a classic scene in the movie *The Blues Brothers*. Two, it's the home of Calumet Fisheries, a stand-alone hutch that has been frying and smoking seafood since 1948, when brothers-in-law Sid Kotlick and Len Toll opened the place. To this day, the Kotlick and Toll families run the joint. It's strictly carryout. No seating, no bathroom, no credit cards. And, if you believe the ominous street sign, no parking. The place draws a working-class, melting-pot crowd and a fair number of amateur fishermen. (The murky Calumet is a good place to find bluegill.) Fried perch, smelts, and frogs' legs are big here, but they also bring in scallops, crab, catfish, and oysters. The fried stuff is very good, but what you really want is the smoked fish, smoldering in the bunkerlike smokehouse around back. Salmon steaks, shrimp, chubs, and trout, all kissed with wood and cooked with care.

CAMP WASHINGTON CHILI

3005 Colerain Avenue
Cincinnati, OH
Owner: John Johnson
2000 AWARD WINNER

Since 1940, Camp Washington Chili has been serving Cincinnati's chili aficionados twenty-four hours a day, every day but Sunday. Current owner John Johnson has been working at at the Queen City eatery from the time of his arrival in America in 1951; he bought the restaurant from its founders, Steve Andon and Anastasios "Fred" Zarmbus, in 1977. Camp Washington set the standard for Cincinnati's very particular style of chili: bean-free, redolent with aromatic spices like cinnamon and cloves, and served most often on a bed of spaghetti with a number of toppings. Despite a move to a new location in 2000, the Midwestern chili parlor ambience and low-key menu have stayed the same. The staple is still the "5 way"—a pile of aromatic chili on fat spaghetti, topped with beans, onions, and bright orange cheese.

KRAMARCZUK'S

214 East Hennepin Avenue
Minneapolis, MN
Owner: Orest Kramarczuk
2013 AWARD WINNER

Minneapolis is known for its Scandinavian heritage, but for more than a century the city's northeast neighborhoods have been a vibrant eastern European enclave. A great deal of that Catholic, blue-collar culture has dissipated during the past twenty years, but some overt traces remain, most notably a dozen or more elaborate churches and Kramarczuk's, the landmark sausage-making company and restaurant. The business dates to 1954, when Ukrainian refugees Wasyl and Anna Kramarczuk purchased Central Provisions, one of the city's oldest butcher shops, and renamed it Kramarczuk Sausage Co. It has been at the same address, just across the Mississippi River from downtown Minneapolis, since 1967. Run today by Wasyl and Anna's son Orest, Kramarczuk's still serves the traditional fare that Anna prepared for her family: gigantic pork- and rice-filled cabbage rolls smothered in a tomato cream sauce, dumplings stuffed with potatoes and cheese and served with a dill pickle, and meat-filled crêpes topped with horseradish-laced sour cream. Of course there's an ever-changing selection of the house specialty, the butcher shop's expertly made sausages, bratwurst, kielbasa, and wieners, swiped with some of the kitchen's zesty mustard and stuffed into sturdy, housemade golden buns. Along with a relatively recent push toward elaborate tortes, cakes, and cream puffs, the bakery continues to turn out delicious kolaches filled with cheese, prunes, apricots, or poppy seeds.

LAGOMARCINO'S

1422 Fifth Avenue
Moline, IL
Owners: Lagomarcino family
2006 AWARD WINNER

Main Street soda fountain Lagomarcino's has served as the spiritual heart of Moline, Illinois, for nearly a century. Italian immigrant Angelo Lagomarcino opened his cafe and fruit stand in downtown Moline in 1908. Angelo and his wife, Luigia, raised their three children—Charlie, Mary, and Tom—behind the counter and in an apartment above the restaurant. Tom and his wife, Betsy, brought up their six kids in the business, and today three of them are preserving their family's rich legacy. In Lagomarcino's yesteryear setting, customers enjoy Green Rivers— housemade lime phosphate sodas— and turtle sundaes amid vintage mahogany booths, milk-glass tabletops, and colorful stained-glass lamps. Tradition is the unspoken daily special at the long stretch of a soda fountain, the place for liver or ham-salad sandwiches on rye, banana-pineapple salad with cinnamon-raisin toast, or a big bowl of chili. As a veteran Multimixer malt machine whirs in the background, fresh-faced teenagers whip up cherry phosphates, egg creams, and, for a few magical weeks every summer, fresh strawberry sodas. The busy basement candy kitchen turns out all manner of treats, like toffee, sponge candy, lemon bark, and—at Easter—chocolate eggs filled with individually wrapped chocolates and candies.

"It's not always about the money, it's about enjoying other people, it's about sharing food. That's what I think of when I think of the American Dream."
—NICK KRAMARCZUK,
Kramarczuk's in Minneapolis, MN

THE PICKWICK

508 East Superior Street
Duluth, MN
Owner: Chris Wisocki
2007 AWARD WINNER

The Duluth beer hall known as the Pickwick has a storied history. Its roots can be traced to the late 1880s, when the Fitger Brewery opened a beer hall. In 1914, the hall moved next door to a splendid new building (the restaurant's present location) and was renamed the Pickwick. In 1919, a year after Prohibition, the brewery's owners sold the Pickwick to manager Joseph Wisocki, a Polish immigrant. It has been in the family ever since. Christopher Wisocki, Joseph's great-grandson, became owner in 2001, following in his father's, uncle's, and grandfather's footsteps. Duluthians flock there for its Lake Superior views, stately supper-club atmosphere, and classic steakhouse menu, which includes a few beloved specialties like house-smoked Lake Superior whitefish, top-notch onion rings, and a breaded and deep-fried cheeseburger.

SOKOLOWSKI'S UNIVERSITY INN

1201 University Road
Cleveland, OH
Owners: Bernard Sokolowski, Mary Balbier, and Michael Sokolowski
2014 AWARD WINNER

In 1923 Victoria and Michael Sokolowski founded a Polish restaurant on a bank of the Cuyahoga River in Cleveland. Today, Sokolowski's University Inn serves edible homages to the city's immigrant-driven industrial past, dishing sturdy comfort foods like the cabbage rolls that once fueled the city's growth. Pierogis, stuffed with whipped potatoes, bathed in butter, and drenched in caramelized onions, are everyday specials. The Sokolowski family does right by midwestern dishes, too. They beer-batter and fry Lake Erie perch. They craft their own bratwurst and smoked kielbasa. Originally a tavern when the Tremont neighborhood was flush with blue-collar steelworkers, Sokolowki's expanded to cafeteria-style service in the 1950s, and has evolved more recently into a touchstone restaurant for Polish families in search of their culinary roots.

ST. ELMO STEAK HOUSE

127 South Illinois Street
Indianapolis, IN
Owners: Stephen Huse and Craig Huse
2012 AWARD WINNER

Open since 1902, St. Elmo is an Indianapolis institution. Sure, Saint Elmo, the patron saint of sailors, is a curious namesake in a city without a navigable river. But this steakhouse, with its bone-in filets and fabled shrimp cocktail, served in a silver-rimmed, ice-lined bowl, has long been the city's special-occasion restaurant of choice. Old guard locals are not the only devotees. If there's a celebrity in town, this is the place to spot him or her, and the restaurant's walls are filled with photos of the stars: former Colts quarterback Peyton Manning reviewed his first contract in St. Elmo's dining room. Ownership has changed hands a few times since the 1940s, but the steakhouse has remained a constant in the lives of Indianapolis locals. And with a recent million-dollar makeover, which added private dining rooms, a wine cellar, and an open kitchen, St. Elmo's is ready for another century of life.

- - - - - - - - - - -

The first chicken dinners at
Stroud's were served during
World War II and cost $0.35.

- - - - - - - - - - -

STROUD'S

5410 Northeast Oak Ridge Road
Kansas City, MO
Owner: Mike Donegan
1998 AWARD WINNER

A Kansas City staple since 1933, Stroud's restaurant was opened by Guy and Helen Stroud as a barbecue roadhouse shortly following the repeal of Prohibition. During World War II, when beef was rationed, Helen began serving fried chicken, and a tradition was born. Today Stroud's has three locations in Kansas City, Wichita, and Fairway—none of them on the original site. But prices have remained low, portions are still hefty and family-style, and chicken, pan-fried to order and served with mountainous mashed potatoes with milky gravy, is still the restaurant's claim to fame.

THREE BROTHERS RESTAURANT

2414 South St. Clair Street
Milwaukee, WI
Owners: Branko Radicevic and Patricia Radicevic
2002 AWARD WINNER

See page 118.

TUFANO'S VERNON PARK TAP

1073 West Vernon Park Place
Chicago, IL
Owner: Joseph DiBuono
2008 AWARD WINNER

Tucked away on a residential side street in what remains of Chicago's Little Italy, Tufano's Vernon Park Tap has been owned and operated by the same family since Joseph DiBuono and Theresa Tufano DiBuono opened their barroom in 1930. The original small table in the bar's kitchen, where Joseph DiBuono worked his culinary magic, has since expanded to include two dining rooms that are regularly packed with businessmen, police officers, families, and pregame sports fans. Today the restaurant is run by Joey DiBuono, the grandson of the original owners, and he has maintained many of the details that ground Tufano's in its history: chalkboard menus, a cash-only policy, and hearty Italian-American fare like fried calamari, eggplant Parmesan, and the DiBuono family's legendary lemon chicken.

WATTS TEA SHOP

761 North Jefferson Street
Milwaukee, WI
Owner: Sam Watts
2011 AWARD WINNER

George Watts & Son is a fifth-generation downtown Milwaukee business that celebrated its 140th anniversary in 2010. The store's first floor is devoted to an astounding inventory of china, glassware, flatware, linens, and tchotchkes. Most of the building's second floor is home to its well-mannered restaurant, Watts Tea Shop. The restaurant's roots date back to the mid-1920s, when then-owner Howard Watts built a beautiful new building to house his family business. His great-grandson, thirty-one-year-old Sam Watts, is now the store's president. The tea shop became a beloved destination among generations of Milwaukee devotees and it remains a quiet mainstay of the downtown lunch scene. Many of the dishes follow recipes that have been used since the 1930s, including the soft whole-wheat bread, the English muffins, and the olive, nut, and chicken salad finger sandwiches.

THE STORIES

THE RECIPES

THE AWARD WINNERS

SOUTHWEST

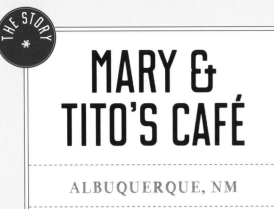

MARY & TITO'S CAFÉ

ALBUQUERQUE, NM

2010 AWARD WINNER

Native New Mexicans and husband-and-wife team Mary and Tito Gonzales opened their adobe café just north of downtown Albuquerque in 1963. Tito was the original cook and creator of the recipes. When he passed away, Mary hired more cooks and continued to run the front of the house, oversee the business, and raise their family. From the worn but clean booths, tables, and a handful of counter stools, diners gaze over family and patron photos, the kids' and grandkids' sports trophies, and other mementos of family accomplishments. Now well past eighty, Mary still comes in daily to greet old friends and new, while her daughter Antoinette manages the café. Other daughters help out too, and various grandchildren wait tables when they're not in school.

MY FATHER OPENED MARY & TITO'S CAFÉ IN 1963. He had no training—he just loved to cook. As a kid he'd been a mama's boy and was always helping his mother in the kitchen, so that's how he learned to cook. The restaurant he opened was real small—it had a bar and maybe four stools and four tables. It was just him, my great-uncle, and a waitress. They ran it like that for a couple of years, before they outgrew the space and moved.

Looking back on it now, it was just so organic. He would let people charge their meals. They would say, "Well, can I charge and I'll pay you on Friday when I get paid?" And he would say, "Yep, go ahead," and would find a ticket and put it in a cigar box. And people would pay him every week.

We all grew up in the restaurant. I didn't think I would work in the restaurant forever—I just thought my mom and my dad would work in the restaurant forever. Why would I? But eventually I knew that this is my place. This is where I'm supposed to be.

My father passed away twenty-six years ago, and my mom and I were running it then. She and I thought, well, everyone was coming to eat here because my father, he was a real character. Customers just adored him. And we thought, "Fair enough, people aren't going to keep coming to this restaurant. They were coming for him." But we stayed very, very busy. Then we knew they weren't just coming for him, they were coming because, you know, the food's pretty good. Probably 90 percent of our customers are regulars.

Our recipes have stayed the same since 1963. They have not changed at all. People will ask, "Well, how many cups of this do you put in this, that, or the other?" And I tell them, "We don't measure." We don't. It's the palm of your hand, that's your measuring cup. Because our recipes stay the same, we want to keep our ingredients the same. One of our challenges is where we get our red chiles. The little farm we get our red chile from is the one that my dad found. They sun-dry their red chiles—most places machine-dry them. This farm has been supplying us for as many years as I can remember, and that can be a challenge, because chile only comes out once a year. It's harvested and that's it, so sometimes by the next August or September, it can be a challenge.

We have some employees that have been with us for a very long time. One cook has been with us thirty-six years; he was taught by my father. And then we have another cook—his brother—and he's been here, I think, thirty-three years. He was also taught by my father. I know that we're still here because of them. I mean, I can do everything in the front, but I can't do everything in the back. That's a hard job. I have done it and know how do to it, but it's hard. They learned straight from my father. And I know that's the biggest part of why we're still here, because they know how to cook the way he did.

—ANTOINETTE KNIGHT

"The kitchen – that was my father's. The whole restaurant was his baby. But his kitchen was his kitchen. He rolled out the tortillas for the first twenty years he was in business."

– ANTOINETTE KNIGHT,
Mary & Tito's Café in
Albuquerque, NM

LOUIE MUELLER BARBECUE

TAYLOR, TX

2006 AWARD WINNER

Step through the squeaky screen door and enter a sepia, smoke-bronzed world where it might well be 1946, the year Louie Mueller opened a meat market and grocery store in this small, cotton-farming town about 45 minutes northeast of Austin. Louie was among the Germans who established the central Texas barbecue tradition, applying old-world smoking skills to the prodigious local supply of beef as a way to prevent spoilage and maintain profits. Mueller passed away in 1992, passing the reins to his son Bobby, who in turn lured his son Wayne away from a job in advertising and back to the family business in 2006. Wayne trained under his father's tutelage until Bobby's death in 2008, and today is dedicated to preserving his grandfather and father's legacy. There's no question that he's doing them proud; the brisket coming out of the pit is a wondrous blackened hunk of heaven, sliced and served up on butcher paper. The Muellers' meat just might be the apotheosis of smoked beef: moist slabs and charred shards of beef, intensely concentrated and explosive on the tongue. Louie's also offers fine, smoke-saturated link sausage and pork ribs, which are listed, true Texas-style, separately from barbecue, which everyone around here knows is brisket. Douse any of it with the thin onion-laced sauce that complements, rather than masks, the meat's magnificence. Just a bite and you'll see why at least one writer has suggested that Louie Mueller's Barbecue be moved lock, stock, and pit to the Smithsonian.

I'M A THIRD-GENERATION PITMASTER AND OWNER of Louie Mueller Barbecue.

Pitmasters, we're specialized cooks who work with open fire, generally. We work with natural fuel, such as wood, to cook proteins of all sorts. In Texas—in central Texas in particular—we're beef-centric.

Barbecue, in essence, uses the natural resources available to your area, usually the cheap and readily accessible resources. The best way I can explain it is that we're like culinary alchemists, if you will. We take what would be lead to an alchemist—these cast-off tough cuts of meat—and through our philosopher's stone, our process of cooking and smoking, we turn that lead into black gold. We make it something scrumptious and juicy and tender and delicious.

Barbecue here in Texas developed in the same way barbecue developed everywhere else—it's just that the protein source that we used was different. The rest of the country really knew barbecue as being pulled pork, and baby back ribs, and pulled hog. This whole idea of beef-centric barbecue was something new. But my grandfather saw beef barbecue as just a twist on an existing cuisine known as steakhouses. He said, "You know, if we're going to do beef, we're going to do it the way it should be done. It shouldn't be chopped and sauced and put on a bun. It should be sliced out like prime rib." He felt that simplicity was best: The rub should be made with the spices that people use every day—salt, pepper, the ones you find most common on all dinner tables—and that the beef was robust enough that it shouldn't be covered in some sort of sauce, or ketchup base, or anything. The beef should stand on its own just as a steak would.

The hardest thing about what we do is not necessarily doing it. It's doing it successfully, in large volume, every single day, and keeping that quality standard high. That's the hard part. The greatest change really has been the volume of people that are coming though and the volume of food that has to be prepared in order to accommodate that, Now, instead of ten people standing in line, there's a hundred people standing in line. We've had to develop new systems. We've had to develop food training methodologies, new holding and preparation methodologies, all to accommodate those changes, but ultimately the end goal is still the same, and that is to produce the same product that we were producing ten years ago, thirty years ago, fifty years ago still.

Louie Mueller is still a quick service. It's still line service. All of that is still the same. The floors, the ceilings, and paint, all of that is exactly as it was. In many ways, I see myself as a curator nowadays as much as a restaurateur, because you see registers come and go, scales come and go. We've seen jukeboxes come and go. We've seen sausage stuffers come and go; old Coke machines and stuff that we've had as part of our history that don't go away. They become iconic pieces in our establishment. None of those things have changed, and I hear people come in who haven't been in in fifteen, twenty, twenty-five years saying, "It still looks the same. It still smells the same. It still tastes the same," and I can't think of a greater compliment.

Barbecue isn't a concept. It's a culture, and it's a way of life in a way that Subway or Olive Garden is not, you know? Those who are the most successful have their full heart and soul in it, and that was really imprinted upon me by my grandfather and most indelibly by my father. You're only going to get out of this what you put into this, and I really am most proud of those men because they molded and shaped not only this place, but me to be who I am so that I would have the right temperament, the right perspective, and the desire to keep this going instead of letting it die.

What has been most meaningful is the fact that I had people before me who created this and had enough foresight to keep it all in its pristine, original, historical, traditional context. And I have this platform by which to promote not just my family history and my family establishment, but something that's bigger than that, something that has become iconically Texas. It's not a family business: It represents a culture.
                                                        —WAYNE MUELLER

CAFE PASQUAL'S

SANTA FE, NM

1999 AWARD WINNER

Cafe Pasqual's owner Katharine Kagel opened the restaurant in 1979 almost on a whim less than a year after moving to Santa Fe. Set on the site of a former Texaco station, the small, forty-eight-seat corner café has always hewn to a commitment to organic and local ingredients that was years ahead of its time. The eclectic menu—breakfast offerings include huevos barbacoa, griddled polenta with chorizo and chile, smoked trout hash, and golden-brown cheese blintzes—is inspired by the culinary traditions of both old and New Mexico, as well as by Kagel's own background and quality-driven preferences. Everything is made by hand: fresh salsas, house-churned ice cream, loaves of bread. With a gallery featuring local artists and Native American pottery adjoining the restaurant, the cozy café is not only a popular gathering place for Santa Fe natives but also a vibrant reminder of the city's unique sensibility and complex, diverse history.

I MOVED TO SANTA FE IN JUNE OF '78. I always called Santa Fe the town of cousins—everybody was related to everybody in those days. You went to the movies, you knew absolutely everyone in the theater. Or you had seen them. Everyone smiled and said something to a passerby. When I first came I thought I was going to open a Japanese antique gallery. Isn't that weird? But the first night I was in town, I was with some old friends and I told them to invite twelve people to a dinner party, and I would make thirteen dishes. Somebody at the table said, "You ought to cater." The next morning I woke up, and I knew. I did all the business in that day: I got a tax number, got a card. I was ready. A few months later, I had two different people suggest I buy the same restaurant at the corner of Water and Don Gaspar. We opened the restaurant on March 31 of 1979—so much for the Japanese antique business. I thought it would be easier to have a restaurant than to have a catering business. I was wrong.

In those days it was difficult to get ingredients, very difficult. You couldn't buy whole-bean coffee in the state of New Mexico, for real. We had to talk to a coffee company that kept a corner of their warehouse in Colorado just for our request of whole-bean coffee. Can you imagine?

In the beginning we were only open for breakfast and lunch because of the liquor laws and also because people here didn't really dine out at night very much. They went out for great family occasions and that was it. From 1979 to 1986 we were just a daytime restaurant. But that was kind of common. It was what I called the town of luncheonettes. We stood out because we served breakfast as well and we served it all day. And we still serve it all day until the close of lunchtime, just because I love breakfast, personally. I think that if you want breakfast you want breakfast. Nothing else will substitute.

Living and cooking in Santa Fe really keeps me aware of nature and of the elements—all the elements are present at all times. It's really enlivening. We don't have the layers that the rest of America has between our sustenance. And, as our general manager likes to say, we give good value at Cafe Pasqual's. People know that everything is made in-house. Everything is made from the best possible ingredients. It's not going to harm them, it's going to enhance their lives. It's very hands on—we seldom open a can. It's fresh. It's truly cared about. People really care about what they do at the restaurant. Our patrons mean a lot to us. They become part of our family.

Because we're small, I think we really get that opportunity. Small is beautiful, there's no doubt about it. Lots of restaurants will say, "Well, I want a second location, a third location," and then everyone groans and says it's not the same as the first. It's not as good. I think we just hold it closely and we hold it dearly and we do our very, very best every day. That's the thing. And it's not easy but everyone does their best.

And they do it, I think, from a really sacred, heart place. I know it sounds corny but it's a real opportunity to live a life of passion and compassion.

—KATHARINE KAGEL

"One person said to me,
'How can you stand to make
chile every day?'
And I was so aghast.
I said, 'How could I not?'"
— KATHARINE KAGEL,
Cafe Pasqual's in Santa Fe, NM

Barbecue

Unlike many other iconic American foods, barbecue styles can't be divided into five (or ten, or even fifteen) neatly defined geographical areas, as any pitmaster worth his weight in hickory wood would tell you. In some states barbecue is so fiercely regional that 'cue conventions vary by county. (In North Carolina, for example, the pig is king, but the state splits down the middle when it comes to how they serve their slow-cooked smoked pork.) An overview of American barbecue styles could easily fill a book (and indeed there are many great ones on the subject), which is more room than we have here. But we can tell you what to expect when visiting the exemplary and distinctive barbecue joints that have received the America's Classics award.

Region	Style of Barbecue	Where to Get It	Words of Wisdom
EASTERN NORTH CAROLINA	Chopped whole hog, including cracklings, dressed with a peppery, vinegar-based sauce	**THE SKYLIGHT INN** Ayden, NC	"At Skylight Inn, they have three things on the menu: slaw, cornbread, and whole-hog sandwiches," says Amy Mills Tuniscliffe, author of *Peace, Love & Barbecue*. "They cook those hogs, seasoned with salt and pepper, over oak and they're chopped. The thing about a whole hog sandwich is that you taste the delicate mixture of flavors of all the parts of the meat. So you get a little bit of the bacon, a little bit of the ham, a little bit of the rib meat. And what they do that's super special is before that hog comes off the fire they put it over direct flame to crisp up the skin. So you get these little bites every now and then of this crunchy, crispy, salty skin, and that is like a little bite of heaven."
WESTERN NORTH CAROLINA	Wood-smoked pork shoulder paired with minced cabbage and a tangy, sweet sauce	**LEXINGTON BARBECUE #1** Lexington, NC	"When you order those shoulders at Lexington, it's good to ask for a little bit of the 'brown' meat, the outside bark, because it has that great smoky flavor," says Mills Tuniscliffe. "They're also known for this red slaw, it's a vinegar-based slaw with a little bit of ketchup in it. It helps cut through the richness of the pork."
ARKANSAS	It's futile to sum up Arkansas barbecue, as it differs throughout the state, but at Jones Bar-B-Q in Marianna it means only one thing: hacked pork shoulder served on white bread with a spritz of vinegary sauce	**JONES BAR-B-Q DINER** Marianna, AR	"The sauce—that's the deal right there. The barbecue sauce," says third-generation proprietor James Jones. "We were told by our daddy—if either one of the boys give up that recipe, he'd come back from the grave and do something to you."
CENTRAL TEXAS	Beef brisket, seasoned only with salt and pepper, along with pork ribs and housemade sausage usually sold market-style, or by the pound, and served without sauce. (See page 186).	**LOUIE MUELLER BARBECUE** Taylor, TX	Beef brisket reigns supreme in Texas and that's in part due to Louie Mueller, a German immigrant who was one of the first to see that his country's native meat-smoking techniques and the area's ample cattle ranches were made for each other.

EPIPHANY MANGO BEET SALAD

CAFE PASQUAL'S

SANTA FE, NM

A trip to an open-air market in the Isthmus of Mexico inspired the creation of this gorgeous, jewel-toned salad. The dressing doesn't contain any oil but you won't miss it: The sweetness of the orange juice balances out the tart lime juice and brings the dish together. Bibb or any other mild lettuce can be used in place of the mixed greens. Keep the beet and mango cubes separate until serving to keep their vibrant colors pristine. **SERVES 4 TO 6**

DRESSING

¼ cup freshly squeezed orange juice

¼ cup freshly squeezed lime juice

Pinch of cayenne pepper

Pinch of kosher salt

SALAD

½ cup coarsely chopped macadamia nuts

6 large red beets

3 ripe mangoes

4 cups mixed greens

½ cup fresh mint leaves

Salt and freshly ground black pepper

TO MAKE THE DRESSING: Whisk together the orange juice, lime juice, cayenne pepper, and salt in a nonreactive bowl and set aside.

TO MAKE THE SALAD: Preheat the oven to 300°F.

SPREAD the macadamia nuts on a baking sheet and toast in the oven until golden brown, stirring occasionally, 8 to 10 minutes. (Watch the nuts closely to make sure they don't burn.) Wrap the toasted nuts in a dishtowel and smash once or twice with an iron skillet to crumble. Set aside. (The nuts can be toasted up to 2 days ahead of time. Store, covered, at room temperature.)

INCREASE the oven temperature to 400°F. Wash the beets and cut the tops off, leaving a 2-inch stem. Wrap individually in foil and roast for 1 to 1½ hours, until fork-tender. Let cool completely. Peel the beets by slipping off the skins, then cut into 1-inch cubes. Set aside. (The beets can be roasted up to 2 days ahead of time and stored covered, in the fridge.)

TO cube the mangoes, hold it with the stem end up and cut straight down on either side of the pit to reveal two pitless halves. Score the mango flesh with the tip of a

paring knife to form 1-inch squares on a grid, cutting downward through the flesh but not through the skin. Turn the mangoes inside out to pop up the mango squares and cut them off. Set aside.

IN a large salad bowl, toss the greens and mint leaves with three quarters of the dressing and season with salt and black pepper. Top the greens with the mangoes and beets, being careful not to overlap the two to avoid coloring the mango. Drizzle the remaining dressing over the salad. Sprinkle with the crumbled macadamia nuts. Serve immediately, as the citrus dressing will wilt the greens.

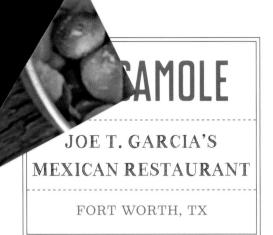

AMOLE

JOE T. GARCIA'S
MEXICAN RESTAURANT

FORT WORTH, TX

There's no better way to spend a balmy Texas night than at a table in Joe T. Garcia's enchanting poolside garden with a pitcher of icy margaritas and a bowl of their legendary guacamole. Use perfectly ripe, small, black Hass avocados to make the dish; buy them a few days ahead of serving so they can ripen on a kitchen counter. If you have the time to make your own chips by deep-frying triangles of corn tortillas, you won't regret the effort.

SERVES 4

2 ripe Hass avocados

½ small white onion, diced

1 tomato, diced

1 serrano chile, seeded and minced

⅓ cup minced fresh cilantro

1 tablespoon freshly squeezed lemon juice

Salt

HALVE the avocados. Remove the pits and scoop out the avocado flesh into a medium bowl. Coarsely mash the avocado with a fork. Add the onion, tomato, chile, cilantro, lemon juice, and salt to taste. Mix well and serve immediately.

SMOKED TROUT HASH WITH POACHED EGGS AND TOMATILLO SALSA

CAFE PASQUAL'S

SANTA FE, NM

To make this beloved breakfast standby, Cafe Pasqual's chef and owner Katharine Kagel tops a crisp potato pancake with two perfectly poached eggs, flakes of smoked trout, and a piquant, spinach-flecked salsa. Be sure to let the potatoes cool completely before grating. You can substitute any smoked white fish of your choice for the trout; smoked bluefish also works beautifully. To keep the salsa on the milder side, omit the chile de árbol, use only one jalapeño, and remove all membranes and seeds from the jalapeño before adding. If fresh chiles de árbol aren't readily available, a fresh Thai or serrano chile can be used instead. Leftover salsa can be eaten as a dip for tortilla chips, drizzled over tacos, soups, and stews, or served atop grilled fish or chicken.

SERVES 4

TOMATILLO SALSA

12 large tomatillos, husked and rinsed

2 jalapeño chiles, stemmed and cut in half

½ small white onion, peeled and coarsely chopped

1 garlic clove, peeled

½ bunch fresh cilantro, stems removed

2 cups spinach leaves

1 fresh chile de árbol, stemmed and seeded

1½ teaspoons kosher salt

HASH BROWN POTATO CAKES

2 pounds russet potatoes, peeled

5 ounces grated Gruyère cheese (about 1 generous cup)

⅓ cup finely minced fresh chives or scallions

2 teaspoons kosher salt

1½ teaspoons freshly ground black pepper

5 tablespoons unsalted butter

8 large organic eggs

1 pound smoked trout, flaked into bite-size pieces

Handful of finely chopped fresh cilantro, parsley, or chives

TO MAKE THE SALSA: Put all the ingredients in a blender and pulse until liquefied. Adjust the seasoning as needed. Transfer to a bowl. You can make the salsa up to 1 day in advance and store it in the refrigerator.

TO MAKE THE POTATO CAKES: Fill a very large pot with enough water to cover the potatoes. Bring the water to a boil and then carefully add the potatoes. Cook for 20 minutes in bubbling water, until the potatoes are just barely fork-tender. Do not overcook or the potatoes will crumble. Drain the potatoes and let cool completely

(continued)

(this can take 3 to 4 hours; the potatoes can also be cooked a day ahead of time and refrigerated).

GRATE the potatoes on a box grater into a large bowl. Add the cheese, chives, salt, and pepper. Using clean hands, gently toss to combine.

PREHEAT the oven to 200°F. Heat a 7-inch nonstick sauté pan over medium-high heat and add one quarter of the butter, tipping the pan to cover the surface. Add one quarter of the potato mixture (about 2 cups) and pat down with a spatula to form a large pancake. Cook for 4 to 5 minutes, using the spatula to loosen the edges of the pancake from the sides of the pan and shake the pan occasionally to make sure the bottom is not sticking. Once the underside is golden brown, flip the pancake over and cook for another 3 to 4 minutes. (Be careful when flipping the pancake to avoid breaking it apart and burning yourself. One way to do this is to place a cake pan on top of the sauté pan, hold both pans together with oven mitts, and turn the whole thing upside down, so that the pancake drops onto the underside of the cake pan. Then, slide the pancake back into the sauté pan so that the uncooked side is on the bottom now. If the pancake breaks apart, just press it back into shape with the spatula.)

SLIP the pancake onto an ovenproof plate and place in the oven to keep warm. Repeat until all four pancakes are made, placing sheets of parchment paper between them.

TO poach the eggs, fill a small saucepan with a couple inches of water. Bring the water to a bare simmer. Cook the eggs one at a time: Crack each egg into a cup, slip it into the water, and cook for 3 to 4 minutes, until the white is opaque but the yolk is still runny. Repeat with the remaining eggs and drain on paper towels.

IN a nonstick skillet over medium-low heat, gently heat the trout until warmed through.

PLACE the poached eggs on top of the potato pancakes. Surround with the warmed trout and drizzle a generous tablespoon of salsa across the eggs. Garnish with herbs and serve with additional tomatillo salsa on the side.

SOPA DE TORTILLA

TORTILLA SOUP

JOE T. GARCIA'S MEXICAN RESTAURANT

FORT WORTH, TX

Topped with diced avocado, Oaxacan-style cheese, and a squeeze of lime juice, this brothy, smoky soup is a meal in itself. It gets much of its rich flavor from the pasilla chile (also known as chile negro), which is the dried form of the chilaca chile, a relatively mild chile that has a pungent, complex taste. If pasillas are not available, an ancho chile can be substituted. The dish also includes epazote, a leafy green with a singular citrus-pine flavor. A combination of cilantro, oregano, and savory can be used instead, or it can be omitted entirely. For a spicier soup, include some of the pasilla chile seeds in the puree.

MAKES ABOUT 6 CUPS; SERVES 6 TO 8

1 dried pasilla chile

4 ripe tomatoes, coarsely chopped

½ onion, coarsely chopped

2 garlic cloves, peeled and crushed

1 tablespoon lard or vegetable oil

6 to 8 cups chicken broth (homemade, if possible)

2 small sprigs fresh epazote, or ½ teaspoon dried (optional)

½ teaspoon salt, plus more to taste

2 cups tortilla chips (homemade, if possible)

2 cups shredded cooked chicken

3 avocados, pitted, peeled, and diced

7 ounces queso Chihuahua (Mexican string cheese, sometimes called "Oaxacan-style cheese"), grated or shredded (about 2 cups)

2 limes, quartered

SPLIT the chile in half. Remove the stem and scrape out and discard the seeds. Put the chile in a bowl of hot water and set aside to rehydrate for 20 minutes.

IN the bowl of a food processor or blender, puree the tomatoes, onion, garlic, and rehydrated chile until smooth.

IN a large saucepan, heat the lard over medium heat, being careful not to let it smoke and burn. Add the puree to the saucepan, bring to a simmer, and cook until it has reduced and thickened, about 15 minutes.

ADD 6 cups of the broth to the saucepan, raise the heat to medium-high, and bring to a boil. Lower the heat and simmer, uncovered, until the liquid has slightly reduced and the flavor has concentrated, 45 minutes to 1 hour. If the soup becomes too thick, add more broth. Add the epazote and simmer for 15 minutes more. Season with salt.

TO assemble, place a handful of chips, chicken, and avocado in a bowl. Ladle the soup into the bowl and top with cheese and a squeeze of lime juice.

Chile Peppers

Chile peppers are indigenous to the Americas, and thus are prominent in several Latin American and Caribbean cuisines; they've since been incorporated into many Asian cuisines as well. But there is nowhere in the United States where people take more pride in their chiles than in the Southwest—and particularly in New Mexico, where the chile pepper is, in fact, an official state vegetable (though technically, of course, it is a fruit). Up to ten thousand acres of chiles are grown annually in New Mexico; festivals and chile roasts mark harvesttime each autumn in several towns. A good number of recipes in this book, particularly in the Southwest chapter, feature the smoky, spicy heat of fresh or dried chiles, some of which might not be readily available in all parts of the country. The following primer provides a brief description of the chiles found in these recipes, along with suggested substitutions, if necessary.

Ancho

Ancho chiles are actually dried poblano chiles. Smoky and subtly sweet, anchos are often reconstituted in hot water to soften and then pureed into sauces, or ground into chile powder to make red enchilada sauce or mole.

SUBSTITUTE: Pasilla chile or dried New Mexico chile

COOK WITH IT: Red Chile Enchiladas (page 184); Enchiladas Mexicanas (page 182)

Cascabel

Small and dark reddish brown, cascabel chiles are sometimes called "rattle chiles" because of the sound they make when shaken. They're very flavorful and have a moderate heat.

SUBSTITUTE: Guajillo chiles

COOK WITH IT: Enchiladas Mexicanas (page 182)

Chile de Árbol

Petite but powerful, this spicy chile is native to Mexico and sometimes referred to as "bird's beak chile." Unlike many other chiles, it retains its bright red color even when dried. A staple in southwestern kitchens, chiles de árbol are often dry-toasted in a hot skillet and then blended or crumbled into dishes.

SUBSTITUTE: Pequin chiles or a smaller amount of cayenne pepper

COOK WITH IT: Smoked Trout Hash with Poached Eggs and Tomatillo Salsa (page 173); Salmon Namban (page 214)

Serrano

A staple ingredient in raw salsas like pico de gallo, serranos have a fresh, zesty flavor and a pleasantly sharp bite. For a milder heat, remove the membranes and seeds before adding the chile to a dish.

SUBSTITUTE: Jalapeños (increase the quantity) or habaneros

COOK WITH IT: Guacamole (page 172)

New Mexico Red Chile

Earthy, flavorful, and hot, New Mexico red chiles are, not surprisingly, a key ingredient in the state's regional cuisine. When dried and coarsely ground to a size and texture similar to red pepper flakes, it's called chile caribe. When finely ground, it's called chile molido. If substituting one for the other, use half as much chile molido as chile caribe.

SUBSTITUTE: California chile or ancho chile (much milder)

COOK WITH IT: Carne Adovada (page 188)

Pasilla

Also known as chile negro because of its color, pasillas are the dried form of the chilaca chile, a thin, moderately hot chile that has a pungent, complex taste. Pasilla chiles are a key ingredient in mole negro.

SUBSTITUTE: Ancho chiles

COOK WITH IT: Sopa de Tortilla (page 176)

Jalapeño

One of the most readily available chiles in the United States, jalapeños have a good kick to them, but aren't overwhelmingly spicy. It's a good idea to taste the jalapeños before cooking with them; their heat level can vary from fruit to fruit and you might want to bump up or decrease the amount used accordingly. Pickled jalapeños are frequently used in Mexican and southwestern cooking and are sold in most supermarkets in whole or sliced form. Or you can make your own by marinating sliced jalapeños in a heated mixture of white vinegar, water, sugar, kosher salt, garlic, and oregano.

SUBSTITUTE: Serranos, though they are hotter than jalapeños, so use less

COOK WITH IT: Smoked Trout Hash with Poached Eggs and Tomatillo Salsa (page 173), Green Chile Hominy (page 189), Estofado de Pollo (page 239; pickled)

Poblano

Large, green, and mild, poblanos are often stuffed with cheese or meat and fried to make chiles rellenos or roasted and tossed with cream and cheese in *rajas con crema*. Poblanos have a thick, waxy skin and are rarely eaten raw; once roasted or charred, however, the chile's flavors deepen and they become easy to peel.

SUBSTITUTE: Anaheim (or California) chiles

COOK WITH IT: Chiles Relleños (page 180); Green Chile Hominy (page 189)

CHILES RELLEÑOS

IRMA'S

HOUSTON, TX

At Irma's, where the menu changes daily, customers know they've hit the jackpot when chiles relleños are an offering. Filled with a savory, cumin-spiked mixture of ground beef, onions, and tomatoes, these mild poblano chiles are dunked in a foamy egg batter and deep-fried until golden brown. Poblano chiles can be found at many supermarkets; make sure to choose medium to large ones so they'll be easier to stuff. If necessary, a toothpick or skewer can be used to seal the chile before frying. The accompanying salsa ranchera—which absolutely makes the dish—is prepared with a combination of fresh and canned tomatoes to deepen the sauce's flavor.

SERVES 6 TO 8

12 medium to large fresh poblano chiles

2 tablespoons canola or vegetable oil, plus more for deep-frying

2 pounds lean ground beef

1 small onion, chopped (about 1 cup)

1 garlic clove, minced

4 tomatoes, diced (about 2 cups)

1½ teaspoons salt

1 teaspoon freshly ground black pepper

½ teaspoon ground cumin

2 cups all-purpose flour

8 large eggs, separated, at room temperature

Salsa Ranchera (recipe follows)

½ cup shredded Monterey Jack cheese

¼ cup chopped fresh cilantro

USING tongs, carefully roast the chiles over a gas flame, turning until blistered and slightly charred all over, about 2 minutes per chile. (If you don't have a gas stove, the chiles can also be placed on a baking sheet and charred under the broiler. Turn the chiles frequently until blistered on all sides, 7 to 10 minutes.) Put them in a heavy-duty resealable plastic bag and set aside to steam for about 10 minutes. Remove the chiles from the bag and peel off and discard their skin. Using a paring knife, make a lengthwise slit through one side of each chile and carefully remove and discard the seeds and membranes. Rinse the chiles and drain well, using paper towels to pat the peppers dry.

TO prepare the stuffing, heat the oil over medium-high heat in a large, heavy-bottomed skillet. Add the meat and cook until lightly browned, about 5 minutes. Add the onion and garlic, stirring to combine, and cook for 1 minute. Add the tomatoes, 1 teaspoon of the salt, the black pepper, and the cumin and cook, stirring constantly, until the tomatoes cook down and most of the liquid has evaporated, about 10 minutes. Set aside to cool. (You should have about 5 cups.)

FILL each chile with about ½ cup of the ground meat mixture. Set aside.

PUT the flour in a shallow bowl and season with the remaining ½ teaspoon salt. In a medium bowl, beat the egg whites until stiff and foamy, about 3 minutes. In a separate bowl, lightly beat the egg yolks. Add the egg yolks to the egg whites and stir to combine.

IN a deep skillet, heat at least 2 inches of oil over medium-high heat. When the oil is hot, dip each stuffed chile into the flour to coat and then the egg mixture. Drop into the hot oil seam side down and fry to a golden brown on both sides, about 3 minutes, working in batches to avoid crowding the pan. Drain on paper towels.

SERVE the chiles relleños topped with salsa, cheese, and cilantro.

SALSA RANCHERA

MAKES 5 CUPS

2 tablespoons canola or vegetable oil

1 large onion, chopped (about 2 cups)

2 red bell peppers, seeded and diced (about 2 cups)

1 garlic clove, minced

⅛ teaspoon ground cumin

4 tomatoes, diced (about 2 cups)

1 (28-ounce) can diced tomatoes

Salt

IN a large, heavy-bottomed skillet, heat the oil over medium-high heat. Add the onion and cook until translucent, about 2 minutes. Add the fresh tomatoes, bell peppers, garlic, and cumin and cook until the peppers begin to soften, 2 to 3 minutes. Add the canned tomatoes and bring the mixture to a boil. Lower the heat and simmer until the sauce is slightly reduced, 10 to 15 minutes. Season to taste with salt.

"I was raised in this area. When I first opened up Irma's, everybody was moving out because the businesses were going out of business. When I was offered the opportunity to open up the restaurant, I wanted to make a difference."

— IRMA GALVAN,
Irma's in Houston, TX

ENCHILADAS MEXICANAS

IRMA'S

HOUSTON, TX

The warm, rich red chile sauce that tops these queso blanco–filled enchiladas is the star of this dish; it gets its deep, smoky flavor from a combination of ancho chiles, which are dried poblanos and should be easy to find, and dried cascabel chiles. Sometimes called "bola chiles" or "rattle chiles" because of the way the seeds rattle when the chiles are shaken, cascabel chiles are small and brown and have a moderate heat. If they're unavailable, guajillo chiles can be substituted, or—in a pinch—the number of ancho chiles can be doubled. The dish is very quick to assemble if the sauce is made ahead of time: the enchiladas are simply rolled up and topped with a ladle of sauce right before serving. The enchiladas are not baked after being rolled, as is traditional, so the queso fresco will not be melted, just slightly warmed from the heat of the sauced tortillas. Irma likes to serve the dish with diced boiled potatoes and peppery diced, blanched carrots.

SERVES 4

1½ pounds fresh queso blanco, crumbled, plus extra for serving

½ small white onion, diced (about ¾ cup), plus extra for serving

Enchilada Sauce (recipe follows)

1½ cups vegetable or canola oil

10 corn tortillas

Diced avocados

Chopped fresh cilantro

IN a medium bowl, combine the cheese and onion. Set aside.

GENTLY reheat the sauce in a wide saucepan.

IN a large, heavy-bottomed skillet, heat the oil over medium-high heat until hot but not smoking. Working in batches and using tongs, submerge the tortillas one by one very briefly in the hot oil to soften, about 1 second per side. (Alternatively, you can warm the tortillas in a 300°F oven for 3 to 5 minutes, but they won't be as pliable and easy to roll.) Remove the tortilla from the oil and immediately dip into the enchilada sauce to lightly coat both sides. Place the tortilla on a plate and repeat with the remaining tortillas.

TO assemble the enchiladas, divide the cheese and onion mixture evenly among the tortillas and roll up each like a cigar. Place 2 or 3 enchiladas on each plate and top with warm enchilada sauce. Top with additional queso blanco and chopped onions, garnish with avocados and cilantro, and serve immediately.

ENCHILADA SAUCE

MAKES ABOUT 4 CUPS

4 tablespoons vegetable or canola oil

5 large dried cascabel chiles

5 large dried ancho chiles

1 cup tomato puree

3 garlic cloves

¼ teaspoon salt

¼ teaspoon freshly ground black pepper

⅛ teaspoon ground cumin

HEAT 2 tablespoons of the oil in a heavy-bottomed skillet over medium-high heat. Add the cascabel and ancho chiles and cook until golden, about 2 minutes per side. Remove from the skillet and set aside. Wipe out the skillet.

IN the bowl of a blender, combine the browned chiles with the tomato puree, garlic, salt, black pepper, and cumin. Blend at medium speed for about 3 minutes, until it becomes a thick paste. Add 2½ cups water and blend again for 2 to 3 minutes, until smooth. Set aside.

HEAT the remaining 2 tablespoons oil over medium-high heat in the skillet. Add the enchilada sauce and cook for 15 minutes. Set aside. The sauce can be made up to 3 days ahead of time and stored in the refrigerator.

- -

"You go in Irma's and there's no menu.
They start rambling off the dishes and
you've got to pay attention, it's like
twelve things. Her flautas are awesome,
just crispy and light and delicious. I
really love a good chicken enchilada, and
then if they could put some mole next to
it and then a little pile of carne asada,
and the rice and beans—I'm in heaven."
—CHRIS SHEPHERD, JBF Award Winner

- -

RED CHILE ENCHILADAS

THE SHED

SANTA FE, NM

Unlike the enchiladas most often served throughout the United States, this version is "flat": each enchilada consists of two tortillas stacked up and covered with spicy red chile sauce and plenty of cheese. The dish is baked until piping hot and topped with a fried egg. All the chiles used at the Shed in Santa Fe are grown exclusively for the restaurant at a farm in southern New Mexico and milled in-house. (The pungent pods should be stored in a dry environment; at the Shed the chile stash is kept in the freezer.) Making the sauce for this dish can be a bit time-consuming (and messy), but it's well worth it: The smoky, richly flavored red chile sauce can be used in enchiladas, spooned over huevos rancheros, added to chile con carne, or even swirled into mashed potatoes. The sauce can be made ahead of time and refrigerated for several days or frozen for up to 3 months.

SERVES 6

1 cup shortening or canola oil

12 (6-inch) blue or yellow corn tortillas

1 bunch scallions, minced (about ½ cup)

1½ pounds sharp cheddar cheese, grated (about 9 cups)

1½ cups Red Chile Sauce (recipe follows)

6 large eggs, fried over easy (optional)

PREHEAT the oven to 450°F.

IN a large, heavy-bottomed pan, heat the shortening over medium-high heat. Working in batches and using tongs, submerge the tortillas one by one very briefly in the hot shortening to soften, 2 to 3 seconds per side. Remove the tortillas and blot with paper towels. Repeat until all the tortillas have been softened.

PLACE 6 tortillas on a large, rimmed baking sheet with at least ½ inch between them. Sprinkle each one with a little less than 1 tablespoon of the scallions and ½ cup of the cheese. Top each one with another tortilla and repeat. Pour sauce over each tortilla stack and sprinkle each with more cheese. Bake until the cheese has melted and the sauce begins to bubble, about 10 minutes. Serve immediately, topped with the eggs if you like.

RED CHILE SAUCE

MAKES 2 QUARTS

8 ounces dried New Mexico red chiles or ancho chiles, stems and seeds removed

2 garlic cloves

1 tablespoon kosher salt

2 tablespoons vegetable shortening

3 tablespoons all-purpose flour

FILL a large pot with water and bring to a boil. Add the chiles to the pot and cover. Simmer for 30 minutes, stirring occasionally to make sure all the chiles soften evenly. Drain.

WORKING in batches, fill a blender two-thirds full with softened chiles. Cover with water and pulse a few times to coarsely blend. Empty the contents of the blender into a large bowl and repeat until all the chiles have been blended.

PASS the blended chile mixture through a food mill, discarding the skins.

ON a cutting board, mince the garlic. Sprinkle the salt on top of the garlic and, using the flat of the knife, scrape the garlic and salt mixture against the cutting board to create a smooth paste. Set aside.

IN a large pot, heat the shortening over medium heat. Add the flour and cook, stirring constantly to prevent burning, until the roux is a rich golden brown, about 5 minutes.

SLOWLY add the chile pulp to the roux and whisk to combine. Be careful, as it might spit. Add the garlic mixture and 2 cups water to the pot and stir. Bring to a boil and then lower the heat to a simmer. Cook, uncovered, until thickened and darker in color, 45 minutes to 1 hour. Stir frequently to avoid burning.

TEXAS-STYLE OVEN BRISKET

LOUIE MUELLER BARBECUE

TAYLOR, TX

It's not often that a world-famous barbecue joint is willing to share one of their recipes, so we jumped at the chance to include this oven-cooked version of Louie Mueller's legendary brisket. With a crackling, peppery crust, this tender, perfectly seasoned meat is as close as one can get to real Texas barbecue when cooking in a home kitchen. The shockingly simple recipe was adapted by Louie's grandson, current owner Wayne Mueller, who tested the recipe himself multiple times to make sure it held up to his family's exacting brisket standards. (There's no question here: It does.) **SERVES 12 TO 14**

1 cup coarsely ground black pepper

2 tablespoons kosher salt

5 to 6 pounds brisket, trimmed, with a layer of fat at least ¼ inch thick, choice grade or higher

MOVE the oven rack to the center position and preheat the oven to 275°F.

IN a small bowl, stir together the pepper and salt. Spread the pepper mixture evenly across a large baking sheet.

REMOVE the brisket from its packaging. Dampen a kitchen towel and rub the wet towel over the entire brisket. Place the brisket, fat cap down, onto the pepper mixture to thoroughly coat with a thick layer. Using clean hands, press the pepper mixture over all sides of the brisket. Flip the brisket over so the fat cap is facing up; make sure that the entire fat cap is covered with the pepper mixture.

PUT the brisket in a roasting pan large enough to hold the brisket without the brisket touching any sides of the pan. (Always use a pan with sides that are at least 3 inches high.) Place the brisket in the oven and bake, uncovered, for 5½ hours, basting with grease from the pan every hour.

At Louie Mueller Barbecue, the brisket is slow-cooked in fifty-year-old brick-and-steel posts over post oak wood.

REMOVE the brisket from the pan and place on a cutting board or other large, flat surface. Immediately wrap the brisket in plastic wrap, making sure no brisket surface is left exposed. Over that, thoroughly wrap the brisket with newspaper, a paper bag, or butcher paper. Place

the brisket in a small, empty, insulated ice chest or cooler that is at room temperature. (A microwave oven can also be used in place of an ice chest.) Allow the brisket to rest in the container, undisturbed, for 1 hour. Remove the brisket from the ice chest or microwave and remove all of its wrapping.

SET the brisket on a carving board, with the point to your left and the flat facing right. Begin carving the brisket, against the grain, on the flat (right) side, moving right to left as you carve. Once you reach the midpoint of the brisket, turn the brisket 90 degrees to the right so that the point is facing away from you and the exposed (cut end) of the brisket is facing you. Begin carving from the right side and continue carving from right to left until the entire point is carved. (Carving the brisket this way will enable you to cut across the grain of both muscle masses, so the meat is as tender as possible.) Serve warm.

CARNE ADOVADA

THE SHED

SANTA FE, NM

A traditional New Mexican dish, carne adovada features succulent chunks of pork slowly braised in an earthy red chile sauce. The Carswell family's recipe calls for chile caribe, which is coarsely ground dried New Mexican red chile that resembles red pepper flakes in size and texture. The sauce can also be made with whole red chile pods or finely ground red chile powder (chile molido). Serve the pork as an entrée along with pinto beans or posole, or roll it up in a flour tortilla and eat it as a burrito.

SERVES 6 TO 8

2 garlic cloves

1 teaspoon salt

½ cup coarsely ground chile caribe

1½ teaspoons dried Mexican oregano

2½ pounds pork shoulder, cut into 1-inch cubes

PUT the garlic, salt, and 2 cups water in a blender and puree. Add the chile and oregano and blend for 30 seconds.

PUT the pork in a large baking dish or Dutch oven and pour the chile sauce over it. Cover and place the pork in the refrigerator to marinate for at least 2 hours or up to overnight.

REMOVE from the refrigerator and let the pork come to room temperature. Preheat the oven to 350°F.

COVER the baking dish with aluminum foil and place in the oven. Bake the pork until fork-tender, 2½ to 3 hours. Season to taste with more salt if needed.

GREEN CHILE HOMINY

PERINI RANCH STEAKHOUSE

BUFFALO GAP, TX

At Perini Ranch Steakhouse, chef and owner Tom Perini harnesses both cowboy culture and native southwestern ingredients in a menu that highlights some of the best Texas has to offer. Like this hominy casserole, which features crisp nuggets of bacon and subtly spicy green chile in every bite. This easy side can be made up to 2 days ahead of time; cook and assemble the dish without baking and then pop it in the oven before serving.

SERVES 8 TO 10 AS A SIDE DISH

12 ounces sliced bacon (about 12 slices)

1 large white onion, chopped (about 1 cup)

2 poblano or anaheim chiles, seeded and diced

6 cups cooked white hominy, or 4 (15-ounce) cans, drained

1 teaspoon apple cider vinegar, or 1 tablespoon brine from a jar of pickled jalapeños

¾ teaspoon salt

8 ounces cheddar cheese, grated (1 cup)

HEAT a large, heavy-bottomed pot over medium-high heat; add the bacon and fry until crisp. Transfer the cooked bacon to a plate lined with paper towels; discard all but 2 tablespoons of the drippings from the pan. Chop the bacon into small pieces and set aside.

LOWER the heat to medium and sauté the onion in the bacon grease until translucent, about 5 minutes. Add the chiles and stir to combine; cook for 2 minutes to soften the chiles. Add the hominy, vinegar, and salt to the pan; stir well to combine. Sprinkle the cheese over the hominy and stir until the cheese has melted.

REMOVE from the heat and transfer the hominy mixture to a serving bowl. Top with the bacon and serve immediately. (To make the dish ahead of time, transfer the hominy mixture to a 9-by-13-inch baking pan before topping with the bacon. Cover and refrigerate for up to 2 days or freeze for up to 1 month. To reheat, thaw in the refrigerator and bake at 350°F for 30 to 40 minutes, until heated through.)

SOURDOUGH BREAD PUDDING
WITH WHISKEY SAUCE

PERINI RANCH STEAKHOUSE

BUFFALO GAP, TX

What's chuckwagon cooking without a nip of whiskey? Tom Perini is known for this rich sourdough bread pudding, which is finished with a generous drizzle of creamy, boozy sauce. Use the best sourdough bread you can get your hands on and don't cut off the crusts; they'll crisp up when cooking, providing an irresistible, crunchy counterpoint to the soft pudding beneath.

SERVES 8

2 large eggs

2½ cups whole milk

2 tablespoons unsalted butter, melted

2 tablespoons vanilla extract (Mexican, if available)

2 cups sugar

3 cups sourdough bread, at least a day old, cut into 1-inch cubes

⅓ cup pecans, finely chopped

Whiskey Sauce (recipe follows)

PREHEAT the oven to 325°F.

IN a medium bowl, beat the eggs. Add the milk, melted butter, and vanilla extract and stir well to combine. Gradually add the sugar and mix thoroughly until the sugar has dissolved.

PLACE the bread cubes in the bottom of a 9-inch round or 8-inch square baking dish. Pour the egg mixture over the bread, making sure all the pieces are fully saturated. Sprinkle the pecans over the bread, pushing them down into the custard. Bake until golden brown, 55 to 60 minutes. Serve with whiskey sauce.

Perini Ranch Steakhouse is located in the tiny town of Buffalo Gap, Texas, which has a population of 463 people.

WHISKEY SAUCE

MAKES ABOUT 1½ CUPS

½ cup sugar

½ cup (1 stick) unsalted butter

½ cup heavy cream

¼ cup whiskey, such as Jack Daniel's

COMBINE the sugar, butter, cream, and whiskey in a medium saucepan. Stir constantly over medium-low heat until the mixture reaches a low rolling boil. Remove from the heat and keep warm. You can make the sauce ahead: cover and refrigerate for up to 2 days. When ready to serve, warm up the sauce over low heat.

CHOCOLATE ICE BOX CAKE

EL CHORRO LODGE

PARADISE VALLEY, AZ

A rich chocolate mousse layered over ladyfingers and topped with whipped cream, this cake needs to chill overnight to set, but otherwise could not be easier to make. The dessert has a homey, rustic look but can be fancied up if desired. To do so, use a 9-inch springform pan, as opposed to a square baking pan, and line the bottom and the sides with ladyfingers. (The ladyfingers around the circumference of the pan should be placed with the round sides facing out.) Instead of serving the additional whipped cream on the side, pipe it on the top of the cake and finish with a sprinkle of grated chocolate.

SERVES 8

2 (4-ounce) bars German's chocolate, coarsely chopped

4 large eggs, separated (see Note)

2 tablespoons confectioners' sugar

½ cup finely chopped walnuts

1 cup heavy cream

1 (7-ounce) package ladyfingers (about 24)

Whipped cream

MELT the chocolate in a double boiler or in a large metal bowl set atop a pot of simmering water (do not allow the bottom of the bowl to touch the water). Add 3 tablespoons water and stir well to combine. Remove from the heat. Add the egg yolks one at a time, beating vigorously to incorporate each one. Add the confectioners' sugar and walnuts and stir well to blend.

IN a large, chilled bowl, beat the heavy cream just until stiff. Set aside.

IN the bowl of a stand mixer fitted with the whisk attachment, beat the egg whites at high speed until stiff peaks form. Using a rubber spatula, gently fold the beaten egg whites and whipped cream into the chocolate until incorporated.

LINE the bottom and sides of an 8-inch square baking pan with the ladyfingers. Top with the chocolate mixture. Chill for 12 to 24 hours. Serve with whipped cream.

NOTE: This recipe calls for uncooked egg yolks and whites. If you're concerned about the safety of raw eggs, pasteurized eggs can be used.

TAHITIAN CHOCOLATE LACE COOKIES

CAFE PASQUAL'S

SANTA FE, NM

Cafe Pasqual's tropical spin on this classic Florentine cookie is made with toasted macadamia nuts, shredded coconut, and chopped dried mango and papaya. A layer of dark chocolate balances out the sweetness of the dried fruit. The cookies can be delicate; baking them on a silicone liner and using a wide spatula will make them easier to handle.

MAKES 36 COOKIES

1 cup unsalted macadamia nuts

¼ cup sweetened shredded coconut

1⅓ cups dried mango

1⅓ cups dried papaya

¼ cup all-purpose flour

⅔ cup heavy cream

⅔ cup sugar

Pinch of sea salt

5 ounces semisweet or bittersweet chocolate, chopped

PREHEAT the oven to 300°F.

IN a shallow ovenproof pan, combine the macadamia nuts and coconut. Place the pan in the oven and roast until the nuts and coconut are golden in color, 12 to 15 minutes, stirring frequently and watching carefully so they don't burn. Set aside and allow to cool for 5 to 10 minutes.

PUT the toasted macadamia nuts and coconut, mango, papaya, and flour in the bowl of a food processor fitted with the steel blade and pulse until the mixture is coarsely chopped. Set aside.

IN a small saucepan, heat the cream, sugar, and salt over medium heat until the sugar has dissolved, stirring occasionally, about 5 minutes. Remove from the heat and let the mixture cool completely. Pour the cream mixture into a medium bowl and add the reserved nut and fruit mixture. Stir to incorporate, cover, and refrigerate until chilled, about 1 hour.

PREHEAT the oven to 350°F. Line four baking sheets with silicone mats or parchment paper. (You could also bake the cookies in batches.)

FORM the dough into 36 balls, using about 2 teaspoons for each one. Place 8 on each baking sheet, about 2 inches apart as the cookies will spread while baking. Bake for 15 minutes. Use a wide spatula to transfer the cookies to a cooling rack to cool.

IN a double boiler or a metal bowl placed over a saucepan of simmering water, melt 4 ounces of the chocolate, stirring frequently. Remove from the heat and stir in the remaining chocolate to melt it. Working quickly and using a small offset spatula or silicone brush, spread the chocolate onto the flat sides of the cookies. Let the cookies cool, chocolate side up, on a cooling rack, but serve them chocolate side down.

The Fry Bread House

Native American Food • Dine in • Take out

"Beans are the main food on my reservation.
We cooked beans every single day and ate
beans every single day when I was small."
– CECILIA MILLER,
The Fry Bread House in Phoenix, AZ

The Award Winners

CAFE PASQUAL'S

121 Don Gaspar Avenue
Santa Fe, NM
Owner: Katharine Kagel
1999 AWARD WINNER

See page 166.

EL CHORRO LODGE

5550 East Lincoln Drive
Paradise Valley, AZ
Owner: Jacquie Dorrance
2005 AWARD WINNER

Joe Miller had no idea what he was getting into when he took a bartending job at El Chorro Lodge in 1952. The rambling, low-slung adobe hacienda, once a girls' school, had been converted into a flourishing western-style restaurant in 1937. Happy hour, complete with carved turkey and roast beef, was a hit from the beginning, and Joe oversaw it with easygoing aplomb. When the original owners chose to gallop off into the sunset, Joe and his wife, Evie, bought El Chorro, pledging to continue its tradition of hospitality. The Phoenix metropolitan area has mushroomed in the decades since—and the property was sold to area philanthropist Jacquie Dorrance in 2009—but sitting on twelve desert acres overlooking the majestic Camelback Mountain, El Chorro feels like an outpost of yesteryear. The mesquite tree–dotted patio is the heart of the property, where the outdoor hearth, burning fragrant juniper, still attracts real cowboys as well as returning snowbirds, corporate executives from downtown high-rises, and a cross-section of other folks in the know. Whatever the diet trend of the moment, diners continue to flock in for the legendary cinnamon-laden sticky buns, an institution for six decades, and the restaurant's hearty aged prime steaks, sizzled under a 1,600°F broiler. You'll also find chateaubriand for two, Rocky Mountain lamb chops, shrimp cocktail, trout almondine, an iceberg wedge with Roquefort crumbles, and scalloped potatoes.

THE FRY BREAD HOUSE

1003 East Indian School Road
Phoenix, AZ
Owner: Cecilia Miller
2012 AWARD WINNER

No trip to Phoenix is complete without a visit to the Fry Bread House, a trim-paneled room on a modest, sun-baked residential street, founded in 1992. The sign outside says, "Native American Food." At the counter inside, you can order exhilarating, complex red and green chile stews that are a primal blast of the Southwest. Owner Cecilia Miller comes from the Sonoran Desert Tohono O'odham Nation, and her all-native staff is drawn from assorted Arizona tribes. Their blissfully delicious specialty is hand-stretched fry bread—downy bronze cushions the size of dinner plates, in both savory and sweet versions. On the savory side: Indian tacos, layered with refried beans and chorizo or beef in red or green chile sauce, garnished with crisp chopped iceberg, shredded cheese, and tart red salsa. For dessert: fry bread baptized with butter and local honey or homemade chocolate sauce. The faithful clientele is wonderfully democratic, from Tohono O'odham friends of the house to hipsters and businessmen and the ever-present lucky traveler.

The adobe hacienda that houses El Chorro Lodge was once an all-girls' school. They make fifteen hundred sticky buns a day in the high season.

H&H CAR WASH AND COFFEE SHOP

101 East Yandell Drive
El Paso, TX
Owner: Kenneth Haddad
2001 AWARD WINNER

This restaurant-in-a-car-wash may well be the only one of its kind, but the story of its genesis is tied to a great, near-lost Texas road-food tradition. When owner Kenneth Haddad's father, Najib Haddad, founded the place with the two eldest of his six sons back in 1958, little roadhouses known as "toddle houses" lined the Texas highways, serving great American food in Lilliputian style. Each had an abbreviated counter, three or four tables, and a minuscule kitchen—everything within arm's reach of the short-order cook. The toddle houses fascinated Najib, so when he opened his car wash, he built his own little eatery instead of a reception area. It was a soda fountain and grill combo that offered the usual American fare: cheeseburgers, fries, and shakes. There were eleven stools and three tables, enough space for just twenty-three customers. By toddle-house standards, it was positively gigantic. Najib eventually got tired of running the eatery and for several years he leased the space. In 1985, Kenneth reopened the café himself. Today the place looks a lot like it did in his father's time, since even the equipment dates back to its beginnings, but the menu of road food, American-style, has been largely supplanted by spot-on Tex-Mex food like chile colorado and enchiladas with salsa verde.

"I don't know much about restaurants, but I do know that half the game is when you put that plate in front of somebody, if it looks good, they're going to enjoy it more."

— KENNETH HADDAD,
H&H Car Wash and Coffee Shop
in El Paso, TX

IRMA'S

22 North Chenevert Street
Houston, TX
Owner: Irma Galvan
2008 AWARD WINNER

If you want to get elected to public office in Houston, you had best start eating lunch at Irma's. Breakfast, too. It's the city's clubhouse, the restaurant that all races and classes claim as home. Open since 1989, Irma Galvan's downtown breakfast-and-lunch spot has long served as an incubator of community and a beacon of vernacular cookery. Among the knick knacks, kitschy artwork, and memorabilia that plaster the walls, business honchos and blue-collar workers sit side-by-side enjoying honest, high-quality Tex-Mex dishes like breakfast tacos, chunky guacamole, enchiladas with chile gravy, and refried beans, all served with Irma's famous fruit-laced lemonade.

JOE T. GARCIA'S MEXICAN RESTAURANT

2201 North Commerce Street
Fort Worth, TX
Owner: Lancarte family
1998 AWARD WINNER

Originally opened in 1935 as a tiny, sixteen-person barbecue stand run out of its founders' family home, Joe T. Garcia's has since grown into a Dallas–Fort Worth Tex-Mex institution capable of seating more than a thousand customers at a time. The restaurant may be sprawling, but it continues to be family-run: Esperanza "Hope" Lancarte, the daughter of original owners Joe and Jesusa Garcia, oversaw the eatery's transformation and operations, with the help of her sister Mary, from 1953 until her death in 2014. Since then Hope's sons and daughter-in-law have been carrying on their grandparents' legacy. Initiated customers still line up to sit on the poolside patio and order without menus for a traditional Mexican dinner. In recent years, the family has also set up Esperanza's, a café and bakery next door.

Irma's Restaurant

LOUIE MUELLER BARBECUE

206 West 2nd Street
Taylor, TX
Owner: Wayne Mueller
2006 AWARD WINNER

See page 164.

MARY & TITO'S CAFÉ

2711 4th Street Northwest
Albuquerque, NM
Owners: Mary Gonzales and Antoinette Knight
2010 AWARD WINNER

See page 162.

THE ORIGINAL SONNY BRYAN'S

2202 Inwood Road
Dallas, TX
Owner: Brent Harman
2000 AWARD WINNER

There is nothing like the Original Sonny Bryan's on Inwood Road, with its no-frills counter service and school-desk seating. Though the restaurant's franchised offshoots expanded to include several locations in the Dallas–Fort Worth area, the original Sonny's is still the most beloved. The menu includes many of the local favorites—smoked brisket, of course, along with pork ribs, pulled chicken, and colossal onion rings—but the incomparably tender and moist beef brisket sandwich is always a hit.

PERINI RANCH STEAKHOUSE

3002 FM 89 #A
Buffalo Gap, TX
Owners: Tom Perini and Lisa Perini
2014 AWARD WINNER

Cowboy cook and rancher Tom Perini made a bold decision in 1983. With oil and cattle prices depressed, he turned a hay barn on his family spread into a restaurant, hoping to draw folks from nearby Abilene. Serving Texas standards with genuine hospitality, he has created a rural roadhouse with grilled steaks at the heart of the menu. Tom knew that if he opted for prime beef, he'd price himself out of the local market. He chose instead to grill the best choice rib-eyes, strips, and filets. The appeal of those steaks owes much to mesquite; the scrubby, thorny trees grow everywhere in this arid terrain, and their coals yield a pungent smoke that perfumes the air. Comfort foods and chuckwagon favorites fill out the offerings, which include green chile hominy and garlicky cowboy potatoes. For dessert, there's whiskey-laced bread pudding.

"I tried to be a cowboy, but being a cowboy is very difficult. I found that I would kind of lean toward cooking lunch and dinner at the ranch chuckwagon."

— TOM PERINI,
Perini Ranch Steakhouse
in Buffalo Gap, TX

THE SHED

113 East Palace Avenue
Santa Fe, NM
Owner: Carswell family
2003 AWARD WINNER

A restaurant begun in a burro shed on a dusty alley in a then sleepy little town might not sound as if it would be—over sixty years later—hailed as a venerable institution. The Shed, though, has become the standard-setter for northern New Mexican fare, Santa Fe charm, and warm hospitality. Thornton and Polly Carswell founded the Shed after homey meals they offered to area skiers proved popular. Their son, Courtney, thought a career in Latin American business lay ahead for him, but Polly's passion for food and cooking was too deeply ingrained. Courtney stayed on to help the growing enterprise flourish, in the roles of cook, host, dishwasher, and, eventually, manager. His wife, Linnea, now the business's financial officer, joined him. Courtney and Linnea helped refine the Shed's reputation for exceptional cooking. While a great burger and salad have long been staples here, the stacked blue corn enchiladas with red chile sauce, green chile stew, soft tacos, white-corn posole, and long-simmered pinto beans are the heart of the menu. And the "number five" plate of enchiladas, bathed in brick-red chile, distills Santa Fe cooking to its core. To ensure the quality of the remarkable chile sauces, the Carswells purchase the entire production of two specific southern New Mexico chile fields each year. The Shed today sits two blocks from the original burro shed location. A rambling seventeenth-century adobe hacienda now houses the restaurant, complete with a courtyard oasis framed by graceful trumpet vines.

WEST

HELENA'S HAWAIIAN FOOD

HONOLULU, HI

2000 AWARD WINNER

With fish-net décor on the walls, bare-topped Formica tables, and bright red stools for seats, Helena's Hawaiian Foods is the most humble of restaurants. Its menu of pipikaula-style short ribs and butterfish collars (the latter is lusciously fried sections of the fish just ahead of the gills), makes it an ultra-rarity in America, scarce even on the Hawaiian Islands—a genuine Polynesian restaurant. No puu-puu platters or parasol-topped libations here. Helena's offers true regional fare such as kalua pig, lomi-lomi salmon, or fried ahi accompanied by poi— fresh, day-old, or sour—ordered à la carte and served without ceremony on weekdays only, to fit the needs of the working people who have been its best steady customers.

Like so many great regional restaurants, Helena's Hawaiian Foods had a single significant culinary force behind it. That was Helen Chock, who opened for business in 1946 and oversaw the restaurant until her death at ninety years old in 2007. The restaurant has also relocated, but remains humble—its new environs are between a radiator shop and the highway. Helen's grandson, Craig Katsuyoshi, now runs the restaurant, which still draws long lines.

MY GRANDMOTHER HELEN OPENED HELENA'S IN 1946 (Helena is the Hawaiian form of Helen). As a female business owner she was a pioneer in her day. She actually took the business over from her brother and when she started, she didn't really know what restaurant work was about. She always told us that she learned to cook when she worked with Hawaiian ladies at the navy shipyard. She worked at the restaurant every day until she was eighty-nine years old.

I started working there in high school, about 1985, busing tables, washing dishes, mopping floors. It was very small. We were just a tiny place, and we served mainly regular customers and the local people. But because of the food's quality and Helen's way of doing the best she could to please people, the restaurant has always been popular.

We serve Hawaiian food. The first Hawaiians would heat up lava rocks, dig a hole in the ground, and put the pork in the hole with the hot rocks. They would wrap the pork with banana leaves and taro leaves—that's how they cooked a lot of things. They didn't have pots and pans. We use a lot of the traditional cooking styles.

We also serve the food that missionaries brought with them. It's still Hawaiian food because it evolved here, but it's centered around ingredients missionaries brought, like beef. The missionaries brought cows, and they started ranching over here, so we have people who are called paniolos, which are Hawaiian cowboys. They would salt things to transport them to the island, so we have things like salted salmon and salted tomatoes. When Chinese immigrants came they brought noodles. All of these foods are on our menu.

This is really a family restaurant. At one point in time everyone in my family worked here and helped. I was the one who came back to run the business. I thought it was going to be my first business—I didn't know it was also going to be my last business. My mom is the cashier right now, my wife comes in. I have nieces working here, and of course we have other people working here, but they're all family now.

We serve comfort food, and we're a part of the community. I remember kids that have come in here: a small little girl whose parents brought her in, she went to school, she graduated from college, she got married, and now she comes in with her kids. There are still customers that come in from when my grandma started the restaurant. The community here hasn't changed much, and we haven't changed much either. I think that's one of the biggest challenges for me, keeping up with the times and yet staying the same. We're in a world of change, but we stay the same.

—CRAIG KATSUYOSHI

Pipikaula short ribs are one
of the most popular dishes at
Helena's Hawaiian Food, which
serves 250 to 300 pounds of the
crisp, slow-cooked meat daily.

MANEKI

SEATTLE, WA

2008 AWARD WINNER

Maneki is a family-owned enterprise whose roots stretch back to the early years of the twentieth century. Some believe it was founded in 1902. Others claim a date of 1911. In any case, it's the only surviving restaurant from Seattle's once bustling Japantown. Since 1974, the Nakayama family has been at the helm, first Kozo, now his wife, Jean. Maneki has long claimed a place at the center of Seattle's Japanese-American community. In the 1930s one of the restaurant's dishwashers was a University of Washington student named Takeo Miki, who later served, from 1974 to 1976, as Japan's prime minister. When Seattle's Japanese Americans were sent away to internment camps during World War II, many stored their belongings in the then-shuttered Maneki. Today the modest eatery specializes in provincial dishes like agedashi tofu and takoyaki as well as sushi and sashimi, satisfying homesick Japanese locals while introducing new generations to traditional Japanese cooking.

MANEKI RESTAURANT WAS OPENED BACK IN 1902. Back then, Maneki was shaped like a Japanese castle, a three-story castle with a terraced garden on the top of a hill here in Seattle. I think the second floor alone would seat five hundred people. It was one of the highlights for dignitaries who came in from Japan, like the first prime minister of Japan who came to Seattle and had dinner there. It was a fancy occasion for the Japanese community back in the early 1900s. Back in the old days, it was mostly Japanese companies who would go and eat at Maneki—it was the center of the Japanese community here. After work there was a lot of drinking, a lot of contracts and things like that, that occurred at Maneki.

The second owner of Maneki was Mr. Soto, and he took over in 1923. I believe he ran the restaurant up until the war, when everyone was interned in camp. After they came back from the camp, the original Maneki had been destroyed. The building that the current Maneki is in was used as storage for all the internees, and Mr. Soto just decided to stay in that space instead of pursuing the bigger, grander kind of Maneki. So we've been in this space since 1946, after the war.

Mr. Soto's daughter eventually took over the restaurant, and she had it until the mid-1970s. My husband was her chef at the time. He was young and he came from Japan, and he took over the restaurant in 1974. As a little girl I used to always eat at Maneki, so we knew all the waitresses and even knew the previous owners, and nothing has really changed. We still have the tatami rooms. It's actually pretty antique now because in Japan they don't have tatami rooms as much as they did in the old days. So we do have some guests that come from Japan and they go, "Oh, how nostalgic. I haven't sat in one of these in years."

The building was sold and remodeled in 1998, and my husband passed away about a year after the remodel. And so I've been running the restaurant since then. Our oldest and longest employee, we call her Mom. She doesn't even know how long she's been there. She'll be eighty-five this year, and she tends bar twice a week and other nights she helps me host. So she's still there and we still have all her friends, they come and visit her while she's tending bar. There's one couple, and every year they celebrate their wedding anniversary at Maneki. They're so cute, the last one they celebrated here was their sixty-fifth anniversary, I think. I'm always satisfied at the end of the day when I hear stories like, "Well, Grandma used to bring me here . . ." and I still remember what they used to eat when they were little and now they're all grown up and have their own kids. We sometimes have three or four generations together in the tatami room. Food is very important—it creates memories.

—JEAN NAKAYAMA

"One thing I strive for is the authenticity of Japanese food. It needs to be traditional, to be something that brings back a memory."
— JEAN NAKAYAMA,
Maneki in Seattle, WA

Sandwiches

There are few faster ways to satisfy hunger than by taking something delicious and wrapping it in bread. It's such a basic and universal food, yet sandwiches, like barbecue, seem to bring out one's sense of loyalty and fierce cultural pride in a way that can be downright competitive. How else to understand the fervor with which Philadelphians debate the source for the best cheesesteak, or the rancor that can develop between corned beef connoisseurs when discussing East Coast versus West Coast delicatessens? People feel strongly about sandwiches. Here are some of the ones that we always get excited about:

Region	Sandwich	Where to Get It	Words of Wisdom
SOUTHEAST	Cuban sandwich	**VERSAILLES** Miami, FL	A special sandwich press called a plancha is used to prepare this warm, toasted sandwich made with Cuban bread stuffed with sweet ham, roast pork, Swiss cheese, pickles, and mustard.
NORTHEAST	Philly cheesesteak	**JOHN'S ROAST PORK** Philadelphia, PA	At this longtime sandwich institution, proprietor John Bucci Jr. has developed his own recipe for what the *Philadelphia Inquirer* decreed the city's best cheesesteak sandwich—a heaping whirl of caramelized-to-order onions; seasoned, thinly sliced rib-eye; and aged provolone crammed inside a hollowed-out crusty roll.
MIDWEST	Bratwurst sandwich	**THE BERGHOFF** Chicago, IL	There's bratwurst and then there's bratwurst. And at the Berghoff, where the brats are as good as it gets, the rich veal sausage is grilled and served with sauerkraut on a Bavarian pretzel roll that takes the dish over the top.
SOUTHWEST	Green chile frybread	**THE FRY BREAD HOUSE** Phoenix, AZ	Spicy, tender chunks of beef simmered in fragrant green chile is served on hand-stretched fry bread—a doughy Native American specialty—and topped with chopped iceberg lettuce, shredded cheese, and fresh salsa.
WEST	Cheeseburger (page 242)	**GOTT'S ROADSIDE** St. Helena, CA	There's no sandwich more all-American than a hamburger, and there are few burger joints as evocative of vintage Americana as Gott's, a roadside burger joint with a '50s-style aesthetic. At Gott's the juicy, secret sauce–slathered burgers are made of Niman Ranch beef and served on tender pain de mie buns alongside fries, shakes, or even kale salad. (It is California, after all.)

SAKURA SALAD

MANEKI

SEATTLE, WA

Maneki debuted the first full-service sushi bar in Seattle in the 1970s, and it's still known for its pristine, beautifully presented fish. This stunning first-course salad is dressed with aromatic grated ginger and a drizzle of ponzu, a tangy Japanese condiment made with rice vinegar, mirin, bonito (tuna) flakes, seaweed, and the juice of a citrus fruit like lime or yuzu. It's often used as a dipping sauce for sashimi and can be a flavorful, complex marinade for chicken or beef. Ponzu can be found in Asian grocery stores or specialty markets.

SERVES 2

2 cups mixed baby greens

4 thin slices tuna (about 4 ounces)

4 thin slices amberjack (about 4 ounces)

4 thin slices avocado

½ teaspoon grated fresh ginger

2 tablespoons citrus soy sauce (ponzu)

1 teaspoon salmon roe

PILE the greens on a serving plate. Place alternating slices of tuna, amberjack, and avocado on top. Sprinkle grated fresh ginger on top of the salad and drizzle with ponzu. Scatter salmon roe on top of the salad.

"One of my all-time favorite Japanese restaurants in Seattle is Maneki. It's one of those places that makes you feel like you're being taken care of at your grandmother's house. It's been a longtime cooks' spot for an incredible meal that doesn't break the bank."
— MARIA HINES, JBF Award winner

SALMON NAMBAN

MANEKI

SEATTLE, WA

In this startlingly good chilled appetizer, cubes of salmon are dusted with potato starch, crisped in hot oil, and then soaked overnight in a piquant soy sauce–based marinade. Potato starch, or katakuriko, can be found in most Asian specialty stores; in a pinch cornstarch can be substituted. The marinade calls for light soy sauce, which is an intensely flavored, slightly sweet Japanese soy sauce to which a bit of mirin, or rice wine, has been added. ("Light," in this instance, does not mean low-sodium.) Dashi is an elemental soup stock used throughout Japanese cooking; it is sold in powdered form at Asian grocery stores, or you can make your own by simmering kombu and bonito flakes in water and then straining the fragrant broth.

SERVES 4

1 cup light (usukuchi) soy sauce

1 cup sugar

1 teaspoon dashi powder, or 2 cups homemade dashi

1 dried red chile pepper, crushed

½ white onion, thinly sliced

½ lemon, sliced into thin half-moons

Vegetable oil for deep-frying

2 tablespoons potato starch (katakuriko)

1 pound salmon, preferably wild sockeye or king, cut into 1-inch squares

Sliced scallions

IN a medium bowl, combine the soy sauce, sugar, dashi powder, and crushed chile pepper with 2 cups water; stir well to combine. (Note: Two cups homemade dashi can be substituted for the dashi powder and water.) Add the onion and lemon slices to the bowl and set the marinade aside.

POUR 1 inch of oil into a large, heavy skillet; heat over medium-high heat.

SPREAD the potato starch on a plate. Add the salmon squares and toss gently to coat. Working in batches to avoid crowding the pan, deep-fry the salmon squares until they are lightly browned, about 3 minutes per side. Do not overcook.

IMMEDIATELY immerse the hot fried salmon squares in the marinade. Cover and refrigerate for at least 1 hour—ideally overnight. Use a slotted spoon to serve and top with scallions.

Maneki means
"the welcome cat"
in Japanese.

SABLEFISH IN SAKE KASU
WITH HONEY SOY SAUCE AND SCALLION OIL

RAY'S BOATHOUSE AND CAFÉ

SEATTLE, WA

Perched at the water's edge, with majestic views of the Puget Sound, Ray's offers the area's most pristine seafood, much of it sourced through local fishermen. This dish is made with sablefish, a buttery fish indigenous to the West Coast. It's marinated for 48 hours: first in salt, which lightly cures the fish, and then in kasu, a paste made from the lees, or yeast deposits, left over from sake production. Kasu has been used in Japan to preserve food for thousands of years, but when mixed with mirin and a little sugar it becomes a delicious marinade that imparts a subtle, earthy sweetness. You'll find kasu paste in Asian specialty markets or sake distilleries. At Ray's, kasu-marinated sablefish is paired with jasmine rice and steamed choy sum, a leafy green similar to bok choy.

SERVES 4

2 to 2½ pounds sablefish fillets (also known as black cod or butterfish), skin on, cut into 4 pieces

⅓ cup kosher salt, or more if needed

¾ cup kasu paste

⅓ cup sugar

2 tablespoons canola oil

Honey Soy Sauce (recipe follows)

Scallion Oil (recipe follows)

PLACE the sablefish fillets skin side down in a shallow glass baking dish. Sprinkle a generous layer of salt over the fish, cover with plastic wrap, and refrigerate for 24 hours.

RINSE the salt from the fish and pat dry. Place the fish skin side down in a clean dish. Using a hand mixer, in a medium bowl, beat the kasu paste and sugar together until smooth. Gradually add ¾ cup water and mix until incorporated. Pour the kasu mixture evenly over the fish, cover, and refrigerate for another 24 hours.

REMOVE the fish from the marinade, allowing the excess to drip off. Heat the oil in a large, heavy pan over medium-high heat. Add the fish to the pan, skin side down. Once the bottom is golden brown, about 5 minutes, turn the fish over and cook until it's just cooked through, about 5 minutes more. (The fish can be grilled instead of pan-seared, if you'd like.) Transfer to individual plates. Serve with honey soy sauce and scallion oil.

HONEY SOY SAUCE

MAKES 1½ CUPS

1⅓ cups honey

¾ cup soy sauce

¼ cup freshly squeezed lime juice

2 tablespoons rice wine vinegar

2 teaspoons arrowroot powder

COMBINE the honey, soy sauce, and lime juice in a saucepan and bring to a boil over medium-high heat. In a small bowl, whisk the vinegar and arrowroot to make a slurry. Add the slurry to the saucepan, stir to combine, and bring the mixture to a boil again. Once the mixture begins to boil and thicken, remove from the heat and let cool.

SCALLION OIL

MAKES 1¼ CUPS

1 teaspoon kosher salt, plus more to taste

1 cup chopped scallion tops (green parts only)

1 cup canola oil

FILL a 2-quart pot three-quarters full of water and add the salt. Bring the water to a rolling boil. Drop in the scallions and stir until bright green, about 10 seconds. Drain the water through a strainer and immediately place the scallions under cold running water. When cool, squeeze out excess water.

IN a blender, combine the blanched scallions, oil, and salt to taste. Blend for 4 to 5 minutes, until well combined. This can be made 1 day in advance and refrigerated in a glass jar or a condiment squeeze bottle. Shake well before using.

OCTOPUS SALAD

SWAN OYSTER DEPOT

SAN FRANCISCO, CA

A lemony vinaigrette dresses this refreshing sea-food salad, which features bites of crunchy diced celery and a generous handful of flat-leaf parsley. According to Kevin Sancimino at Swan Oyster Depot, this recipe has been passed down through his family's Sicilian lineage for several genera-tions. Prior to cooking the octopus he likes to freeze it for at least a day to make it less chewy, but he notes that this step isn't necessary if you don't have time. He also boils his octopus with a cork in the water, an old Mediterranean trick that many chefs swear is the key to keeping the octopus tender. This recipe uses octopus tentacles only; the mantle of the octopus would be too chewy if prepared this way, so save it for another dish. (Note: The dish can be made with any cephalopod; Calamari, cuttlefish, and sepia will all work well, though the cooking times will vary.)

SERVES 6 TO 8

2 pounds frozen octopus tentacles, preferably 1 inch in diameter

Coarse sea salt

1 lemon, halved

¼ cup olive oil

2 tablespoons red wine vinegar

½ tablespoon Dijon-style mustard

½ teaspoon salt

Freshly ground black pepper

Pinch of cayenne pepper

2 celery ribs, diced

2 garlic cloves, minced

½ red onion, thinly sliced (about ½ cup)

½ cup fresh flat-leaf parsley, finely chopped

PUT the still-frozen octopus tentacles in a large stockpot or a Dutch oven and cover with cold water. Add 2 tablespoons coarse sea salt, a lemon half, and a clean wine cork to the water and bring it to a boil over medium-high heat. As soon as the water comes to a boil, begin timing; octopus tentacles that are 1 to 1½ inches in diam-eter at their thickest point will cook in 25 to 30 minutes. Adjust the cooking time for smaller or larger tentacles (tentacles that are 2 inches in diameter at their thick-est point will take closer to 30 minutes). The octopus is done when it's tender when pierced with a knife at the thickest part of the tentacle. You can also cut off a piece and give it a taste: it should still have a bite to it, but shouldn't be chewy.

WHILE the octopus is cooking, prepare an ice water bath in a large bowl. Drain the cooked octopus and immerse it in the ice water bath; this will cool it down and

prevent it from overcooking and will also make it easier to remove some of the skin. Discard the lemon half and wine cork. Let the octopus cool in the ice bath for about 5 minutes.

REMOVE the tentacles from the ice bath and pat them dry with paper towels. Some of the skin will come off as you dry it; discard, but try not to remove all of the skin as it has a lot of flavor. Run your hands or a small, clean brush over the tentacles to make sure they're clean. Slice the tentacles into thin rings, ¼ inch thick or less.

IN a large bowl, whisk together the oil, vinegar, the juice of the remaining ½ lemon, the mustard, salt, black pepper to taste, and cayenne. Add the octopus, celery, garlic, onion, and parsley and mix well. Chill for at least 20 minutes before serving.

CREAM OF ARTICHOKE SOUP

DUARTE'S TAVERN

PESCADERO, CA

Tucked back in an old farming village east of the scenic Highway 1, Duarte's Tavern is set right in the middle of artichoke country, and its owners have long showcased their town's prized crop in dishes such as chilled artichokes with aïoli, artichoke omelet, and this creamy artichoke soup, one of their acclaimed dishes. To make the dish with fresh artichokes, trim all the leaves, thistle, and any outer green part from 10 artichokes, placing the trimmed artichoke hearts in lemon juice–spiked water while you work. When ready to cook, put the artichoke hearts in a large pot and fill with water, ¼ cup olive oil, and 1 peeled smashed garlic clove. Bring to a boil and cook until the artichokes are tender. Drain and allow to cool before proceeding with the recipe.

SERVES 4

10 cooked artichoke hearts, or 1 pound frozen artichoke hearts, defrosted and drained

3 cups chicken broth, preferably homemade

1 tablespoon unsalted butter

½ teaspoon kosher salt, or more if needed

½ teaspoon freshly ground white pepper

2 teaspoons chicken base, or 1 chicken bouillon cube (optional)

2 garlic cloves, minced

¼ cup cornstarch

½ cup heavy cream

WORKING in batches, puree the artichoke hearts in a blender with 3 cups water. Pour into a large, heavy-bottomed pot or Dutch oven and add the broth, butter, salt, white pepper, chicken base (if using), and garlic. (If not using chicken base or bouillon, add an extra ½ teaspoon salt to the broth mixture.) Bring to a boil, then reduce the heat to low and simmer, uncovered, for 1 hour.

IN a small bowl, whisk together the cornstarch and ¼ cup warm water to make a slurry. Slowly add the slurry to the simmering soup. Stir until the soup has thickened. Remove from the heat and add the cream, stirring to combine. Serve hot.

PESTO-GARNISHED MINESTRONE

NICK'S ITALIAN CAFÉ

MCMINNVILLE, OR

When second-generation owner Carmen Peirano and her husband, Eric Ferguson, took over the running of Nick's Italian Cafe, the talented restaurant alums completely revamped the menu. One of the only original dishes they kept was this layered minestrone soup. The recipe calls for fresh green beans and shell peas, but chopped zucchini, diced potatoes, shredded kale, or other in-season green vegetables can be substituted or added. To stretch the dish, add a handful of cooked pasta to each bowl before serving. Extra pesto can be tossed with pasta, stirred into scrambled eggs, or added to vinaigrette.

SERVES 8

3 carrots, peeled and trimmed

1 yellow onion, coarsely chopped

1 celery rib, coarsely chopped

½ green bell pepper, coarsely chopped

6 garlic cloves, coarsely chopped

Leaves of ¼ bunch fresh parsley, chopped

8 ounces lean salt pork

1 (14½-ounce) can diced tomatoes

½ cup tomato paste

2 beef bouillon cubes, or 2 cups rich beef stock

1 tablespoon dried oregano

1 teaspoon freshly ground black pepper, or more to taste

8 ounces green beans, trimmed and cut into 1-inch pieces

1¼ cups shelled fresh or frozen peas

Salt and freshly ground black pepper

Pesto (recipe follows)

COARSELY chop 1 of the carrots and put it in the bowl of a food processor. Add the onion, celery, bell pepper, and garlic and pulse until the vegetables are finely chopped. Transfer the chopped vegetables to a large, heavy-bottomed pot. Add the parsley, salt pork, and 12 cups water and bring to a boil over medium heat. (If using beef stock instead of bouillon cubes, use only 10 cups water in this step.) Reduce the heat to medium-low and simmer, covered, for 2 hours.

USING a slotted spoon, transfer the salt pork to a food processor and process until the fat liquefies and the meat turns into a paste, about 30 seconds. Pass the salt pork through a sieve back into the pot, using a rubber spatula to press as much paste through the sieve as possible. Stir well to combine. Using a metal spoon, skim off and discard the fat from the broth. Add the tomatoes, tomato paste, bouillon cubes (if using), oregano, and black pepper to the pot. Simmer over medium-low heat, covered, for 1 hour.

ADD 2 cups water to the pot, increase the heat to medium-high, and bring to a boil. Meanwhile, thinly slice the 2 remaining carrots into discs, then add to the pot. Add the green beans and peas (if using fresh), reduce the heat to medium, and simmer the soup, partially covered, until the carrots, beans, and peas are soft, about 30 minutes more. If using frozen peas, add them after the carrots and beans have softened and stir to heat through. Season to taste with salt and black pepper. Serve each bowl topped with a spoonful of pesto.

PESTO

MAKES ¾ CUP

Leaves of ½ bunch fresh basil (about 1 cup tightly packed leaves)

Leaves of ½ bunch fresh parsley (about 1 cup tightly packed leaves)

¼ cup freshly grated Parmigiano-Reggiano

¼ cup freshly grated Pecorino Romano

2 teaspoons pine nuts

2 tablespoons extra-virgin olive oil, plus more if desired

Salt and freshly ground black pepper

PUT the basil, parsley, Parmigiano-Reggiano, Pecorino Romano, pine nuts, and oil in a food processor and process until smooth. Season to taste with salt and pepper.

When Nick's Italian Café opened in McMinnville, Oregon, in 1977, there were six wineries open in the area. Now there are hundreds.

CABBAGE SOUP

LANGER'S DELICATESSEN-RESTAURANT

LOS ANGELES, CA

This sweet-and-sour soup is made with hearty eastern European ingredients like cabbage, paprika, and sauerkraut, but it gets its distinctive tart flavor from citric acid crystals, also known as sour salt. Citric acid crystals are used in many Ashkenazi Jewish recipes, most likely because they were infinitely more readily available than lemons in eighteenth-century Poland and Russia. Today sour salt can usually be found in the grocery store (look with the canning supplies or in the bulk herbs section if there is one)—and occasionally the pharmacy—but if you can't find it, substitute ½ cup freshly squeezed lemon juice.

SERVES 8

12 cups chicken broth, preferably homemade

5 pounds green cabbage (about 2 medium heads), cored and thinly sliced

1½ cups granulated sugar

7 tablespoons ketchup

7 tablespoons tomato puree

¼ cup light brown sugar

1¾ tablespoons salt

1¾ tablespoons citric acid crystals

1¼ tablespoons monosodium glutamate (optional)

1 tablespoon sweet or Hungarian paprika

1¼ cups stewed tomatoes, crushed

1 cup sauerkraut

1 carrot, chopped

8 ounces Yukon Gold or other boiling potatoes, cooked and cubed (about 1 cup)

IN a large, heavy-bottomed pot or Dutch oven, stir together the broth, cabbage, granulated sugar, ketchup, tomato puree, brown sugar, salt, citric acid crystals, monosodium glutamate (if using), and paprika. Cover and bring to a boil over medium-high heat. Lower the heat and simmer until the cabbage is almost tender, 25 to 30 minutes. Add the stewed tomatoes, sauerkraut, and carrot. Return to a boil, lower the heat, and simmer for an additional 15 minutes. Add the potatoes and stir to heat through. Remove from the heat and adjust the seasoning to taste. The soup should taste both sweet and sour, with the bites of creamy potato mellowing the tang of the tomatoes and sauerkraut.

ORIGINAL #19 HOT PASTRAMI SANDWICH

LANGER'S DELICATESSEN-RESTAURANT

LOS ANGELES, CA

The hot pastrami sandwich at L[...] so good it has inspired fierce de[...] lovers, among them Nora Eph[...] homage to it in the *New York[...]* tender but chewy, peppery but sour, [...] tangy," she wrote of Langer's version of the qu[...] essential deli dish. "It's a symphony orchestra, different instruments brought together to play one perfect chord." The restaurant steams the well-spiced cured meat for hours before hand-cutting it into thick, tender slices. To make this popular variation, Langer's layers the hot meat on twice-baked rye bread, still warm from the oven and slathered with Russian dressing, and tops it with Swiss cheese and a scoop of their sweet-and-sour coleslaw. (If you prefer your coleslaw less sweet, you can reduce the amount of sugar to suit your taste.)

MAKES 4 SANDWICHES

8 slices seeded rye bread

2 pounds pastrami, sliced

4 tablespoons Russian dressing (recipe follows)

4 slices Swiss cheese

1 cup Coleslaw (recipe follows)

PREHEAT the oven to 300°F. Wrap the bread in aluminum foil; bake for 10 to 12 minutes, until the bread is warmed through.

MEANWHILE, to steam the pastrami, bring a pot of water fitted with a steamer basket to a boil. Wrap the pastrami in aluminum foil and place in the basket; cover and allow to steam for 15 to 20 minutes, until all the slices are thoroughly heated.

TO assemble each sandwich, spread ½ tablespoon Russian dressing on one slice of warm rye bread. Add ½ pound of hot pastrami to the same slice, overlaying the Russian dressing. Top the hot pastrami with 1 slice of Swiss cheese and ¼ cup coleslaw. Spread ½ tablespoon Russian dressing on another slice of rye bread and place it on the sandwich. Slice in half.

Langer's Delicatessen-Restaurant has served more than 4 million pounds of pastrami.

RUSSIAN DRESSING

MAKES ABOUT 2 CUPS

1 cup mayonnaise

1 cup sweet pickle relish

¼ cup ketchup

1½ tablespoons buttermilk

IN a large bowl, combine the mayonnaise, relish, ketchup, and buttermilk. The dressing can be made in advance. Leftovers will keep for several days in the refrigerator.

COLESLAW

MAKES ABOUT 6 CUPS

1¼ cups mayonnaise

½ cup sour cream

¼ cup plus 2 tablespoons granulated sugar

1 tablespoon white vinegar

2 teaspoons salt

1 small head cabbage, shredded (about 2 pounds)

½ red bell pepper, julienned

½ carrot, julienned

WHISK the mayonnaise, sour cream, sugar, vinegar, salt, and ¼ cup water in a medium bowl.

IN a large bowl, combine the mayonnaise mixture with the cabbage, bell pepper, and carrot and stir to combine. The coleslaw can be made up to 1 day in advance and refrigerated.

Salmon Tip to Tail

At the Gustavus Inn in coastal Alaska, proprietors JoAnn, David, and Dan Lesh buy whole king, sockeye, and coho salmon directly from local fishermen. The fish is so fresh and pristine, they don't want to let an ounce of it go to waste. Knives sharp, they break down the head-on salmon, which has been cleaned and gutted, and put every single edible part to good use. Here they provide step-by-step instructions for replicating this process at home. The first step, of course, is to procure top-quality fish. Look for whole wild Alaskan salmon that's been flash-frozen.

How to Fillet a Whole Salmon

1. With the fish lying with its back toward you, cut the head off just above the collars (the fins next to the head). Trace the tip of the knife around the circumference of the cheek socket and lift out the cheek meat; repeat on the other side. (The cheeks will need to be skinned before cooking.) Set the head aside for stock.

2. Remove the collars and set aside. (This prized, fatty cut is delicious when brushed with ponzu sauce or teriyaki glaze and broiled.)

3. Place the fish backbone toward you with the head on the side of your dominant hand. (If you're a right-handed person, the head should be on your right.) With your sharpest and longest knife, start filleting just above the backbone, cutting through the ribs where they attach to the backbone. Continue down the backbone by feel, using your left hand to keep the belly open and hold the fish in place. Lay the fillet skin side down.

4. With the fish in the same position, fillet the flesh underneath the backbone the same way, cutting the ribs where they meet the backbone and above the dorsal fin. Set the backbone aside.

5. There is a line of bones running down the top of the fish that includes the dorsal fin; this needs to be removed. To do so, run your knife just under the fin and along the fillet to remove this strip of bones. Set aside.

6. Using a thin, more flexible knife, fillet off the rib bones, being careful not to remove the belly strip. Portion the fish into desired sizes; keep very cold until needed.

7. If you want to have skinless fillets, use a pair of pliers to hold just a bit of skin on the tail end of the fillet. Keeping your knife flat, slide it just under the skin, slicing back and forth to remove. Use the pliers to pull out the pin bones.

8. Using a soup spoon, scrape the flesh off the reserved backbone and strip of bones from the back of the salmon. Keep this meat to use for stock, fish cakes, or tacos. Save the bones to use for stock (recipe follows).

SALMON STOCK

MAKES 8 TO 10 CUPS

PUT the bones and trimmings from 2 king salmon or 3 to 4 smaller salmon such as coho or sockeye in a deep stockpot along with 4 celery ribs, 4 carrots, 5 scallions, 1 quartered white onion, 10 garlic cloves, a handful of fresh herbs (parsley, oregano, basil), 10 black peppercorns, a few whole cloves, and a bay leaf. Cover with water (about 8 to 10 cups) and bring to a simmer very slowly to avoid burning the fish on the bottom of the pan. Simmer for just 20 minutes (fish cartilage breaks down quickly) and strain through a fine-mesh strainer while still hot. Let cool before freezing.

GUSTAVUS INN SALMON CHOWDER

SERVES 6 TO 8

IN a soup pot, sauté chopped scallions, crushed garlic, and chopped celery in olive oil. Add 8 cups salmon stock (see above), 2 (16-ounce) cans diced or crushed tomatoes, bay leaves, oregano, basil, and salt and pepper to taste. Bring to a boil, then lower the heat and simmer for 20 to 30 minutes, until slightly reduced and flavorful. Just before serving, add 1½ pounds cubed fresh salmon, or 2½ cups flaked leftover cooked salmon, and the juice of 1 lemon. Return the soup to a boil, remove from the heat, and serve immediately. Garnish with chopped fresh chives if desired.

BARBECUED SALMON

SERVES 4

PREPARE a grill (the Lesh family uses charcoal and adds a few small chunks of alder wood for flavor). If using charcoal, use enough to cover the grill evenly with just a thin layer, so it doesn't burn too hot.

COMBINE 1 cup (2 sticks) unsalted butter, ⅔ cup brown sugar, the juice of 1 lemon, and ¼ cup soy sauce in a saucepan over medium heat and stir until the sugar has dissolved.

PLACE 4 (8-ounce) skin-on salmon fillets skin side down on the grill rack directly over the heat. If the grill heats unevenly, try to place the thicker fillets over the hotter areas. Baste with the sauce. Grill, covered but vented, until done, 10 to 15 minutes, basting two or three times during cooking. Do not turn the fillets while cooking. The salmon is done when an instant-read thermometer inserted into the thickest part of the flesh reads 120°F. Serve with additional sauce and lemon wedges.

BARBECUED SALMON DIP

MAKES ABOUT 5 CUPS

COMBINE 3 cups flaked leftover barbecued salmon (see above) with 1 cup mayonnaise, 1 cup sour cream, and ⅓ cup chopped fresh parsley or chives. Stir well and serve chilled as a dip for crackers.

CEDAR PLANK SALMON

RAY'S BOATHOUSE AND CAFÉ

SEATTLE, WA

The Pacific Northwest tradition of cooking fish on a wood plank likely originated centuries ago with the region's Native American population, and it is carried on today for good reason: the wood—usually cedar or alder—flavors the fish as it gently cooks, imbuing it with a subtle smokiness. Few recipes as simple as this one, made with sugar-brined salmon fillets, garner such impressive results. The technique also makes the fish easier to handle while it grills or bakes. To prevent your plank from going up in flames, make sure to use wood that is at least $3/4$ inch thick and has been soaked for several hours. For a lovely finishing touch, serve roasted lemon halves alongside the planked salmon.

SERVES 4

4 (8-ounce) fillets of king salmon

2 cups light brown sugar

1 cup kosher salt

SOAK two 4-by-8-inch thin cedar planks (or one cedar plank large enough to fit the 4 fillets) in water for several hours. (The water can be flavored with herbs and citrus, if desired.)

IN a medium bowl, combine the brown sugar and salt with ½ cup water and stir until dissolved. Rub the brine on both sides of each salmon fillet. Place the salmon in front of a fan or allow to air-dry until the brine feels tacky on the fish, about 2 hours. Give the fillets a quick rinse to remove most of the brine and pat dry.

PREHEAT the oven to 350°F. Place the salmon fillets skin side down on the cedar planks. Place in the oven and cook for 10 to 12 minutes, until just barely done (the fish should still be slightly translucent at the center). Serve on the planks.

CRAB CIOPPINO

DUARTE'S TAVERN

PESCADERO, CA

Cracked Dungeness crabs, their sweet meat still in the shell, practically spill out of Duarte's famous cioppino. Piled in a bowl of light, parsley-flecked tomato soup, the crab is flanked by a generous smattering of clams, jumbo prawns, and chunks of white fish. Dungeness crab is native to the West Coast, but is sold frozen at fishmongers across the country. Serve this main-course soup with crusty sourdough bread.

SERVES 6 TO 8

3 whole Dungeness crabs, lightly cooked, cleaned, and cracked

8 ounces white fish, such as snapper, tilapia, or black sea bass, cut into 6 pieces

Cioppino Sauce (recipe follows)

⅓ cup dry white wine

12 jumbo prawns

12 clams

PUT the crabs in a large, heavy-bottomed pot or Dutch oven. Top with the fish. Ladle the cioppino sauce over the seafood and add the wine to the pot. Cover and bring to a boil over medium-high heat. Lower the temperature to maintain a simmer and cook until the fish is beginning to turn opaque, about 5 minutes. Add the prawns and clams and cook until the fish and prawns are cooked through and the clams are open, 3 to 5 minutes more. Serve at once.

- -

"Duarte's has always been a destination; I probably went there for the first time in the early sixties with my parents. Our coast up here is foggy a lot, or else it's sunny until two P.M. and then this frostbiting fog comes rolling in and everybody has to leave their beach day and head for someplace where they can get something warm and wonderful. So you go to Duarte's and you have artichoke soup and some sand dabs and a berry pie."

— NANCY OAKES, JBF Award winner

- -

CIOPPINO SAUCE

MAKES 6 CUPS

1 (28-ounce) can diced tomatoes

1 (15-ounce) can tomato sauce

1 yellow onion, diced

4 celery ribs, diced

2 garlic cloves, minced

2 teaspoons salt

1 bay leaf

1 teaspoon dried oregano

1 teaspoon dried basil

1 teaspoon Italian seasoning

1 teaspoon ground cumin

½ teaspoon crushed red pepper flakes

½ cup fresh parsley, chopped

COMBINE the diced tomatoes, tomato sauce, onion, celery, garlic, salt, bay leaf, oregano, basil, Italian seasoning, cumin, and crushed red pepper in a large stock-pot. Bring to a boil over medium-high heat, then lower the heat and simmer for 1 hour, or until the tomatoes are falling apart and the onion and celery are tender. Stir in the parsley and adjust the seasonings to taste.

SHRIMP DUMPLINGS

YANK SING

SAN FRANCISCO, CA

Known as "har gow," these translucent shrimp dumplings are a staple offering from the busy dim sum carts at Yank Sing. They're made with wheat starch, a flourlike ingredient that contains almost no gluten and is what gives these dumpling wrappers their signature chewy texture and see-through "crystal" skin. Traditionally, Chinese chefs press out the thin, stretchy wrappers by using the oiled, flat side of a cleaver against a wooden surface. But with a little practice, a rolling pin—or even a tortilla press—will work too.

These dumplings freeze well, so you might want to enlist some help and make a double or even triple batch. If you make the dish with fresh bamboo shoots, which are available at many Asian markets, look for the smaller winter shoots and be sure to blanch or boil them before use as they contain toxins that are destroyed by cooking.

MAKES ABOUT 20 DUMPLINGS

8 ounces small or medium raw shrimp, peeled and deveined

¼ cup fresh prepared and boiled bamboo shoots (or canned whole), finely diced

½ tablespoon cornstarch

½ teaspoon salt

½ tablespoon sugar

Pinch of freshly ground white pepper

½ teaspoon sesame oil

Shrimp Dumpling Skins (recipe follows)

CUT each shrimp into two or three pieces; drain any extra moisture.

PUT the shrimp, bamboo shoots, cornstarch, and salt in a medium bowl and mix well. Press hard on the shrimp with the back of a spoon or the palm of your hand to break down the shrimp slightly, but be sure to leave chunks. (If you have a stand mixer with the paddle attachment, mix for 2 minutes on low speed.)

ADD the sugar and white pepper and mix well. Add the sesame oil and stir to incorporate thoroughly. Cover and refrigerate the mixture until ready to use. (The filling should not be made more than a few hours ahead of time.)

TO wrap, place a heaping teaspoon of filling in the center of one dumpling skin and loosely fold into a half-moon shape. Holding the dumpling in one hand, use the other hand to pinch the edges together, making 10 to 12 equally spaced pleats along the top of the half-moon; press along the pleats to ensure that the dumpling is sealed. Be careful not to tear the dough; this will take some practice. If you're finding it difficult, start with fewer pleats and work your way up to 12. (If making the dish ahead of time, the uncooked dumplings can be frozen on a waxed paper–lined baking sheet. Once frozen, transfer to resealable plastic bags and freeze for up to 3 months.)

TO cook, steam on a piece of cheesecloth in a bamboo or metal steamer over a wok of simmering water until translucent and cooked through, about 8 minutes.

SHRIMP DUMPLING SKINS

MAKES ABOUT 20 DUMPLING WRAPPERS

¾ cup wheat starch

1 tablespoon tapioca starch

½ tablespoon shortening

Vegetable oil for rolling

SIFT the wheat starch and tapioca starch into a medium heatproof bowl and add the shortening. Quickly pour ½ cup boiling water into the bowl and immediately mix vigorously with a spoon. When you can no longer incorporate any more flour by stirring, turn the dough out onto a clean work surface and knead until it is smooth, about 3 minutes. The dough will be slightly sticky.

"Yank Sing has been one of my favorite spots in San Francisco since moving here in 1991. It was around the corner from Rubicon, so before we opened the restaurant we regularly frequented Yank Sing for a delicious lunch while plotting the opening."

— TRACI DES JARDINS, JBF Award winner

ROLL the dough into a sticklike cylinder about 9 inches long and 1 inch in diameter. Cover with a damp paper towel and let rest for 15 minutes.

SLICE the cylinder into 20 pieces, each just under ½ inch thick. Using your hands, roll each piece into a ball and cover with a damp paper towel until ready to use.

TO form the wrappers, oil your hands, a small rolling pin, and a wooden work surface. Using the heel of your hand, gently press down on each ball to flatten. Then, using the rolling pin, carefully roll out a thin round, 3½ inches in diameter. Don't use any flour. If the dough is cracking around the edges, knead each ball a bit before rolling it out.

SHANGHAI DUMPLINGS

SOUP DUMPLINGS

YANK SING

SAN FRANCISCO, CA

There's a method to eating soup dumplings: You place the dumpling on your soup spoon and gently bite off the doughy nub in the center, releasing a stream of hot soup. Sip the soup out of the thick dumpling wrapper and then eat the pork filling within, drizzled with black vinegar, if you want, to cut the subtle sweetness. There's a method to making them, too: A clear, expertly seasoned aspic is added to the filling; when the dumplings are steamed the aspic melts, becoming the heady broth that gives this classic Shanghai dish its name. Ask your butcher for the pork skin to make the aspic. If it's not available, a fatty cut of pork such as pork belly can be substituted.

MAKES ABOUT 18 DUMPLINGS

8 ounces ground Kurobuta pork

¾ tablespoon cornstarch

1½ tablespoons Shaoxing wine

1 tablespoon soy sauce

½ tablespoon sesame oil

2 scant teaspoons sugar

¾ teaspoon salt

Pinch of freshly ground white pepper

8 ounces (about 1 cup) Shanghai Dumpling Aspic (recipe follows)

2 teaspoons minced scallion

1 tablespoon plus ¾ teaspoon grated fresh ginger

Shanghai Dumpling Skins (recipe follows)

PUT the pork and cornstarch in the bowl of a food processor and mix until the pork resembles a paste. Transfer the pork mixture to a large bowl; add the wine, soy sauce, sesame oil, sugar, salt, and white pepper and mix thoroughly. Gently fold in the aspic, scallion, and ginger and stir to combine; do not overmix. Cover and transfer the filling to the refrigerator until ready to make the dumplings.

TO wrap, place a heaping teaspoon of the filling in the center of one dumpling skin. Hold the dumpling in one cupped hand (you can also use a very small prep bowl to hold the dumpling) and use the other hand to make small folds around the circumference of the dough, pleating the edge of the dough like an accordion, and moving in a circle until reaching the end, all the while twisting the top together so the pleats spiral around. At the end, the dumpling should be completely sealed; it will resemble a little coin purse. The dumpling should be circular and well pleated with a small piece of dough sticking up in the center.

TO cook, steam on a piece of cheesecloth in a bamboo or metal steamer over a wok of simmering water until cooked through, about 8 minutes.

SHANGHAI DUMPLING ASPIC

MAKES ABOUT 13 OUNCES (1½ CUPS)

2 ounces pork skin, cut into 1-inch cubes

4 ounces chicken bones (the backbone and wing tips from one chicken)

1 small slice fresh ginger

1 (3-inch) piece of scallion

¾ teaspoon Shaoxing wine

IN a large, heavy-bottomed pot or Dutch oven, combine the pork skin and chicken bones and cover with cold water. Bring to a boil over high heat, then immediately remove from the heat. Drain and return the pork skin and chicken bones to the pot; add 2 cups water, the ginger slice, scallion, and wine. Bring to a boil, then reduce the heat to low. Cover and very gently simmer for 2½ hours.

REMOVE from the heat, allow to cool, and strain the liquid into a bowl. Once cooled, cover and refrigerate overnight. The aspic will gel and become very thick as it chills.

(continued)

SHANGHAI DUMPLING SKINS

MAKES ABOUT 18 DUMPLING WRAPPERS

1 cup all-purpose flour, plus more for rolling
½ teaspoon vegetable oil

PUT the flour in a medium bowl and add 6 tablespoons warm water, 1 tablespoon at a time, mixing after each addition. Add the oil and stir to combine. When you can no longer incorporate more flour by stirring, turn the dough out on a work surface and knead the rest of the flour into the dough until it is well blended, soft and smooth, and bounces back slowly when pressed, about 5 minutes.

DIVIDE the dough into two pieces. Roll each piece into a sticklike cylinder about 9 inches long and 1 inch in diameter. Cover the two pieces with damp paper towels and let rest for 15 minutes.

SLICE each cylinder into pieces ½ inch wide; roll each piece into a ball and cover with a damp paper towel until ready to use.

TO form the wrappers, very lightly flour your hands, a small rolling pin, and a wooden work surface. Using the heel of your hand, gently press down on each ball to flatten. Then, using the rolling pin, carefully roll out a thin round, 3 inches in diameter. Keep the work surface dusted with flour while rolling out each piece of dough.

The words *Yank Sing* mean "City of the Ram," a reference to the southern Chinese city of Guangzhou (Canton), which is said to have the best dim sum in the world.

ESTOFADO DE POLLO

CHICKEN ESTOFADO

GUELAGUETZA

LOS ANGELES, CA

"Customers love this dish because it reminds them of dinnertime at home back in Oaxaca," says Bricia Lopez of Guelaguetza. Unlike a mole negro, a traditional Oaxacan recipe that's usually served at big celebrations, like weddings or quinceañeras, *estofado*—or "stew"—is a more quotidian dish. That doesn't mean this gently simmered chicken, served in a spiced tomato sauce enriched with blended almonds and sesame seeds, is any less deserving of attention, however. "The *estofado* is by far my personal favorite," says Lopez, who notes that the dish has been served since the day the restaurant opened. Serve with rice and warm corn tortillas.

SERVES 6

1 (3½- to 4-pound) whole chicken

8 garlic cloves, peeled

¾ medium onion

1½ tablespoons salt

4 tablespoons vegetable oil

½ cup whole unblanched almonds

¼ cup sesame seeds

¾ cup raisins

¼ cup dried oregano

2 tablespoons dried thyme

6 whole black peppercorns

½ Mexican cinnamon stick (about 1 inch long)

1 whole clove

3 large tomatoes, cut into quarters

3 tomatillos, husked and rinsed

2 sprigs fresh parsley

¼ cup sugar

¼ cup green olives, pitted

2 to 3 whole pickled jalapeños, or ¼ cup sliced pickled jalapeños

PUT the chicken, 3 of the garlic cloves, ¼ onion, and 1 tablespoon of the salt in a stockpot with 8 cups water. Cover and bring to a boil over medium-high heat; immediately lower the heat and simmer until the chicken is tender and fully cooked, 30 to 45 minutes. Remove the chicken from the pot and let cool. Cut the chicken into 8 to 10 pieces; set aside. Strain the broth and set it aside; discard the garlic and onion.

WHILE the chicken is cooking, heat 2 tablespoons of the oil in a large skillet over medium heat. Add the almonds and fry, stirring frequently, until they begin to brown and are fragrant, about 5 minutes. Watch them carefully to make sure they don't burn. Using a slotted spoon, remove the almonds from the skillet; set aside. Add the sesame seeds to the skillet and repeat the process, stirring frequently until they begin

(continued)

to brown, about 2 minutes. Remove from the skillet immediately and set aside. Add the raisins to the skillet and cook until plump and beginning to brown, about 5 minutes; set aside.

IN a comal or on a griddle, toast the oregano, thyme, peppercorns, cinnamon, and clove over low heat until aromatic, just under 1 minute; set aside. Raise the heat to medium-high and add the remaining onion half to the griddle, cut side down; cook until the onion is beginning to char on the outside, about 7 minutes. Set aside. Cook the remaining 5 garlic cloves on the griddle until light brown, about 2 minutes. Set aside.

PUT the tomatoes and tomatillos in a medium saucepan with 2 tablespoons water and cook over medium-high heat, stirring occasionally, for about 10 minutes, until the tomatoes are broken down and the tomatillos are tender. Transfer the tomato mixture to a blender and puree. Strain the blended tomato mixture through a sieve and set aside.

IN a food processor, combine the almonds, raisins, sesame seeds, oregano, thyme, peppercorns, cinnamon, clove, grilled onion, grilled garlic cloves, and parsley and process until the mixture forms a finely pureed paste.

IN a large stockpot, heat the remaining 2 tablespoons vegetable oil over medium-high heat. Add the pureed almond mixture and bring to a boil; cook over high heat for 5 minutes, stirring constantly. Add the tomato mixture, sugar, remaining ½ tablespoon salt, and 1½ cups of the strained chicken broth. Bring the mixture to a low boil over medium heat and cook for 10 minutes, stirring occasionally. Add the olives and pickled jalapeños; stir to combine. Remove from the heat.

PLACE the reserved cooked chicken on a platter and ladle the estofado sauce over it. Serve with additional pickled jalapeños, if desired.

PIPIKAULA SHORT RIBS

HELENA'S HAWAIIAN FOOD

HONOLULU, HI

At once salty, sweet, and irresistibly toothsome, these outstanding short ribs are a specialty at Helena's. The chefs there make this classic *paniolo* (Hawaiian cowboy–style) dish the traditional way: after an overnight marinade, the short ribs are hung over the stove in the restaurant's kitchen and left to dry for 4 to 6 hours, until the meat takes on a slightly chewy, jerkylike texture. This recipe has been adapted for home kitchens; instead of being hung, the short ribs are dried for several hours on low heat in the oven.
SERVES 6 TO 8

⅔ cup soy sauce

1 tablespoon sugar

1 tablespoon sea salt

1 garlic clove, minced

5 pounds bone-in, flanken-style short ribs (at least 1 inch thick)

Vegetable oil for frying

IN a saucepan, combine the soy sauce, sugar, salt, and garlic and bring to a boil; cook until the sugar and salt have dissolved, about 2 minutes. Remove from the heat and set aside to cool.

PUT the short ribs and cooled marinade in a large bowl and toss to combine. Cover the bowl and marinate in the refrigerator for 8 hours or overnight, flipping the meat over halfway through so both sides are exposed to the marinade.

PREHEAT the oven to 180°F. Place an oven roasting rack on top of a baking pan. Lay the short rib strips on top of the roasting rack, trying not to let them touch. Put in the oven for 4 hours, turning the meat over halfway through, until the meat is beginning to look a bit leathery on the outside. Remove from the oven and allow the meat to cool for at least 15 minutes. Cut each short rib between the bones; each length of ribs will yield between 3 and 5 pieces, depending on the number of bones.

POUR 1 inch of oil into a large, heavy skillet; heat over medium-high heat. Working in batches to avoid crowding the skillet, fry the dried short ribs in the hot oil until browned and crisp on both sides, about 3 minutes per side. (The dried ribs can also be finished on a hot grill.) Serve hot.

CHEESE-BURGER

GOTT'S ROADSIDE

ST. HELENA, CA

The secret to this superlative cheeseburger is, of course, the condiment-spiked secret sauce, but also the carefully selected ingredients, from the soft pain de mie buns and sweet Early Girl tomatoes to the Niman Ranch Angus beef. Serve with a thick chocolate shake or a bottle of locally brewed craft beer, as they do at this singular roadside burger joint. Leftover sauce can be used as a dipping sauce for homemade oven fries or spooned onto meatloaf or roast beef sandwiches.

MAKES 4 CHEESEBURGERS

1⅓ pounds ground beef

4 pain de mie buns, or preferred hamburger buns, sliced in half

2 tablespoons unsalted butter, melted

4 tablespoons Secret Sauce (recipe follows)

2 Early Girl or beefsteak tomatoes, cut into ¼-inch slices (8 slices needed)

12 dill pickle chips

4 small iceberg lettuce leaves, rinsed and dried

Kosher salt and freshly ground black pepper

8 slices American cheese

DIVIDE the meat into 4 equal portions. Gently shape each portion into a 1-inch-thick circular patty, about 4 inches in diameter. (Try not to overhandle the patty, as it can make the meat tougher.) Make a depression in the middle of each burger with your thumb or the back of a spoon; this will help prevent the burger from puffing up in the middle as it cooks. Set the patties aside.

PREHEAT a charcoal grill or griddle. Brush melted butter onto the cut sides of all the hamburger buns. Toast on the grill or griddle until golden brown; set aside.

SPREAD 1 tablespoon of secret sauce on the cut sides of each toasted bun (½ table-spoon per cut side). Place 2 tomato slices on the top cut side of each bun and 3 pickle chips on top of the tomatoes. Place a lettuce leaf on the bottom cut side of each bun, folded to fit the bun.

SPRINKLE the beef patties evenly with salt and pepper and place on the preheated grill or griddle. When juice starts to appear on the tops of the patties, flip them; top each patty with 2 slices of American cheese and cook to desired doneness (about 10 minutes total for medium-rare).

PLACE the cooked patties on the lettuce-lined bottom buns, and cover the top buns with tomatoes and pickles. Serve immediately.

SECRET SAUCE

MAKES ABOUT 1 CUP

½ cup mayonnaise

¼ cup ketchup

¼ cup sweet pickle relish

1 tablespoon yellow mustard

1 tablespoon Worcestershire sauce

1 teaspoon Tabasco sauce

½ teaspoon kosher salt

¼ teaspoon freshly ground black pepper

IN a medium bowl, whisk together the mayonnaise, ketchup, relish, mustard, Worcestershire sauce, Tabasco sauce, salt, and pepper.

GRANOLA

NORA'S FISH CREEK INN

WILSON, WY

Jackson Hole skiers fuel up on this hearty, nutty granola made with a molasses-sweetened blend of oats, walnuts, almonds, peanuts, sunflower seeds, and sesame seeds. This will make a big batch—enough for four people to nibble on for two weeks at least—and it can easily be doubled if you're hosting a brunch. It also makes a lovely gift for friends and family when packed up in mason jars. Mix in a handful of chopped Turkish apricots or dried cherries if desired and serve spooned over Greek yogurt or sprinkled on top of ice cream.

MAKES ABOUT 8 CUPS

1 cup light brown sugar	6 cups old-fashioned rolled oats	½ cup raw almonds, coarsely chopped
¼ cup molasses	1½ cups sweetened shredded coconut	½ cup roasted peanuts, coarsely chopped
2 teaspoons salt	¾ cup sunflower seeds	½ cup sesame seeds
½ tablespoon ground cinnamon	½ cup walnuts, coarsely chopped	
½ tablespoon vanilla extract		

PREHEAT the oven to 275°F.

IN a medium saucepan, combine the brown sugar, molasses, salt, cinnamon, vanilla, and ¾ cup water. Bring to a boil, lower the heat, and simmer for 3 minutes. Set aside to cool.

IN a large bowl, combine the oats, coconut, sunflower seeds, walnuts, almonds, peanuts, and sesame seeds. Add the cooled brown sugar mixture to the bowl. Using clean hands, mix to combine.

LIBERALLY coat two rimmed baking sheets with non-stick cooking spray. Divide the granola mixture between the sheets, using a spatula to spread evenly. Bake for 1 hour, stirring occasionally. The granola should be golden brown on all sides. Remove from the oven and let cool completely. Store in airtight containers at room temperature for up to 2 weeks.

"People said, 'Nora, nobody will ever travel those seven miles from Jackson to here to eat.' I said, 'Well, you watch.'"

— NORA TYGUM, Nora's Fish Creek Inn in Wilson, WY

GATEAU BASQUE

NORIEGA'S

BAKERSFIELD, CA

A traditional dessert from the Pays Basque region of France, gateau Basque is made by layering a rich pastry dough with custard, pudding, or jam. Usually made in a round cake or tart pan, this rectangular version has decidedly less petite proportions and can easily feed twenty people. Noriega's owner Rochelle Ladd bakes it for special occasions, such as when the restaurant hosts handball tournaments on the onsite courts. She notes that the batter for this cake is actually quite thick, more like cookie dough. "I've eaten it as a bar-type cookie with my hands, when I'm in a hurry," she says. Pernod, which is added to both the cake batter and the pudding filling, has a strong anise flavor; if preferred, amaretto can be substituted. To make a smaller version, halve the recipe and use a 9-inch round cake pan instead of the jelly roll pan. When using the round pan, don't spread the pudding all the way to the edge of the cake; leave a ⅓-inch border of batter around the edge of the cake.

SERVES 20 TO 24

1 (3-ounce) package vanilla pudding mix (not instant)

3 cups milk

¼ cup plus 3 tablespoons Pernod or amaretto

2 cups granulated sugar

1½ cups (3 sticks) unsalted butter, at room temperature

4 large whole eggs, plus 1 egg white for the glaze

2 tablespoons dark rum, such as Myers's

4 cups all-purpose flour

1 teaspoon baking soda

¼ teaspoon salt

2 tablespoons turbinado or raw washed sugar (optional)

"You sit with everybody else. Everybody comes in at the same time, everybody eats the same thing. It's a lot of food."

— ROCHELLE LADD,
Noriega's in Bakersfield, CA

PREHEAT the oven to 350°F.

TO make the pudding, combine the vanilla pudding mix and milk in a heavy saucepan; stir well. Let the mixture stand for 5 minutes, then cook over medium heat, whisking often, until the pudding has thickened, about 10 minutes. Remove from the heat and let cool slightly. Add ¼ cup of the Pernod; stir to combine and set aside to cool completely.

TO make the cake batter, beat the granulated sugar and butter in a large bowl until light and fluffy. Add the 4 whole eggs one at a time, beating until well

incorporated after each addition. Add the remaining 3 tablespoons Pernod and the rum; stir well to combine.

IN a medium bowl, combine the flour, baking soda, and salt and stir. Add the flour mixture to the butter mixture and beat until the flour is fully incorporated, about 2 minutes. The batter will be thick, like cookie dough.

LINE a 10½-by-15-inch jelly roll pan (or a small cookie sheet with 1-inch sides) with waxed paper and spread half the batter onto the waxed paper to coat the bottom of the pan. (This is challenging, but the waxed paper is a key part of the layering process.) Cover the batter with another piece of waxed paper and place the pan in the freezer to chill for 15 minutes. Once chilled, remove from the jelly roll pan and keep cold in the refrigerator while you assemble the cake. Keep the pan at hand.

TO assemble the cake before baking, spread the remaining half of the batter onto the jelly roll pan. Try to smooth the batter out and line it evenly along the bottom of the pan and about ¼ inch up the sides. Spread all of the cooled vanilla pudding on top of the batter.

REMOVE the chilled batter layer from the refrigerator. Peel off the top piece of waxed paper and carefully flip the layer of stiff batter over and place it on top of the pudding. Peel off the second layer of waxed paper.

IN a small bowl, lightly beat the egg white. Gently brush the top of the cake with the beaten egg white and sprinkle with the turbinado sugar (if using). Bake until the entire surface is golden brown, 35 to 40 minutes. Remove from the oven and let cool for 30 minutes. Cut into squares before serving.

HAUPIA

HELENA'S HAWAIIAN FOOD

HONOLULU, HI

This creamy, coconut milk–based dessert is a typical offering at luaus and other Hawaiian celebrations. The amount of cornstarch can be adjusted depending on how firm you prefer the dish. As written, the recipe will yield a dessert that's firm and easy to slice and cube; more like a gelatin-based dish. With a tablespoon or so less cornstarch, the haupia will be on the softer side and more similar to pudding. To add texture, top the chilled squares with toasted coconut flakes.

MAKES 16 (1-INCH) SQUARES

3 cups unsweetened coconut milk (about 2 [13.5-ounce] cans)

6 tablespoons sugar

½ cup cornstarch

IN a medium saucepan, bring the coconut milk and sugar almost to a boil. Meanwhile, in a small bowl, mix the cornstarch with ½ cup water and whisk to combine thoroughly. Pour the cornstarch slurry into the coconut milk mixture and whisk to combine. Cook over very low heat, whisking often, until the mixture is smooth and thick, 5 to 10 minutes.

REMOVE from the heat, pour into an 8-inch square baking dish, and allow to cool at room temperature for 10 minutes. Cover with plastic wrap and refrigerate until firm, 1 to 2 hours. Use a sharp knife to cut into 1-inch squares before serving.

The Award Winners

DUARTE'S TAVERN

202 Stage Road
Pescadero, CA
Owners: Duarte family
2003 AWARD WINNER

Frank Duarte brought his first barrel of whiskey to Pescadero, California, in 1894 and sold it at his bar for ten cents a shot. Today, four generations later, the Duarte family—Ron, Lynn, Tim, and Kathy—is still pouring shots and serving up just-caught fish and garden produce in Pescadero, a dusty coastal town of 670 on the San Mateo County coast, about thirty miles south of San Francisco. Over its 109-year history, the saloon has morphed into a café. Frank's original bar still remains, and the other three dining rooms are chockablock with rickety antique tables and a Formica counter that's seen so many elbows its wood-grain pattern has worn to yellow. Since Duarte's began serving food, the family-tended garden has supplied much of the produce. Pescadero is also a prime fishing spot, and the Duartes continue to work with local fishermen for their daily catches, including the much-coveted abalone. Another renowned item, cioppino, a seafood stew that was once served all over the Bay Area, harks back to the family's Portuguese roots. In the 1930s, the Duarte women started baking fruit pies, and in the 1960s, Emma Duarte discovered the olallieberry—a type of local blackberry—and the pie quickly became the best seller. Now the Duartes make at least thirty pies a day to feed the townspeople, nursery workers, and tourists stopping by on their way down the coast.

EMMETT WATSON'S OYSTER BAR

1916 Pike Place #16
Seattle, WA
Owner: Thurman Bryant
1998 AWARD WINNER

Opened by longtime Seattle columnist Emmett Watson in 1979, Emmett Watson's Oyster Bar was at the time the first oyster bar in the city. The checked-tablecloth spot across the street from Pike Place Market has always kept it simple: The menus are handwritten. The oysters, which are phenomenal, come with a lemon wedge and cocktail sauce. And the beer is plentiful and cheap. Watson sold his share of the restaurant to his partner, Sam Bryant, in 1987; he passed away in 2001. Despite a tourist-heavy location, the spot is still a local favorite for dishes like fish and chips, clam chowder, steamed mussels in garlic broth, and, of course, oysters on the half shell.

FRANK FAT'S

806 L Street
Sacramento, CA
Owners: Fat family
2013 AWARD WINNER

Frank Fat's is a political landmark in California, once known as the "Third House" and one of Sacramento's oldest restaurants. It serves Chinese-American food and is renowned for honey-walnut prawns; Frank's-style New York steak (grilled, sliced, and smothered in sautéed onions and oyster sauce); Fat's brandy-fried chicken; and banana cream pie. Kevin Hefner, writing about the restaurant's seventieth anniversary in 2009 in *Capitol Weekly*, said, "The restaurant often was the site of political meetings that, according to some, sometimes accomplished more than those in the Capitol. The most notable of these deals was the 'Napkin Deal' of 1987, written on the back of a napkin by the participants that defined a multimillion-dollar pact between the lawyers, insurers, doctors, and business interests over tort reform." Willie Brown, former assembly speaker and San Francisco mayor, recalls that it was the place legislators would go to find a "pigeon"—a lobbyist who would buy them a meal. That's changed a bit with political reform, but it's still a popular hangout and a local favorite. The founder, Frank Fat, came to California from China in 1919 as a sixteen-year-old. He worked various odd jobs for twenty years, mostly in Sacramento, before opening his namesake restaurant in 1939 near the capitol. Today the Fat family also operates three other successful restaurants in the Sacramento region: Fat City in Old Sacramento and Fat's Asia Bistro in Folsom and Roseville.

> "My dad was very personable.
> Didn't matter whether you were
> a Republican or Democrat—
> he treated everybody the same."
>
> — JERRY FAT,
> Frank Fat's in Sacramento, CA

Frank Fat

GOTT'S ROADSIDE
(FORMERLY TAYLOR'S AUTOMATIC REFRESHER)

933 Main Street
St. Helena, CA
Owners: Duncan Gott and Joel Gott
2006 AWARD WINNER

Lloyd Taylor opened Taylor's Refresher in 1949 on Main Street in St. Helena, and over the past fifty-plus years this walk-up burger stand has become a social center for locals and tourists alike. On any given day you're likely to find winemakers, chefs, and sports celebrities standing in the egalitarian line waiting to place their order. Once the food arrives, everyone finds a seat at one of the umbrella-shaded tables on the perimeter. The family business is now being run by a new generation: brothers Joel and Duncan Gott, who took over in 1999, initially changing the restaurant's name to Taylor's Automatic Refresher and then, more recently, to Gott's Roadside. If the Gott name sounds familiar, it's because Joel produces his own line of well-respected wines, which is why this is probably the only burger stand in the country where you can get a great glass of Cabernet or a fine bottle of Zinfandel to wash down the popular bacon cheeseburger and garlic fries. But this is California, after all, so the menu also includes such standouts as an ahi burger with ginger-wasabi mayo, fish and vegetable tacos, corn dogs, and seasonal salads like tender baby greens tossed with a lemon vinaigrette, cherry tomatoes, toasted pine nuts, and Parmesan cheese. And for dessert, legions swear by the espresso milk shake. In recent years the Gott brothers have opened new locations in Napa, Palo Alto, and in the Ferry Plaza Building on the Embarcadero in San Francisco.

GUELAGUETZA

3014 West Olympic Boulevard
Los Angeles, CA
Owner: Lopez family
2015 AWARD WINNER

See page 204.

GUSTAVUS INN

1270 Gustavus Road
Gustavus, AK
Owners: JoAnn Lesh and Dave Lesh
2010 AWARD WINNER

Three generations of the Lesh family have welcomed guests to this farmhouse at the edge of a meadow overlooking Alaska's Icy Strait. Jack and Sally Lesh opened the inn in 1965, operating it as a drop-in restaurant, grocery store, and hotel. For many years it was also the town's weather station, airline counter, and radio and telephone contact. From 1976 to 1979 their daughter Sal and her husband, Tom McLaughlin, continued these services, supporting the crew building nearby Glacier Bay Lodge. Dave and JoAnn Lesh took over as innkeepers in 1980 and raised their three sons and daughter there. Over the years, the town has acquired power, phones, and city status, allowing the Gustavus Inn to rely more on serving tourists to Glacier Bay National Park during the summer months. Supper is served family style and usually features local catches like Dungeness crab, salmon, halibut, and sablefish, as well as produce from the inn's garden. Despite the challenges of a short growing season, that garden produces berries, potatoes, rhubarb, myriad greens, and edible flowers. In addition to just-caught seafood, the inn is known for sourdough pancakes with homemade spruce tip syrup and halibut caddy ganty, often called halibut Olympia, a rich mix of fish cooked with onions, sour cream, and mayonnaise.

> "Salmon are an inspiration
> for cooking and living. They are
> born in our streams, head out
> to sea to feed, and bring back the
> ocean's nutrients and
> energy when they spawn,
> enriching our forests and tables."
>
> — JOANN LESH,
> Gustavus Inn in Gustavus, AK

HAMURA'S SAIMIN STAND

2956 Kress Street
Lihue, Kauai, HI
Owner: Lori Tanigawa
2006 AWARD WINNER

In 1952 Aiko Hamura opened the Saimin Stand in Lihue, a sleepy little town on the island of Kauai. Back then, as it is still today, saimin was a popular island dish, a steaming bowl of Chinese egg noodles in a Japanese-style broth, topped off with Chinese roast pork, Spam, and scallions. It's a specialty of Hawaii found nowhere else in the world and it reflects the island state's varied ethnic population. What became known as Hamura's Saimin Stand continues to serve up this delicious local dish, a couple of thousand bowls a day, seven days a week. Aiko's daughter Hazel Hiraoka eventually took over the business. Patrons remember her standing over the special noodle cooker and cauldron of broth, expertly concocting the small, medium, large, and special bowls served to patrons sitting on humble stools at the orange Formica counter. Many places in Hawaii serve up saimin; what makes Hamura's saimin special is the broth, with its pleasing balance of flavors and ingredients, and the crinkly noodles that are cooked just enough so they don't get mushy sitting in the hot broth. Those noodles are made fresh daily on the spot, as is the feathery light lilikoi (passion fruit) chiffon pie, a traditional Kauai dessert. Hazel passed away in August 2005 and now her daughter Lori Tanigawa does the cooking and tends to customers with the help of nephews who represent the fourth generation.

> "Hamura's still has the same mom-and-pop feel that it had when it first opened. There's really a feeling of going back in time to Old Hawaii, and it evokes a sense of nostalgia for a lot of people."
>
> — ALAN WONG, JBF Award winner

HELENA'S HAWAIIAN FOOD

1240 North School Street
Honolulu, HI
Owner: Craig Katsuyoshi
2000 AWARD WINNER

See page 206.

LANGER'S DELICATESSEN-RESTAURANT

704 South Alvarado Street
Los Angeles, CA
Owners: Norm Langer and family
2001 AWARD WINNER

Located in the unlikely MacArthur Park district, Langer's Delicatessen-Restaurant rivals—some would say bests—any New York deli. Members of the Langer family, beginning with pastrami patriarch Al Langer and, later, his son Norm, have been hand-cutting the meat for their ten varieties of hot pastrami sandwiches in this very spot since 1947. Over the years, three major renovations have greatly expanded the original, pint-size space. Why are Angelenos so passionate about Langer's pastrami sandwiches? Norm thinks he knows. First, the processed pastrami is kept in a steam bath until it is actually cut. This way, it can be sliced by hand, against the grain, guaranteeing tender pastrami. Then the meat is sandwiched between slices of fabulous double-baked rye from Fred's Bakery in West Los Angeles (another second-generation family-run business). It's an unbeatable combination. The loaves are delivered unsliced and are "baked" a second time in the ovens at Langer's before they are sliced for the sandwiches. The Langers' attention to ingredients is such that they even mix their own deli-style cream soda. Al Langer passed away in 2007, shortly after his legendary restaurant turned sixty, but Norm and his wife and daughter have kept the legacy going. At lunchtime any day of the week, you'll still see a faithful flock of executives from downtown L.A. chomping on pastrami sandwiches, or perhaps finishing up with a slice of the deli's justly famous strawberry shortcake—a hunk of buttery pound cake resting on a puddle of strawberries in syrup, and topped with two scoops of vanilla ice cream and a cloud of whipped cream.

MANEKI

304 Sixth Avenue South
Seattle, WA
Owner: Jean Nakayama
2008 AWARD WINNER

See page 208.

"The dish I always get [at Maneki]
is the sakana dinner, which is
salt-broiled mackerel served
with sashimi and tempura. The
mackerel is fried whole and it has
such crispy skin on the outside
with the luxurious, melt-in-your-
mouth flesh on the inside. It's a
soulful food experience."

— MARIA HINES, JBF Award winner

NICK'S ITALIAN CAFÉ

521 NE 3rd Street
McMinnville, OR
Owners: Nick Peirano, Carmen Peirano,
and Eric Ferguson
2014 AWARD WINNER

When Nick Peirano, a third-generation Italian-American, opened a serious Italian restaurant in the farming town of McMinnville in 1977, he had no previous restaurant experience. No matter. His restaurant soon became the place where Oregon winemakers hung out when there were just a dozen or so. Now there are hundreds, and Nick's is still their clubhouse. Nick's daughter, Carmen Peirano, and her husband, Eric Ferguson, took over day-to-day operations in 2007. They updated the menu to include wood-fired pizzas and housemade charcuterie, but Nick's Dungeness crab and pine nut lasagna and his pesto-garnished minestrone remain favorites. And you'll find Nick himself shooting pool most nights in the Backroom Bar. Nick's has forged a marriage of Oregon wine country and northern Italian cooking that's as worthy of pilgrimage and patronage as the Oregon Pinot Noirs on their superb wine list.

NORA'S FISH CREEK INN

5600 WY-22
Wilson, WY
Owners: Nora Tygum, Trace Tygum,
and Kathryn Tygum Taylor
2012 AWARD WINNER

Head west on Highway 22 toward the Idaho border at the base of Teton Pass. Take your GPS. Look for the packed parking lot and the sign on top of the log cabin: a twenty-foot trout that covers almost the entire front of the roof. Seven miles from Jackson Hole, Wyoming, in Wilson (population 250), Nora's Fish Creek Inn is a gathering spot for both locals and tourists. When Nora Tygum opened the doors in 1982, she served sandwiches built on bread she'd baked herself. Nora's has been a Jackson Hole destination ever since. People flock here for huevos rancheros, pancakes nearly as big as the plate, and, of course, pan-fried local trout with eggs. The future of the restaurant, now in its fourth decade, is secure. Nora's son, Trace, and daughter, Kathryn, manage the business. More important, Kathryn is the resident pie and cobbler maker. "Some customers come in just for her banana cream or chocolate pecan pie," says her brother.

NORIEGA'S

525 Sumner Street
Bakersfield, CA
Owners: Linda Elizalde McCoy and Rochelle Ladd
2011 AWARD WINNER

The Noriega Restaurant and Hotel has been the hub of Kern County Basque culture since Faustino Noriega opened its doors in 1893. In 1931 the Elizalde family took over, and has run the restaurant ever since. Originally founded as a home away from home for shepherds, today the institution showcases the Basque culture of California's San Joaquin Valley. Located in a warehouse district just east of downtown, Noriega's has a façade that could be mistaken for a neighborhood bar. A jai-alai court (a form of Basque handball) is built into the structure. Parties are individually called into the dining room, where they take their places at long tables covered in checkered oilcloth. The dinner that ensues is always multicoursed and abundant, but it is a generosity marked by great care. The tongue is pickled in-house and thin-sliced. The roast leg of lamb, served on Fridays, is herb-flecked and tender. Big wedges of creamy blue cheese close the meal. With very fair pricing (children are charged only a dollar per year up to age 12), a meal at the Noriega is accessible to all. What you get is a dinner that is invariably imbued with the simmered note of home cooking, a glimpse into a community that has played an important role in this agricultural region for over a century, and a sense, through seasoning and ingredients, of how a people adapted to a new culture while being true to their own.

- - - - - - - - - - - - - - - -

Every dinner at Noriega's includes soup, salad, beans, bread, salsa, pickled tongue, cottage cheese, either lamb stew, beef stew, or oxtail stew, spaghetti, a hot vegetable, French fries, and the main meat entrée.

- - - - - - - - - - - - - - - -

Noriega's

ORIGINAL PANCAKE HOUSE

8601 Southwest 24th Avenue
Portland, OR
Owners: Highet family
1999 AWARD WINNER

Les Highet and Erma Hueneke founded the Original Pancake House in 1953. It later became a favorite of James Beard, a Portland native. Today the pancake palace has over a hundred franchises, but the original location continues to keep its customers satisfied with bottomless cups of good coffee and specialties such as the Dutch baby, served with lemon, whipped butter, and powdered sugar, and an impressive cinnamon-glazed apple pancake. Buttermilk, buckwheat, and potato pancakes are available as well as appetite-conquering servings of eggs Benedict and strawberry waffles.

PHILIPPE THE ORIGINAL

1001 North Alameda Street
Los Angeles, CA
Owner: Richard Binder
1999 AWARD WINNER

When you visit Philippe the Original, which opened in 1908 and is located today on the edge of L.A.'s Chinatown, there's no need to look at the menu. The restaurant is the apocryphal home of the French dip sandwich, a hot, meaty sandwich—usually roast beef, though Philippe sells several variations—served on a baguette dipped in jus right before serving. (The sandwiches are served doused in broth either once, twice, or until the sandwich is "wet.") Alongside the main course customers are offered the choice of tangy coleslaw, homemade potato and macaroni salads, beet juice–pickled eggs, several different kinds of pickles, olives, and hot peppers.

RAY'S BOATHOUSE AND CAFÉ

6049 Seaview Avenue NW
Seattle, WA
Owners: Ross Wohlers, Earl Lasher,
Elizabeth Gingrich, and Jack Sikma
2002 AWARD WINNER

Ray Lichtenberger's bait house and boat rental lured fishermen to the shore of Shilshole Bay when it opened in 1939. Six years later, Ray expanded his business to include a waterfront café, and a Seattle dining tradition was born. Since it was hoisted and lit, Ray's towering red-neon sign has provided a beacon for boaters and a magnet for locals and tourists drawn to the boathouse that would write the blueprint for Seattle seafood restaurants. Thanks to the dedication of a seafood enthusiast, Russ Wohlers, who gathered a group of like-minded investors and bought the place in 1973, Ray's Boathouse has fueled an addiction for Northwest seafood. It was here, in view of Puget Sound and the Olympic Mountains, that diners came to appreciate the taste of fresh, line-caught fish, and were introduced to the unctuous delights of Copper River salmon, the tiny, briny Olympia oyster, and the sweet meat of Alaska's superior spot prawns. In 2012 the dining room underwent a complete overhaul, and the menu was also given a lift. However, Ray's commitment to fresh seafood and the wines that go with it remains a clear reflection of the Northwest's salty spirit.

SWAN OYSTER DEPOT

1517 Polk Street
San Francisco, CA
Owners: Sancimino family
2000 AWARD WINNER

The magic of Swan Oyster Depot? Its dining facilities consist of nothing more than a twenty-seat marble counter. But what fun it is to join the merry chit-chat that never ends among the Sancimino family (proprietors since 1946) and their happy customers. Although the broad front window displays a wide array of sparkling local seafood to take home and cook, the eat-here menu is pretty much limited to raw or steamed fare: oysters on the half-shell, cracked Dungeness crab, prawn or lobster salad, smoked trout and salmon, all accompanied by good sourdough bread and washed down with Anchor Steam beer. About the only complicated cooking goes into the chowder, a buttery-creamy brew that is labeled Boston-style, but is in fact—like everything else you can eat here—exemplary of the Pacific Northwest. The San Francisco stalwart has resisted pressure to expand: a visit there is the same as it was decades ago, and is still worth the wait.

Swan Oyster Depot

TADICH GRILL

240 California Street
San Francisco, CA
Owners: Steven Buich and Michael Buich
1998 AWARD WINNER

Established in 1849 by Croatian immigrants to serve patrons during the California gold rush, Tadich Grill claims to be not only the oldest restaurant in San Francisco, but also the oldest in California. One of the winners of the America's Classics award the very first year of the honor's existence, the Tadich Grill was an easy choice. The restaurant began as a coffee stand that sold grilled fish to dockworkers, sailors, and merchants on Long Wharf pier. It evolved into one of the city's most iconic seafood restaurants, serving local catch like sand dabs, Dungeness crabs, and petrale sole to locals and history-seeking clientele.

"When I was a kid, we used to drive up to the city and eat at Tadich's. I still remember the excitement of being on California Street and hearing the cable cars rumble past. And then entering the warm restaurant with the packed bar, coats and hats hanging at the edge of the tucked-away, secret booths. We would eat cracked crab or a crab cocktail, petrale sole and sand dabs, my grandfather and parents would drink martinis, and we would have the time of our lives."

— TRACI DES JARDINS,
JBF Award winner

YANK SING

101 Spear Street
San Francisco, CA
Owner: Vera Chan-Waller
2009 AWARD WINNER

Henry Chan has made it his life's work to "uplift dim sum." At San Francisco's Yank Sing he has been serving dim sum classics like har gow and Shanghai dumplings alongside newer innovations such as phoenix shrimp and cabbage salad with honeyed walnuts to thousands of diners every day for over half a century. His mother opened Yank Sing's original Chinatown location in 1958. Even as a young man, Henry knew what the restaurant needed to do in order to set itself apart, expand its appeal, and reach a larger audience. By moving to the financial district and creating a more upscale atmosphere, Yank Sing became a favorite among San Francisco's movers and shakers and a must-visit restaurant for tourists. Now a third generation is at the establishment's helm. Henry's daughter Vera Chan-Waller is in the kitchen every day, ensuring that Yank Sing maintains its high quality and traditions—and keeps growing along with the Bay Area's vibrant food culture.

YUCA'S HUT

2056 Hillhurst Avenue
Los Angeles, CA
Owner: Socorro Herrera
2005 AWARD WINNER

Great Mexican restaurants dot L.A. like the ubiquitous
tall palm trees. The best of them become beloved institutions, landmarks amid the city's expanse. But none
is more beloved than Yuca's Hut on Hillhurst Avenue
in Los Feliz. The tiny venue, standing in the middle of
a parking lot, was opened in 1976 by Socorro Herrera
and her husband, Jaime, natives of Merida, Yucatán.
In recent years Herrera has also opened Yuca's on
Hollywood, a sit-down venue that delivers, but not much
has changed at the original location. The minimalism
of the setting highlights the power of the food; in Yuca's
offerings one can always sense the home kitchen from
which their inspiration springs. Tacos, strewn with diced
onion and cilantro, have an uncompromising simplicity, while shredded beef machaca is soulfully powerful.
Cochinita pibil, pork slowly cooked in banana leaves, can
be enjoyed here in a taco, burrito, or, most originally, on
a French roll with a dab of mayo. No matter how you eat
it, the pork is always falling-apart tender with a subtle
achiote seasoning and a lingering intensity that is all its
own. On Saturday mornings the atmosphere at Yuca's
switches from the weekday rush to something akin to
a social club. The entire neighborhood seems to turn
out for vaporcitos, supremely thin tamales steamed
in banana leaves and finished with a delicate tomato
sauce. Sitting at the plastic tables, people all but inhale
the contents of their little savory bundles.

A Strategy for Eating Prince's Hot Chicken

Hot chicken here is a religious thing. There are all different places; each place is like a church, and you choose your worship area. It's such a source of pride for Nashvillians because it belongs to Nashville. That changes everything—when something belongs to a city it becomes something emotional, and that's what's happened here with the hot chicken.

If you have friends coming to town, the first thing you do is go to Prince's. There's this nostalgic thing about it: it's a bit far out of town, it's in a shopping mall, and the place just fits. It's like an old honky-tonk or a juke joint—you can't just build those things. The soul's not there. That's what Prince's has; it has that soul, that vibe you can only get from a place that's been there forever.

I usually order it hot. You get zero respect if you go there and get mild. You might as well not have gone. If you don't order it hot you're wasting everybody's time. That's pointless. Go to Kentucky Fried Chicken. If you're going to eat hot chicken, eat hot chicken—don't eat mild chicken. But when you order it extra-hot, you feel it going through your veins. You feel it in your blood. My ear starts ringing, my left arm goes numb; I start thinking I'm going to die. But it's so delicious. It's crazy delicious. I eat hot chicken once a week, maybe twice a week. It becomes this real addiction, and everyone in Nashville has the fever.

HERE'S WHAT I RECOMMEND TO ANYONE TRYING IT FOR THE FIRST TIME:

1. **ORDER EXTRA PICKLES.** I always get two extra sides of pickles and then you have to get three sweet teas, because their sweet teas are these tiny little things, which is torture. So you've got your pickles, which give you that acid to cut the heat, and then you've got the sweetness of the tea to get you through it.

2. **DO NOT EAT THE BREAD.** They put white bread underneath the chicken, and you think the bread's going to help—but that bread's been sitting there soaking up all that cayenne grease, so it does the opposite: It lights you right back up. So either don't eat the bread or order it on the side.

3. **GET YOUR PAPER TOWEL GAME DOWN.** You have to have two piles, one on the left, and one on the right. The one on the left is for hands only. The one on the right: sweaty face only. You do not want to mix them up.

4. **YOU CAN'T WASH YOUR HANDS ENOUGH.** You can wash your hands and think they're clean and safe, and you'll go to the bathroom two hours later and you'll be picking up some new dance moves. I squeeze lemon juice over my hands.

5. **DON'T DRIVE HOME.** Your brain is so confused that you're distracted and driving a car is not a good idea. You have to have a designated hot-chicken driver.

Most important:

Before you go, put a roll of toilet paper in the freezer. They're not joking when they say it burns twice.

—SEAN BROCK, JBF AWARD WINNER

America's Classic Award Winners

SOUTHEAST

Arnold's Country Kitchen
605 8th Avenue South
Nashville, TN
(615) 256-4455

Beaumont Inn
638 Beaumont Inn Drive
Harrodsburg, KY
(859) 734-3381

Bowens Island Restaurant
1870 Bowens Island Road
Charleston, SC
(843) 795-2757

The Bright Star
304 19th Street North
Bessemer, AL
(205) 424-9444

Crook's Corner
610 West Franklin Street
Chapel Hill, NC
(919) 929-7643

Doe's Eat Place
502 Nelson Street
Greenville, MS
(662) 334-3315

Hansen's Sno-Bliz
4801 Tchoupitoulas Street
New Orleans, LA
(504) 891-9788

Joe's Stone Crab
11 Washington Avenue
Miami Beach, FL
(305) 673-0365

Jones Bar-B-Q Diner
219 West Louisiana Street
Marianna, AR
(870) 295-3802

Jumbo's
7501 Northwest 7th Avenue
Miami, FL
closed

Lexington Barbecue #1
100 Smokehouse Lane
Lexington, NC
(336) 249-9814

Mosca's
4137 U.S. 90
Avondale, LA
(504) 436-8950

Mrs. Wilkes Dining Room
107 West Jones Street
Savannah, GA
(912) 232-5997

Prince's Hot Chicken Shack
123 Ewing Drive
Nashville, TN
(615) 226-9442

Sally Bell's Kitchen
708 West Grace Street
Richmond, VA
(804) 644-2838

The Skylight Inn
4618 South Lee Street
Ayden, NC
(252) 746-4113

Versailles
3555 Southwest 8th Street
Miami, FL
(305) 444-0240

Weaver D's
1016 East Broad Street
Athens, GA
(706) 353-7797

Willie Mae's Scotch House
2401 St. Ann Street
New Orleans, LA
(504) 822-9503

NORTHEAST

Al's French Frys
1251 Williston Road
South Burlington, VT
(802) 862-9203

Anchor Bar
1047 Main Street
Buffalo, NY
(716) 883-1134

Aunt Carrie's
1240 Ocean Road
Narragansett, RI
(401) 783-7930

Bagaduce Lunch
19 Bridge Road
Brooksville, ME
(207) 326-4197

Barney Greengrass
541 Amsterdam Avenue
New York, NY
(212) 724-4707

Ben's Chili Bowl
1213 U Street Northwest
Washington D.C.
(202) 667-0909

C.F. Folks
1225 19th Street Northwest
Washington, D.C.
(617) 536-7669

Charlie's Sandwich Shoppe
429 Columbus Avenue
Boston, MA
closed

Chef Vola's
111 South Albion Place
Atlantic City, NJ
(609) 345-2022

Doris & Ed's Seafood Restaurant
348 Shore Drive
Highlands, NJ
closed

Durgin Park
340 Faneuil Hall Marketplace
Boston, MA
(617) 227-2038

Frank Pepe Pizzeria Napoletana
157 Wooster Street
New Haven, CT
(208) 865-5762

Grand Central Oyster Bar and Restaurant
89 East 42nd Street
New York, NY
(212) 490-6650

John's Roast Pork
14 East Snyder Avenue
Philadelphia, PA
(215) 463-1951

Keens Steakhouse
72 West 36th Street
New York, NY
(212) 947-3636

Le Veau d'Or
129 East 60th Street
New York, NY
(212) 838-8133

Maison Marconi
106 West Saratoga Street
Baltimore, MD
closed

Mario's
2342 Arthur Avenue
Bronx, NY
(718) 584-1188

Moosewood Restaurant
215 North Cayuga Street
Ithaca, NY
(607) 273-9610

Mustache Bill's Diner
8th Street and Broadway
Barnegat Light, NJ
(609) 494-0155

Olneyville New York System
18 Plainfield Street
Providence, RI
(401) 621-9500

Peter Luger Steak House
178 Broadway
Brooklyn, NY
(718) 387-7400

Polly's Pancake Parlor
672 NH-117
Sugar Hill, NH
(603) 823-5575

Primanti Brothers
46 18th Street
Pittsburgh, PA
(412) 263-2142

Prime Burger
5 East 51st Street
New York, NY
closed

2nd Avenue Deli
162 East 33rd Street
New York, NY
(212) 689-9000

Sevilla Restaurant & Bar
62 Charles Street
New York, NY
(212) 929-3189

Shady Glen
840 Middle Turnpike East
Manchester, CT
(860) 649-4245

Totonno's
1524 Neptune Avenue
Brooklyn, NY
(718) 372-8606

Waterman's Beach Lobster
343 Waterman Beach Road
South Thomaston, ME
(207) 596-7819

White House Sub Shop
2301 Arctic Avenue
Atlantic City, NJ
(609) 345-1564

MIDWEST

Al's Breakfast
413 14th Avenue Southeast
Minneapolis, MN
(612) 331-9991

Archie's Waeside
224 4th Avenue Northeast
Le Mars, IA
(172) 596-7011

The Berghoff
14 West Adams Street
Chicago, IL
(312) 427-3170

Breitbach's Country Dining
563 Balltown Road
Sherrill, IA
(563) 552-2220

Brookville Hotel
105 East Lafayette Avenue
Abilene, KS
(785) 263-2244

Calumet Fisheries
3259 East 95th Street
Chicago, IL
(773) 933-9855

Camp Washington Chili
3005 Colerain Avenue
Cincinnati, OH
(513) 541-0061

Kramarczuk's
215 East Hennepin Avenue
Minneapolis, MN
(612) 379-3018

Lagomarcino's
1422 Fifth Avenue
Moline, IL
(309) 764-1814

The Pickwick
508 East Superior Street
Duluth, MN
(218) 623-7425

Sokolowski's University Inn
1201 University Road
Cleveland, OH
(216) 771-9236

St. Elmo Steak House
127 South Illinois Street
Indianapolis, IN
(317) 635-0636

Stroud's
5410 Northeast Oak Ridge Road
Kansas City, MO
(816) 454-9600

Three Brothers Restaurant
2414 South St. Clair Street
Milwaukee, WI
(414) 481-7530

Tufano's Vernon Park Tap
1073 West Vernon Park Place
Chicago, IL
(312) 733-3393

Watts Tea Shop
761 North Jefferson Street
Milwaukee, WI
(414) 290-5720

SOUTHWEST

Café Pasqual's
121 Don Gaspar Avenue
Santa Fe, NM
(505) 983-9340

El Chorro Lodge
5550 East Lincoln Drive
Paradise Valley, AZ
(480) 948-5170

The Fry Bread House
1003 East Indian School Road
Phoenix, AZ
(602) 351-2345

H&H Car Wash and Coffee
Shop
101 East Yandell Drive
El Paso, TX
(915) 533-1144

Irma's
22 North Chenevert Street
Houston, TX
(713) 222-0767

Joe T. Garcia's Mexican Food
Restaurant
2201 North Commerce Street
Fort Worth, TX
(817) 626-4356

Louie Mueller Barbecue
206 West Second Street
Taylor, TX
(512) 352-6206

Mary & Tito's Café
2711 4th Street Northwest
Albuquerque, NM
(505) 344-6266

The Original Sonny Bryan's
2202 Inwood Road
Dallas, TX
(214) 357-7120

Perini Ranch Steakhouse
3002 FM 89, #A
Buffalo Gap, TX
(325) 572-3339

The Shed
113 East Palace Avenue
Santa Fe, NM
(505) 982-9030

WEST

Duarte's Tavern
202 Stage Road
Pescadero, CA
(650) 879-0464

Emmett Watson's Oyster Bar
1916 Pike Place #16
Seattle, WA
(206) 448-7721

Frank Fat's
806 L Street
Sacramento, CA
(916) 442-7092

Gott's Roadside
(formerly Taylor's Automotive
Refresher)
933 Main Street
St. Helena, CA
(707) 963-3486

Guelaguetza
3014 West Olympic Boulevard
Los Angeles, CA
(213) 427-0608

Gustavus Inn
1270 Gustavus Road
Gustavus, AK
(800) 649-5220

Hamura's Saimin Stand
2956 Kress Street
Lihue, Kauai, HI
(808) 245-3271

Helena's Hawaiian Food
1240 North School Street
Honolulu, HI
(808) 845-8044

Langer's Delicatessen
704 South Alvarado Street
Los Angeles, CA
(213) 483-8050

Maneki
304 Sixth Avenue South
Seattle, WA
(206) 622-2631

Nick's Italian Café
521 Northeast 3rd Street
McMinnville, OR
(503) 434-4471

Nora's Fish Creek Inn
5600 WY-22
Wilson, WY
(307) 733-8288

Noriega's
525 Sumner Street
Bakersfield, CA
(661) 322-8419

Original Pancake House
8601 Southwest 24th Avenue
Portland, OR
(503) 246-9007

Philippe the Original
1001 North Alameda Street
Los Angeles, CA
(213) 628-3781

Ray's Boathouse and Café
6049 Seaview Avenue NW
Seattle, WA
(206) 789-3770

Sam Choy's Kaloko
78-6831 Alii Drive
Kailua-Kona, HI
closed

Swan Oyster Depot
1517 Polk Street
San Francisco, CA
(415) 673-2757

Tadich Grill
240 California Street
San Francisco, CA
(415) 391-1849

Yank Sing
101 Spear Street
San Francisco, CA
(415) 781-1111

Yuca's Hut
2056 Hillhurst Avenue
Los Angeles, CA
(323) 662-1214

Conversion Chart

All conversions are approximate.

LIQUID CONVERSIONS

U.S.	METRIC
1 tsp	5 ml
1 tbs	15 ml
2 tbs	30 ml
3 tbs	45 ml
¼ cup	60 ml
⅓ cup	75 ml
⅓ cup + 1 tbs	90 ml
⅓ cup + 2 tbs	100 ml
½ cup	120 ml
⅔ cup	150 ml
¾ cup	180 ml
¾ cup + 2 tbs	200 ml
1 cup	240 ml
1 cup + 2tbs	275 ml
1¼ cups	300 ml
1⅓ cups	325 ml
1½ cups	350 ml
1⅔ cups	375 ml
1¾ cups	400 ml
1¾ cups + 2 tbs	450 ml
2 cups (1 pint)	475 ml
2½ cups	600 ml
3 cups	720 ml
4 cups (1 quart)	945 ml (1,000 ml is 1 liter)

WEIGHT CONVERSIONS

U.S./U.K.	METRIC
½ oz	14 g
1 oz	28 g
1½ oz	43 g
2 oz	57 g
2½ oz	71 g
3 oz	85 g
3 ½ oz	100 g
4 oz	113 g
5 oz	142 g
6 oz	170 g
7 oz	200 g
8 oz	227 g
9 oz	255 g
10 oz	284 g
11 oz	312 g
12 oz	340 g
13 oz	368 g
14 oz	400 g
15 oz	425 g
1 lb	454 g

OVEN TEMPERATURES

°F	GAS MARK	°C
250	½	120
275	1	140
300	2	150
325	3	165
350	4	180
375	5	190
400	6	200
425	7	220
450	8	230
475	9	240
500	10	260
550	Broil	290

Index

Acknowledgments

To James Beard Foundation Restaurant and Chef Award committees, past and present, for continuing to recognize the historic influence of local restaurants around the country with the prestigious America's Classics Awards.

To those who wrote the America's Classics descriptions for James Beard Foundation publications, which now appear in this book, including Brett Anderson, R. W. Apple Jr., Michael Bauer, Pat Brown, Lourdes Castro, Providence Cicero, Andrea Clurfeld, Alison Cook, John T. Edge, Amy Evans, Andrew Harris, Gwen Hyman, Cheryl Alters Jamison, Patric Kuh, Corby Kummer, Christiane Lauterbach, Nancy Leson, Ed Levine, Rick Nelson, James Oseland, William Rice, David Shaw, Tom Sietsema, Jane and Michael Stern, and Phil Vettel.

To the Beard Award winners who shared their memories of the beloved restaurants featured in this book, including Justin Aprahamian, April Bloomfield, Sean Brock, Andrew Carmellini, Jose Garces, Maria Hines, Traci Des Jardins, Paul Kahan, Donnie Madia, Nancy Oakes, Chris Shepherd, Rick Tramonto, Amy Mills Tunnicliffe, and Alan Wong.

To Matt and Ted Lee, for graciously providing us with a vintage photo of Lexington Barbecue that originally appeared in *The Lee Bros. Southern Cookbook*.

To the Southern Foodways Alliance, who contributed restaurant descriptions and oral history transcripts for the Southeast chapter, as well as words of wisdom and guidance as we started this project.

To author Anya Hoffman, JBF contributing editor, for her creative writing skills, her editing, and her passion for this project.

To Ashley Kosiak, JBF program coordinator, who interviewed the restaurateurs, wrote the oral histories, and solicited the recipes and archival images for this book. And to Maggie Borden, JBF assistant editor, for her recipe-hunting prowess.

To the in-studio photography team—photographer Ben Fink, food stylist Suzanne Lenzer, and prop stylist Maya Rossi—and photographer James Collier for the on-location images that appear in this book.

To our recipe testers, Stephanie Bourgeois, Maia Cheslow, and Yewande Komolafe.

To copy editor Liana Krissoff, proofreader Ivy McFadden, and indexer Cathy Dorsey.

To those at Rizzoli, especially Charles Miers, publisher, for giving support in all stages, and Christopher Steighner, our editor, for expertly guiding us through the process of putting this book together.

And to the restaurateurs and the families of the James Beard America's Classics restaurants and their families for providing the recipes, archival images, and stories that appear in this book.

From Rizzoli International Publications:
To those at the James Beard Foundation who made this book possible, especially Susan Ungaro, president, for sharing her passion for the project and gentle guidance; Mitchell Davis, executive vice president, for having faith and shaping the concept; and Alison Tozzi Liu, editorial director, for steering the book's journey with reassuring aplomb and organizational prowess.

To Alison Lew, at Vertigo Design, for creating attractive pages that unite the book's many components.

ABOUT THE JAMES BEARD FOUNDATION

Founded in 1986, the James Beard Foundation (JBF) celebrates, nurtures, and honors America's diverse culinary heritage through programs that educate and inspire. A cookbook author and teacher with an encyclopedic knowledge about food, the late James Beard was a champion of American cuisine. He helped educate and mentor generations of professional chefs and food enthusiasts, instilling in them the value of wholesome, healthful, and delicious food. Today JBF continues in the same spirit by administering a number of diverse programs that include educational initiatives, food industry awards, scholarships for culinary students, publications, chef advocacy training, and thought-leader convening. The foundation also maintains the historic James Beard House in New York City's Greenwich Village as a performance space for visiting chefs. For more information, please visit jamesbeard.org.

First published in the United States of America in 2016
by Rizzoli International Publications, Inc.
300 Park Avenue South
New York, NY 10010
www.rizzoliusa.com

© 2016 The James Beard Foundation

Photographs © 2016 Ben Fink: pages 23, 41, 45, 47, 73, 91, 95, 99, 125, 133, 145, 151, 175, 177, 193, 213, 227, 231, 245. Photographs © 2016 James Collier: pages 2, 6t, 9, 13, 14, 18, 20, 27, 34, 52, 54, 57, 69, 80, 103tl, 103b, 105, 107, 120, 141, 161, 164, 168, 183, 187, 196, 199t, 200, 203, 208, 210, 215, 219, 220, 233, 237, 238, 248, 249, 253, 257, 258, 259, 260, 264, back cover.

2016 2017 2018 2019 / 10 9 8 7 6 5 4 3 2 1

Distributed in the U.S. trade by Random House, New York

Printed in China

ISBN-13: 978-0-8478-4746-4

Library of Congress Control Number: 2015953473